Busch/Kassung/Sieck (Hrsg.)
Kultur und Informatik: Mixed Reality

Carsten Busch / Christian Kassung /
Jürgen Sieck (Hrsg.)

Kultur und Informatik

Mixed Reality

Verlag Werner Hülsbusch
Fachverlag für Medientechnik und -wirtschaft

C. Busch[*]/C. Kassung[**]/J. Sieck[*/**] (Hrsg.):
Kultur und Informatik: Mixed Reality

Anschriften der Herausgeber:

[*] Hochschule für Technik und Wirtschaft
FB 4, Forschungsgruppe INKA
Wilhelminenhofstr. 75a, 12459 Berlin

[**] Humboldt-Universität zu Berlin
Interdisziplinäres Labor „Bild Wissen Gestaltung"
Hermann von Helmholtz-Zentrum für Kulturtechnik
Sophienstraße 22a, 10178 Berlin

Bibliografische Information der Deutschen Bibliothek
Die Deutsche Bibliothek verzeichnet diese Publikation in der Deutschen
Nationalbibliografie; detaillierte bibliografische Daten sind im Internet unter
http://d-nb.de abrufbar.

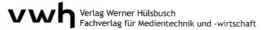

Die Publikation wird ermöglicht durch den Exzellenzcluster „Bild Wissen
Gestaltung". Ein Interdisziplinäres Labor der Humboldt-Universität zu Berlin
(Fördernr. EXC 1027/1) und die finanzielle Unterstützung durch die Deutsche
Forschungsgemeinschaft im Rahmen der Exzellenzinitiative.

© Verlag Werner Hülsbusch, Glückstadt, 2017

vwh Verlag Werner Hülsbusch
Fachverlag für Medientechnik und -wirtschaft

www.vwh-verlag.de

Umschlag: design of media, Lüchow
Druck und Bindung: SOWA Sp. z o. o., Piaseczno

Printed in Poland

– Als Typoskript gedruckt –

ISBN: 978-3-86488-119-0

Content

Preface

Culture and Computer Science – Mixed Reality

The 15th edition of the "Culture and Computer Science" conference series brings into focus best practice examples, challenges and future trends in the fields of Mixed, Augmented and Virtual Reality, media integration, cross media technologies, modelling, visualisation and interaction. The conference targets professionals working within cultural and creative industries, communication and cultural scientists, designers, artists as well as computer scientists and engineers, who conduct research and development on cultural topics.

The central questions of the conference "Culture and Computer Science 2017 – Mixed Reality" include the analysis, design, use, advantages, as well as challenges of hybrid objects. These key issues are not only discussed during the conference, they are part of an ongoing academic discourse on merging the analogue materiality of objects and the digital versatility of data i.e. at the Cluster of Excellence "Image Knowledge Gestaltung. An Interdisciplinary Laboratory" at the Humboldt-Universität zu Berlin, the V&A Research Institute (VARI) at the Victoria and Albert Museum in London, or at the University Lüneburg in the research centre "Medienkulturen der Computersimulation (MECS)". In this context, museums are not only static memory spaces for material objects with some additional selected, and hence also static, knowledge. On the contrary, we are beginning to see and to design the consequences of a constructivist approach in which objects are no longer just prerequisite but also an effect of our interactions with them. Objects are what we know about them, how we measure them, how we design and exhibit them, and how they interact with the surrounding space. We create objects to the same extent as they create us.

With this in mind, the key challenge for tomorrow's museums is to create flexible constellations between collections, research facilities, museums and exhibition spaces, in which objects are modelled as hybrid, (inter-)active structures in order to circulate them, to aggregate and to evaluate the resulting data. The implementation of hybrid objects in Mixed Reality environments has to be explored and the theoretical fundamentals and best practice examples of their strengths, weaknesses and innovative content must be discussed.

In this field, the contributions collected in this volume represent multifaceted approaches towards hybrid exhibition strategies and analyse, demonstrate, and, in particular, discuss current research and developments around "Mixed Reality". The authors of this volumes come from 15 different countries and hence give an extensive international overview of fundamental theories as well as best practice applications of information management, communication, interaction, visualisation, Mixed, Augmented and Virtual Reality, audio technology, multimedia, streaming and data processing, and design within a specific cultural context.

The contributions analyse and discuss the following key topics:

- Mixed Reality;
- Augmented Reality;
- Virtual Reality;
- Design;
- Participatory design;
- 3D technologies;
- Digitalisation in the cultural and creative industries;
- Visualisation and interaction technologies;
- Interactive multimedia solutions for museums, concert halls, exhibitions etc.;
- Virtual reconstructions;
- Digital storytelling;
- Indigenous knowledge;
- Interdependence between culture and computer science;
- The media-compatible treatment and enhancement of information; and
- Social and ethical issues in computer science.

Based on best practice examples, recent developments and requirements are presented in the areas of Mixed, Augmented and Virtual Reality, the use of live data sources for augmentation as well as their visualisation and interaction in concert halls, exhibitions and museums. To present content only in the form of texts, films and stories no longer matches the requirements of today's visitor. Instead, there is an urgent need for new approaches to interconnect the analogue and the digital realm and to find fluid modes of visualisation and interaction between these two worlds. Contemporary museum visitors no longer want to experience objects or to consume information. The wish to be an active and formative element of the knowledge space, affecting the museum in the same way as the presence of the objects. This interaction of visitors, objects and data space is the focus in many of the papers, including concrete ideas on technical solutions.

In addition to four invited keynote papers, more than 50 papers were submitted. Each paper was reviewed by three different members of the international programme committee. Our thanks go to the members of the programme committee for their assistance in reviewing the numerous submissions.

The international programme committee selected 23 papers and grouped the contributions, together with the four keynotes, into the areas:

- Mixed Museum;
- Mixed and Augmented Reality Technology;
- Mixed and Augmented Reality Applications;
- Creating and Presenting Content;
- Mixed Reality and Interaction; and a
- Pecha Kucha session.

The stunning abundance of possibilities, which users have in present multi-media environment, virtual and real worlds, confronts both planners and computer scientists with new challenges. In order to allow cultural institutions to create new socio-digital environments, fluid knowledge spaces need to be established without neglecting the aims of imparting knowledge and cultural education. The papers in this volume will present different approaches and best practice examples to meet these challenges.

This and the previous editions of the series "Culture and Computer Science" are only possible with the continuous support by the "Staatliche Museen zu Berlin". We thank in this context particularly the staff and the curators of the "Bode-Museum", in whose premises we hold the conference "Culture and Computer Science – Mixed Reality". The special atmosphere of the surroundings will certainly continue to have a lasting effect on all speakers and participants. In particular, we would like to thank Prof. Dr. Eisenhauer, Prof. Dr. Weisser and Bernd Rottenburg from the "Staatliche Museen zu Berlin" for their support of and engagement with the conference.

Our special thanks go to all authors, without whose creativity, ideas and hard work it would not be possible to run a wonderful conference and to produce these very interesting and inspiring proceedings.

This and all previous conferences "Culture and Computer Science", as well as this publication, would not have been possible without the commitment of the staff and colleagues of our research group INKA at the University of Applied Sciences HTW Berlin. In particular, we would like to thank Kerstin Remes, Elisabeth Thielen and Michael Thiele-Maas.

Carsten Busch, Christian Kassung and Jürgen Sieck

Berlin, May 2017

This publication was made possible by the Cluster of Excellence "Image Knowledge Gestaltung" at the Humboldt-Universität zu Berlin (sponsor number EXC 1027/1) with financial support from the German Research Foundation as a part of the Excellence Initiative.

Co-Creating Taxonomies with Indigenous Knowledge Holders in the Digital Zone

Tariq Zaman

Faculty of Computer Science and Information Technology
Universiti Malaysia Sarawak (UNIMAS)
94300 Kota Samarahan, Sarawak, Malaysia
zamantariq@gmail.com

Abstract

Knowledge representations and conceptualisations of the world differ profoundly across cultures and indigenous knowledge systems. Current technology designs are deeply anchored in a Western epistemology, which is often conflicting with indigenous paradigms. Thus we pursue a locally situated approach to co-creating a new digital reality with indigenous knowledge holders in Malaysia.

This paper covers our experiences of community driven design process and especially the insights and challenges in the design and development of indigenous knowledge management systems in a rural site of Malaysian Borneo. We also highlight the results of different attempts for establishing abstract structures unfamiliar to indigenous people yet necessary for digitalisation. Our endeavors lead us to question the validity of techniques and interpretations of interactions originating from a Western scientific paradigm and pursue the creation of an indigenous HCI paradigm to frame design methods.

1   Introduction

Over the last two decades, there has been an increasing interest in designing information and communication technology (ICTs) systems for "traditional/ indigenous" knowledge which represents the "other" forms of knowledge that differ from those that dominate in producing ICTs. [Van10] classified these systems and solutions into two categories: knowledge-centred and knower-centred. The knowledge-centred approach focuses on "contents" while knower-centred approach focuses more on "tools" enabling knowledge representation in more informal ways. The role of the "engagement" and "participation" of knowledge holders in designing technologies is widely acknowledged, however, frequently overlooked [Bal14] [Cham13]. The concepts of "community engagement" and "user involvement" in design activities are context specific and vary greatly from case to case which has often contended in developing technologies "for" indigenous knowledge that can be used by indigenous people.

In our long term partnership with indigenous communities of Malaysia, we practiced system-centred approach to integrate a more holistic view in designing technologies for indigenous knowledge conceptualisation and representation. In system-centred approach, the context defines local and situational parameters related to design process that are then aligned with social, cultural, structural, and human attributes.

The collaboration and partnership in co-designing processes results in creating a shared space where the indigenous community of Long Lamai is constructing new identity in the digital zone. For theoretical base, we levereged on prior research of [Carter15], which defines information technology identity as *the extent to which an individual views use of an information technology as integral to his or her sense of self.*

2   Context and Collaboration

Institute of Social Informatics and Technological Innovations (ISITI) Universiti Malaysia Sarawak (UNIMAS) is one of the active implementers of ICTD and ICT4D projects in highly isolated and remote locations in Malaysia. The Key strength of ISITI is to bridge the technology-people's gap, in particular, encompassing technological innovations for indigenous communities. To facilitate this, ISITI, has developed a strong relationship with indigenous communities, where all its sites' population comprise different indigenous groups of different social and cultural settings.

One of the project sites is Long Lamai, a remote rural Penan village in Malaysian Borneo. The community in Long Lamai consists of approximately 598 individuals with limited infrastructure and communication facilities [Zaman15a]. The Penans in Long Lamai were nomadic, but have settled down in the area for over 50 years. They still return to the forest to hunt and to gather forest produce. Since 2008, the Long Lamai community is partnering with UNIMAS in different Information and Communication Technologies (ICT) related projects such as using the Internet to market their tourism products and activities, to document indigenous botanical knowledge, to create an online Penan language dictionary and to develop mobile apps by integrating their unique forest sign language [Zaman15b].

In traditional development discourse and narrations of "modernization", the Penans have been portrayed as a traditional tribe fighting against aggressive timber operations and opposing development [Ibrahim15]. However, the Penans of Long Lamai are very consciously countering the mainstream narrative by adopting technologies in their indigenized cultural revitalisation movement and "creating their own information technology identity".

3 System-Centred Approach and Evolution of Community

The social and cultural interconnectedness and mobility across space, time and geography impact technology use and design [Shklovski10]. In international design teams it is very common that the developers and users originate from different socio-cultural backgrounds which sometimes results in contradictory and incompatible understanding of common reality [Wins10]. To develop a system-centred, community based co-design approach and to analyse the other relevant approaches, literature from design, anthropology, information systems and Human-Computer Interaction was explored. Based on our literature review and community narratives (their experiences with other development projects) we designed a four-tier framework to analyse the community evolution in partnership (Fig. 1). The first level is where the community plays the role of a *user* and the designer expects community participation as users of the system only. The second level is where the community participates in the design process as *informed users*. The designer decides to let the community know about the wider context of the project and the community can provide suggestions to improve the system design. The third level is where the community performs their role as *content creators*. They are not part of the design process but they populate the designed system by contributing their contents. The ideal scenario is fourth level where the community participates and is recognised as *co-designers*. The fourth level can be depicted as Collaboration + Skills + Information = Participation.

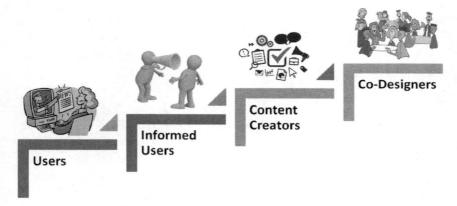

Fig. 1: Evolution of community in design process and partnership

4   Our Digital Endeavours for Cultural Revitalisation

In 2009, after the telecentre inauguration, Long Lamai community got access to Internet and telecommunication services. For one and half years, the researchers trained local community on using ICT tools and Internet. After that, the community identified digitization of local botanical knowledge as a "next step" within the collaboration. For the next two years, a team comprises of community members and researchers from UNIMAS worked together and co-designed eToro, a digital platform to manage indigenous botanical knowledge of the Penans [Zaman15]. The design of the system is based on the community's conceptualisation of their indigenous botanical knowledge management (BKM) (Fig. 2). Later on, it is translated into formal requirement specification documents (Fig. 3) and implemented within a mainstream technology such as an android based application for data collection (ODK) and a content management system to support the data management.

Fig. 2: Community conceptualisation of BKM

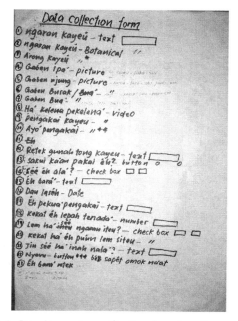

Fig. 3: Requirement specification form for eTor system

In 2014, as a second digital endeavour, Long Lamai community initiated partnership with researchers from UNIMAS and Namibia University of Science and Technology for digitization and preservation of Oroo', a unique forest sign language. As a first step, we initiated the documentation of Oroo' signs, followed by designing multiple digital solutions such as PC based Oroo' Adventure Game [Zaman 15b] and Oroo' Tangibles for mobile devices [Plimmer15]. In the third attempt, we co-designed the Penan Oroo' Short Messages Signs (PO-SMS) app with a group of Penan youth in Long Lamai [Zaman15c].

Another attempt was to co-create an indigenous persona of Penans in digital zone by engaging Penan youth in social media. It is evident that new technologies are emerging, changing communication landscape and indirectly changing lifestyle in local and indigenous communities. Unfortunately, it is leaving behind people endowed with rich culture but "poor" in access. Penan youth living in urban cities normally become socially and culturally "visible" and suffer from an inferiority complex [Ibrahim15]. Access to digital technologies and social media provides them a space for interaction and opportunities to be part of "the community" in digital space. By engaging 25 youth participants (diaspora) for a month in a Facebook group, we constructed a representative indigenous cultural persona in digital world as a counter narrative (Fig. 4).

Fig. 4: Penan Indigenous cultural persona co-created by Penans youth

5 Discussion and Conclusion

Our long term partnership in co-designing of ICT tools for cultural revitalisation leads us to develop the following guiding principles for researchers, designers and students working with remote rural and indigenous communities. If we comprehend all our learning from the field in one word then it would be "Active Participation".

Collaboration + Skills + Information = Active Participation.

Collaboration of stakeholders is the key to active participation. Long Lamai is a semi-nomadic community and still depends on their forest for hunting and gathering their livelihoods. In all hunter-gatherers communities, collaboration and solidarity have been the most important values. According to the village headman Wilson Bian Bilare, *"anyone who wishes to partner with Long Lamai should engage in detailed negotiations with the community elders and community members beforehand. They should discuss the process and outcome at the very start, everyone in the community must agree and only then the partnership can be developed."*

In orthodox participatory design methods mere the participation of key users is sufficient though it may be counter productive from the perspective of an egalitarian community such as Long Lamai where one need to engage the community members at three different levels: local liason, community elders or gate keepers and then users. After the collaboration, *skills development* and mutual learning is the next important principle of active participation. The community members can only participate in and inform the design process if they have the skills to understand new systems, articulate their needs and contribute their insights. "What after?" designing and deployment of technology is a fundamental question for Long Lamai community. Hence, the community always prefer to have a set of community members sufficiently familiar with the technology to repair and maintain it independently of the outside partner. We observed that the community members mutually enjoy "being participated" and interaction with researcher makes them ready to face the outside world. In all the three above stated digital endeavours, the community volunteered to be part of the co-designing process as they considered it a good opportunity for learning and developing new skills.

Along with skills the next important principle is access to "related information". The community members should be part of the discussion from very initial phase of the design endeavours, to ensure long-term sustainability of the project. The partners should discuss in detail the possible challenges, opportunities and potential effects of external interventions. According to Wilson, *"there is a common perception about the Penans that they are not good at maintaining the provided facilities and this case can augment that wrong perception. The community could handle the situation better if they were aware about the possibilities and options."* From the headman's perspective, we can gather that for Penans of Long Lamai participation in design endeavours is not just a one-time activity but they feel it closely related to their identity. Hence, the ultimate goal of participation is not just "fun" but it contributes to revitalise their indigenous identity. It is also important to probe alternative technologies in exploring the best fit within a specific context.

In conclusion, though focusing only on one indigenous community but in long term partnership, our study offers a window into insights from different technology design projects and key learnings. It may help the researchers and designers working with other indigenous, remote and rural communities who have similar desire of partnership for designing ICT tools for indigenous knowledge representation.

Literature

[Bal14]   Balestrini, M., Bird, J., Marshall, P., Zaro, A. and Rogers, Y. Understanding Sustained Community Engagement: A Case Study in Heritage Preservation in Rural Argentina, In Proceedings of the SIGCHI Conference on Human Factors in Computing Systems (Toronto, Canada), ACM Press, (2014): pp. 2675–2684.

[Cham13]   Chamberlain, A., Crabtree, A., and Davies, M. Community engagement for research: Contextual design in rural CSCW system development. In Proc. Int. Conf. on Communities &Technologies 2013 (Muenchen, Germany, July1-2, 2013), ACM Press, (2013): pp. 131–139.

[Carter15]   Carter, Michelle, and Varun Grover. "Me, My Self, and I (T): Conceptualizing Information Technology Identity and its Implications." Mis Quarterly 39, no. 4 (2015): pp. 931–957.

[Ibrahim15] Ibrahim, Z. From island to nation-state formations and developmentalism: Penan story-telling as narratives of "territorialising space" and reclaiming stewardship. International Journal Advances in Social Science and Humanities, (2015) 3(3), pp. 1–15.

[Plimeer15] Plimmer, Beryl, Liang He, Tariq Zaman, Kasun Karunanayaka, Alvin W. Yeo, Garen Jengan, Rachel Blagojevic, and Ellen Yi-Luen Do. "New interaction tools for preserving an old language." In Proceedings of the 33rd Annual ACM Conference on Human Factors in Computing Systems, pp. 3493–3502. ACM, 2015.

[Shklovski10] Shklovski, I., Lindtner, S., Vertesi, J. and Dourish, P. Transnational times: locality, globality and mobility in technology design and use. In Proc. 12th ACM international conference adjunct papers on Ubiquitous computing – Adjunct, ACM (2010), pp. 515–518.

[Van10] Van Der Velden, Maja. "Design for the contact zone. Knowledge management software and the structures of indigenous knowledges." (2010): pp. 1–18.

[Wins10] Winschiers-Theophilus, Heike, Shilumbe Chivuno-Kuria, Gereon Koch Kapuire, Nicola J. Bidwell, and Edwin Blake. "Being participated: a community approach." In Proceedings of the 11th Biennial Participatory Design Conference, pp. 1–10. ACM, 2010.

[Zaman15a] Zaman, Tariq, Narayanan Kulathuramaiyer, and Alvin W. Yeo. "eToro: Appropriating ICTs for the Management of Penance' Indigenous Botanical Knowledge" Indigenous People and Mobile Technologies 31 (2015): p. 253.

[Zaman15b] Zaman, Tariq, Heike Winschiers-Theophilus, Alvin W. Yeo, Lai Chiu Ting, and Garen Jengan. "Reviving an indigenous rainforest sign language: digital Oroo'adventure game." In Proceedings of the Seventh International Conference on Information and Communication Technologies and Development, p. 69. ACM, 2015.

[Zaman15c] Zaman, Tariq, and Heike Winschiers-Theophilus. "Penan's Oroo'Short Message Signs (PO-SMS): co-design of a digital jungle sign language application." In Human-Computer Interaction, pp. 489–504. Springer International Publishing, 2015.

A Contemporary Cultural Expression of Marginalised Namibian Youth Through Re-appropriated Technologies

Heike Winschiers-Theophilus, Michael Chamunorwa,
Shilumbe Chivuno-Kuria, Rosetha Kays
Faculty of Computing & Informatics
Namibia University of Science & Technology
hwinschiers@nust.na, chamunorwamichael@gmail.com,
{schivuno, rkays}@nust.na

Susanna Immonen, Hanna Stenhammar
Aalto University
{susanna.immonen, hanna.stenhammar}@aalto.fi

Daniel G. Cabrero
University of West London
Daniel.Gonzalez-Cabrero@uwl.ac.uk

Hedvig Mendonca
University of Namibia
hmendonca@unam.na

Abstract

This paper presents two interactive digital games re-designed by marginalised youth in Windhoek through a series of participatory design
workshops. While the two games were originally designed to enhance
user experiences in the cultural heritage sector by the INKA group, HTW
Berlin, the youth appropriated the content to showcase the challenges

they face in their current lives on a daily basis, and the future they visualize for their community and themselves. The aim was to engage the youth in co-designing a digital contemporary cultural self-representation. The re-purposed interactive games were displayed at a youth day event with the intent to raise public awareness of the desperate situation of unemployed youth in informal settlements. A brief reflection on the co-design process and outcome are presented in this paper.

1   Introduction

Game Design is a key approach to address diverse issues in societies in an array of cultures and sites around the World. Using participatory design allows end-users and lay designers to become part of the digital adaptations of self-representation encapsulating the cultural values of participants during the workshop sessions. Preceding research with youth applied Participatory Design (PD) methods and tools with positive results [Ongw14, Wins15]. The owners of the problems must be given the ability to contribute to the design and participate in the development of solutions at all stages [Giac08]. This allows them to explore and contribute fully towards a solution to the problem and, a chance to "contribute in a manner appropriate to their ability" [Aria00]. Any complex design problem requires relevant knowledge. That knowledge is usually spread across the participants. Once put together a shared understanding is created. This leads to new solutions, ideas, artefacts and is therefore called participatory or collaborative design [Giac08]. "Having different viewpoints helps one discover alternatives and can help uncover tacit aspects of problems" [Aria00].

Thus, we have engaged a number of unemployed Namibian youth in a technology adaptation endeavour, enabling the youth to become creators of their own design as promoted by [Roge13]. In the spirit of "Ubuntu", an African philosophy, the technology design unfolded by manifesting strong group cohesion with decisions being considerate of others and beneficial to the whole community. The most outstanding cultural treasure of Ubuntu is in the form of values such as compassion, caring and sharing, which would be reflected in the technologies. The aim thus, was two-folded: (1) for the youth to engage in self-reflection and digital cultural expressions and (2) to create a public awareness and empathy of their difficult situation through the display of the interactive games.

2   Context

2.1   Namibian unemployed Youth in Havana

Namibia, with a population of approximately 2 million, is a multi-cultural country with as many as 11 ethnic groups speaking their own languages. Promoting a united Namibia, it holds a democratic status and a peaceful political stability. However, Namibia also holds one of the highest uneven income distributions in the world, with an alarming youth unemployment rate of 39.2% in 2014 according to the Labour Force report 2014 (Namibia Statistics Agency). In hope to find employment in urban areas, many migrate from their rural homes to town, where they stay mostly in informal settlements at the outskirts of town. One of those settlements in Windhoek is known as "Havana", consisting of approximately 4000 houses and shanties. Basic infrastructures are mostly absent, thus households have no access to running water, electricity, sanitation, telecommunication or other services.

2.2   The "Youth for Youth" day

In September 2015 under the motto "Youth for Youth", achievements of colla-borations with the Youth were celebrated as a one-day event at the Namibian Business Innovation Centre. The audience consisted of potential donors such as ambassadors, managers from private and public organisations, diplomats, managers and staff from the university, Havana fellows and general members of the public. The aim of the event was to display a contemporary cultural expression of marginalised youth as an interactive exhibition to create public awareness and to attract funders for further youth projects.

2.3   Preparations towards the "Youth for Youth" day

Havana and other unemployed youth from Windhoek together with resear-chers, undergraduate students and RLabs organisers had two months to prepare the day-event. A total number of 27 participants comprising 19 youth, 4 students and 4 researchers took part in the overall project. After a first event planning workshop governed by unoriginal ideas, a visiting academic from the University of Berlin presented several exhibiting concepts he had or created and showcased in the past years [Siec15a,b]. From the displayed exhibitions, two were chosen by the youth to adapt to their context, imagination, and epistemic understanding of the world. Both games were technology-based – the one being the Race Game; the other was a Picture Identification Game. The latter consisted of hidden rock art canvas which could be inspected through a movable hole. The player can guess the animal by selecting street art representations of it. The Race Game was a mobile phone-based game whereby the user chooses an agent for which s/he would then shake a mobile phone, which in turn would make the agent to race to finish line in a virtual running contest projected on the wall. Two sub-groups consisting of one researcher, one student and at least 2 youth participants were responsible for a prototype each, as outlined below.

3   The "Hole of Change" Games

The "Rock Art/Street Art" system designed by the INKA group [Siec15a,b] was utilized as a creative inspiration and as a starting point for the "Hole of Change" game. Two versions of this game were designed, namely the *Havana Game* representing current challenges in Havana, and the *Training Game* conveying discrete youth stories. The games were designed to raise awareness of current challenging issues regarding unhealthy living environments and unskilled youth (see http://rlabsnamibia.org/edutainment.html).

3.1   Design Intention

In the *Havana Game* there was a mediated level of self-representation, as the youth could communicate their views through their living environment: what Havana currently looked like and which improvements they would suggest. In the *Training Game* the youth could convey their self-representations more directly through real-life stories: what they have been going through, what is the role of the RLabs trainings in their lives, and how they see their future. Thus while for the general audience, the games could create awareness, for the attending youth, the intent was to inspire behavioural change. By showing youth viewers samples on how other youth have changed their lives by participating in RLabs trainings. The focus was in empowering them via inspirational means to actively think about their lives, and to take their own control and change if they felt so. Also, the intention of the games was to generate empathy, especially cognitive empathy. Cognitive empathy is about knowing how the other feels like [Pete14]. By playing the games and seeing the images and stories in them, the youth's aim was for the audience to start feeling how joblessness life in Havana really is.

3.2   Game Development

Developing the *Havana and Training Game* included several phases. First, the youth planned the game and chose the problems that were going to be depicted. Then the development group conducted a field walk in Havana to take photos to use in the game. Then the youth designed the texts for the game, and lastly the IT students finalized the programming of it.

3.3   Game Description

Both games, *Havana Game* and *Training Game*, have the same basic idea and logic behind. They consisted of one large image on a digital screen, which was covered with a black layer, and accompanied with six smaller images below it as thumbnails. The player of the game could take a look at the hidden picture only via a small existing hole. Such holes were moved with a cursor or, when using a mobile device, with one finger. The idea was that the player could only see a small part of the picture at a time. When the player clicks some of the thumbnails below a pop-up window opens with that picture and a text.

In the *Training Game* the large image presents the youth before they started to participate in RLabs trainings: bored and with no hope or meaning for life (black and white pictures), while the six smaller thumbnails introduce people who have taken part in RLabs training (joyful colour pictures). When the player clicked on one of the thumbnails, the story behind the person appeared with an explanation of how the training has contributed to change their lives.

Fig. 1: Training game (left and middle) and Havana Canvas Collage (right)

In the *Havana Game* the big picture on top showcases the current state of Havana with its challenges such as improper road system, poor sanitation, poor water supply, improper shack houses, no recreational facilities for the kids and inadequate community centre. The thumbnails underneath included the youth's future scenario of the area, where problems were now being solved. When clicking individual pictures, a pop-up window opened with an image of the solution and a small text explaining how the enhancement was done.

4   Race Game

The Race Game was adapted from the Animal Race app mentioned above. The aim was to physically engage event visitors into feeling the youth's efforts of leaving a desperate life behind.

4.1   Design Intention

The idea behind this game relates to the Havana project and its aim in empowering unemployed youth to get employed [Wins15]. It underlines the importance to support others in the same community in order to be successful all together in the spirit of Ubuntu. The start line in the race represented the situation before the youth got jobs, including themes of poverty and poor living standards. In turn, the finish line represented the dream situation in Havana after youth have worked hard, got employed, and as such improved their living standards. Engaging visitors in a way that could make them relate to the youth's plight was crucial. Thus, the following design values were identified: empathy, entertainment, teamwork and physical activity.

Empathy

The exhibition made use of posters and presentations from the youth so as to make visitors understand their feelings and, perhaps, to think of ways to assist in empowering them.

Entertainment

To ensure the environment was conducive for interaction between the unemployed youth and visitors, the mood had to be lightened-up. The race game provided a relaxed atmosphere that allowed the youth to mingle freely and "race together" with visitors, thereby increasing the chances of continuing the interaction after playing the game.

Teamwork
The game allowed for more than one person to choose the same racing character at a time. This lead to players participating as a team and not as individuals, thereby fostering a semblance of communal teamwork.

Physical activity
The Race Game involved shaking a mobile device to move a character towards the finishing line. The researchers and the youth agreed that this was the best way to mimic the hard work that an individual carries out to realize their goals in life. The pain and fatigue from shaking one's arm for approximately one minute (the time it approximately takes to complete the race) was to represent the trials and tribulations youths go through on a day-to-day basis as they work to achieve their goals.

4.2   Game Development
The original racing game used animals as avatars for the racing characters. Youth and researchers discussed which ones would be the most appropriate avatars to use in the game in place of the default animal avatars. It was agreed to make use of human avatars, as these would easily and readily represent participants. Four different avatars were chosen to represent the diverse youth with diverse talents who are found in the community. The avatars racing against each other helped show the differences in each player's strength and also the difference in the paths they choose in life, as represented by the race tracks in the game which had different colour schemes.

Fig. 2: Visitors play and evaluate the game at the Youth for Youth Day.

4.3   Game Description

The *Racing Game* had four avatars displayed on a web browser of any computer (main screen). These avatars have a coloured track designated to each of them. Each player could choose an avatar by pressing a button on the browser of their mobile phone. Each of the buttons had a colour that corresponded to the track colours on the main screen. The game was initiated and played by shaking a connected mobile phone via Bluetooth, and the chosen avatar moved at the rate at which the player shook his phone. The player who crossed the finishing line first was declared a winner. On conclusion of the race, four more players could use their mobile devices to play against each other. Youth and researchers set up the venue of the game to have the same appearance as the game and they added the race tracks on the floor of the venue with the same colour as the tracks in the game. These tracks would guide visitors to the main game staging area. In addition to the race tracks, there were also posters on the walls, which allowed visitors to get information on the aim of the exhibit in that venue.

The first poster was near the entrance and depicted a starting line. This poster showcased the challenges the youth in Havana currently faced e.g. lack of employment, poor living conditions and lack of education facilities.

The second poster "Shaking mobile phone" was aimed at emphasizing the importance of hard work and teamwork, which was an underlying theme in the Havana project. This poster consisted of several texts and pictures from the Havana project. The aforementioned content described the aim of the Havana project, the work that had been done during the project, and future hopes on a general level.

A third and final poster, Finish Line, represented a situation whereby all the goals had been achieved. There were three people standing on a rostrum together on the poster. That symbolized achieving goals as a team - not as an individual. In addition, the poster presented two youth members from the group who answered a question "What's your goal?"

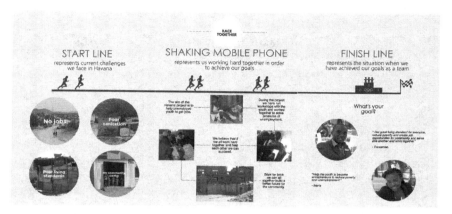

Fig. 3: The final versions of the posters Start line, Shaking mobile phone, Finish line

Right next to the third poster was the board that offered an opportunity to the visitors to write down their own goals using Post-It™ notes. All the Post-It™ were visible to the others and were included as part of the exhibition. The purpose of this was to increase feelings of empathy. Since the third poster presented youth's goals, it aimed to bring the same question close to visitors' own lives. Eventually visitors came to the game area and were enticed to play the Race Game. Youth and the developers assisted visitors to connect their mobile phones to the game. Each game required two to four players. After visitors had played the game, they were given medals with QR codes leading to the RLabs' website.

Our initial idea was to change game mechanics so that succeeding in the game would require teamwork with other players. However, due to technical difficulties it was not realised.

4.4   Game evaluation

The medals created and handed out to participants in the race served several purposes: Firstly, they were mementos that participants could keep as reminders of their participation in the *Youth for Youth* day-event. Secondly, they had a QR Code that contained a link to the RLabs Namibia homepage. This link was linked to a Google analytics account to enable the tracking of all redirections to the website that occurred as a result of the use of the QR Code. Thirdly, the total number of medals printed was known, as it also was the remaining medals after the race. This enabled us to have an exact number of

individuals who had taken part in the race. As a result, tracking the percentage of people who accessed the site via the QR Code was simplified, as
we basically had to count the number of hits from Google analytics vs. the
number of medals awarded.

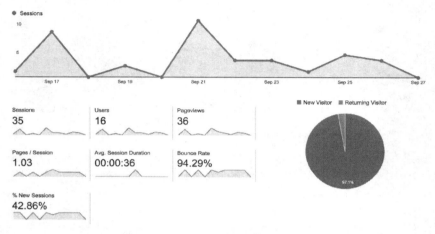

Fig. 4: Analytics performed upon the Racing Game

5   Reflection

5.1   Game changing design

Game design has presented an opportunity to innovatively address the issue
of youth unemployment in Namibia. Therefore, we argue that co-designing
games with the youth enables them to organically participate in design
processes, thus in providing of an input to the design of games that, moreover, can hold cultural values. Since we work in locales where the epistemic
spirit is based upon "Ubuntu", we expect collaborative aims and ways of
working. The outcome of the collaborative game co-design process presented
in this paper was thus compounded of a number of games reflecting inputs
of all participants' contributions to creating public awareness to the issues of
unemployment. The aim of creating public awareness was to create empathy
and self-reflection, especially from the public's point of view. Empathy for
self-realisation of both young and not, poor and not, as well as for working

together to achieve better outcomes that alleviates youth unemployment in Namibia or its effects. Funders approached us and the youth after the event to support long term collaborations in uplifting marginalised youth, thus we conclude that the interactive exhibition was successful.

5.2   The Control Game

Throughout the design process, the researchers/facilitators of the workshops had been exercising control and laisser faire. While at the beginning the facilitators have been passive in the ideation phase, later on measures were taken to ensure the event consisted of interactive technologies as showcases. At all times the facilitation was a delicate act of infusion and withdrawal. While the local youth is generally lacking exposure to innovative designs, their ideas are equally constrained. Thus, it was the facilitators' role to infuse innovative ideas yet without prescribing solutions. However, once the groups engaged in telling the Havana youth story, the youth become more active.

5.3   A Learning Game

Following a PD approach with the Namibian youth has been fruitful, although at the beginning, researchers had to step in and encourage the youth with gaining confidence and ideas beyond the ordinary. Once the youth had been provided with exemplified tools, they were able to spark their own creativity by the thinking of tools and methods that could engage the wider society in the issues that they faced. The event preparation process allowed the youth to work together, explore different techniques and come up with a plan of action. The youth did not only learn how to work in a team, but also learnt how to explore new ideas and how to digitally represent themselves. The youth deliberated on the different activities, which were presented by the different groups into which they were divided. After the deliberations, the youth were able to choose the activities that they felt were representing them and sending the right message to their audience. They also learned a lot from the other participants who had other abilities and talents in the preparations workshops such as dancing and playing instruments.

6   Conclusion

This paper has presented two interactive digital games re-designed by, and towards achieving game changing conditions for Namibia's extensively unemployed youth. The youth's message was elegantly weaved in the interactive games with the purpose of creating public awareness about their desperate living conditions, as well as their collaborative intent of changing all affected youth's livelihood situation. The youth learned new skills throughout the participatory design sessions. We learnt that collaborating with the youth needed an external technology idea inspiration as a starting point for a joint creative design.

7   Acknowledgments

We would like to thank all the participants and students for their commitment and contributions to this research. We would also like to thank the ELCIN leadership in Havana for allowing us to use their premises as well as RLabs. This research was also made possible under a bilateral grant awarded by NCRST, as well as the student exchange funded under the UFISA project.

8   References

[Aria00]   Arias, E., Eden, H., Fischer, G., Gorman, A., & Scharff, E. (2000). Transcending the individual human mind—creating shared understanding through collaborative design. ACM Transactions on Computer-Human Interaction (TOCHI), 7(1), pp. 84–113

[Giac08]   Giaccardi, E., & Fischer, G. (2008). Creativity and evolution: a metadesign perspective. Digital Creativity, 19(1), pp. 19–32

[Ongw14] Ongwere, T., Winschiers-Theophilus, H., Iipito H, & Chivuno-Kuria, S. (2014). Youth empowering the youth through participatory service design, Proceeding of Design, Development and Research (DDR) 2014 international conference. Cape Town, South Africa.

[Pete14]   Peters, D. & Calvo, R. (2014). Compassion vs. Empathy: Designing for Resilience. Interactions, 21 (5), pp. 48–53.

[Roge13]   Rogers, Y., Marsden, G., (2013), Does he take Sugar? Interactions, July & August

[Siec15a]   Sieck, J. (2015). Information and Communication Technology in Culture and Creative Industries. In EVA 2015, Saint Petersburg, pp. 31–33.

[Siec15b]   Sieck, J., & Wündisch, D. (2015). Collaborative Interactions on Media Facades. Electronic Imaging & the Visual Arts. EVA 2015 Florence: 13–14 May 2015, p. 49.

[Wins15]   Winschiers-Theophilus, H., Keskinen, P., Cabrero, D., Angula, S., Ongwere, T., Mendonca, H., Ngolo, R. & Chivuno-Kuria, S. (2015). ICTD within the Discourse of a Locally Situated Interaction: The Potential of Youth Engagement. In 9th IDIA conference, Zanzibar, Tanzania, November 2015.

Movable Books As Animated Machines

Creating 3D-Models of Historical Children's Books

Marius Hug

Staatsbibliothek zu Berlin – Preußischer Kulturbesitz

Marius.Hug@sbb.spk-berlin.de

http://www.sbb.berlin/beweb3d/

Abstract

The project BeWeB-3D[1] deals with specific paper-made objects: movable or pop-up books. It aims at designing a computer-made model of 19th century paper-engineered objects, which facilitates interaction. Contrary to ordinary books these objects contain what you could call an interface. Therefore, interaction is a main goal of our 3D realization. BeWeB-3D was launched in February 2017. It is located at Staatsbibliothek zu Berlin (Berlin State Library) and funded by Germany's Federal Ministry of Education and Research (BMBF).[2] Aside from theoretical questions the technological part of the project is a challenging task. This is particularly so for the following (four) reasons. 1) Our average scientific user demands a low-threshold handling which asks for at least a plug-in free solution. 2) The quality of the original invites to reflect on how to live up to this standard best. 3) The implementation as a dynamical 3D model necessitates the use of game-engines like Unity. 4) The research context requires sustainability, long-term preservation and an open international standard.

---

1   http://www.sbb.berlin/beweb3d/.
2   https://www.bmbf.de/foerderungen/bekanntmachung-1197.html.

1   Movable books – Frontend

Thinking about the digitization of cultural objects – following the theoretical concept of the material turn[3] and especially the BMBF announcement entitled "eHeritage" from June 15, 2016[4] – one has in mind a wide range of objects from museums, collections and archives etc. rather than books. There is a long tradition of referring to books as two-dimensional objects resp. texts. Putting it differently: Making a book for a long time meant reducing any content – be it speech or any other subject – to the two dimensions of a page, usually made of paper.

The present project deals with paper-objects, too. However, these objects serve a third dimension. Pop-up books or movable books (see fig. 1) contain what you could call an interface. Whereas one can talk of interaction between the reader and the object as early as reading is concerned – reading a multi-paged book makes necessary the turning of pages[5] – the objects of our project are rather machines than books.

Fig. 1: What you see is the different states of the movement of an animated paper lion triggered by the reader, who is pulling a strip of paper. Source: Meggendorfer, Lothar. Nah und Fern: ein Tierbilderbuch zum Ziehen. München: Braun & Schneider, 1887.

One the one hand machines are machines as long as they are working, or to put it more generally: Movement is an essential requirement for any machine. On the other hand they are black-boxes:[6] Something goes in, something comes out, what exactly happens in between, how exactly they are *working* remains unknown. As this cybernetical concept leaves behind quite a lot of

---

3   See e.g. Hicks (2010).
4   Richtlinie zur Förderung von Forschungs- und Entwicklungsvorhaben zur Digitalisierung von Objekten des kulturellen Erbes (Guidelines for the Promotion of Scientific and Development Projects for the Digitization of Objects of Cultural Heritage), available at https://www.bmbf.de/foerderungen/bekanntmachung-1197.html.
5   Cf. Schulz (2015). This technique has to be referred to as historical, as the codex obviously has a predecessor without the need of page turning, the scroll.
6   Cf. Ashby (1956), pp. 86-117.

subjects in an unhappy state, the wish to whiten these black boxes or to open them in order to find out what is going on inside, is quite comprehensible.[7] The movable books in our project allow for both of these requests. We are modeling animated 19th century paper-engineered objects. The aim of the project is not a digitized 3D-book but a computer-made model, which enables interaction. A central requirement for reconstructions is the "simulation of their functionality".[8] The human actor has to be put in a position to trigger the movement of the model. Furthermore we are aiming at giving the visitor the chance of catching a glimpse of the inward parts of the model using computed tomography scanners. So, whereas the trigger point is as trivial as pulling a strip of paper, the impact of this action is rather complex.

2   Movable books – Backend

Opening the black-box reveals the mechanism behind (see fig. 2). Whereas the reader just pulls one strip of paper, he activates a fairly complex stage-setting, controlled by ribbons and joints. In the 1880s and 90s the German illustrator Lothar Meggendorfer became one the most famous actors within this discipline worldwide. Referring to Carola Pohlmann, head of the department of literature for children and young people at Berlin State Library, one of the most striking characteristics of Lothar Meggendorfer is his satirical sight towards the world of adults. During a time of pedagogical papers for courteous children, he is making fun of grown-ups in the presence of kids.[9] His handmade children's books with sophisticated fold-up, pulling and transforming mechanisms enjoyed great popularity.[10] Some of them were sold in various editions of up to 10.000 copies. Today, due to their purpose of being toys to play with[11] they are a rare find and therefore very costly to acquire.

As clearly defined our project is referring to its materiality, the conceptual outcome is to remain as open as possible. Therefore, the project aims at deve-

---

7   See e.g. Kassung/Kümmel-Schnur (2008).
8   Kümmel-Schnur (2010), p. 364.
9   Pohlmann (2000), p. 9.
10 Bachmann (2016), p. 11.
11 Peter Goßens points to the interconnection between play and the dissemination of knowledge within the hybrid-medium movable book. See Goßens (2016), p. 61.

loping a *generic concept*,[12] which shall be the foundation for other ventures, likewise dealing with movable parts made out of paper.[13]

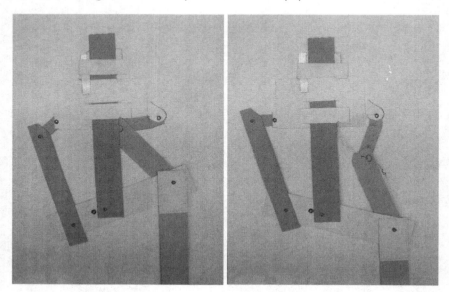

Fig. 2: Two stages of the mechanism of a movable book. Source: Meggendorfer, Lothar. Lustiges Automaten-Theater: ein Ziehbilderbuch. Eßlingen: Schreiber, 1890.

At any point one has to keep focusing on the research which is to be affiliated to the gained realization. Therefore, what is an adequate implementation of the human-machine interaction as far as virtual movable books are concerned? What role do they play in the context of animated objects of the 19th century in general?[14] To what extent one has to regard malfunctioning as something to be implemented in a digitized version of such objects? What are implications of the binary functioning of toy books – e.g. to the question of what is movement – referring to the fact that they often do have two privileged states in which the model remains? What impact, if any, does the industrialization have on the making of animated toy books considering that all movable books up to the present contain handmade parts? Or the other way

12   http://blog.sbb.berlin/beweb-3d/.

13   Surprisingly the history of making books is full of examples. The earliest proven book, the Chronica Majora, dates back to the first half of the 13th century and was a teaching tool for adults by the monk Matthew Paris (http://www.bl.uk/manuscripts/Viewer. aspx?ref=royal_ms_14_c_vii_f157r).

14   The phenakistiscope, zoetrope, thaumatrope, praxinoscope, mutoscope all are instruments of animated motion of the 19th century.

round: What impact does this handmade character have on the digitization of the objects? Finally, what are the conditions of possibility of making movable books a component of – 19th as well as 20th and 21st century – playrooms?

3   The technology behind BeWeB-3D

The project aims at modeling a representative quantity of what one could call animated paper-engineered toy books.[15] The technological side of the project is realized by the Berlin-based Center for Digital Cultural Heritage in Museums (ZEDIKUM).[16] Here we are challenged in different respects:

1. Our average scientific user demands a low-threshold handling which asks for at least a plug-in free solution, e.g. browser technologies based on WebGL.
2. The outstanding haptic quality of the analogue original invites to reflect on how to live up to this standard best.[17]
3. The implementation as dynamical 3D model may necessitate the usage of game-engines like Unity or Blender.[18]
4. The research context requires sustainability, long-term preservation and an open international standard, e.g. CIDOC-CRM[19], which guarantees interoperability as well.[20]

Due to the complexity of our objects – they are books made of pages including text and illustrations and as such quite ordinary elements of library catalogues, but they are animated objects as well, which as far as a digitized presentation is concerned call for an advanced 3D-solution – a systematic proceeding is stringently required. Therefore, one of the first working steps was to categorize the different types of movable books according to the level of interaction: Some of them contain, as mentioned above, strips of paper to

---

15   The English but mainly the German language has some difficulties in finding a precise denomination, particularly as there are about 25 different types, gradually incremented concerning the degree of interactivity.
16   http://www.zedikum.de/.
17   At beginning of the project one conceivable solution aims at a mixed reality implementation.
18   https://unity3d.com/de resp. https://www.blender.org/.
19   Conceptual Reference Model (CIDOC-CRM, ISO 21127), http://www.cidoc-crm.org/.
20   The new DFG guidelines give some suggestions as far as 3D objects are concerned, cf. http://www.dfg.de/formulare/12_151/12_151_de.pdf, p. 26ff.

pull at, others contain volvelles, which one can turn, another type includes flaps which can be folded out and so on.

ZEDIKUM is specialized on 3D-digitization of cultural heritage, for instance using the Structure from Motion technology (SfM). But as this treatment is rather costly and time-consuming and not all of our movable books contain a spatial third dimension it is necessary to reassess which of the objects require this procedure.

Whether advanced 3D-digitization technologies or rather ordinary flatware-scanning will be deployed, the crucial point is the presentation of the data, as a requirement for the desired interactive animation. In this respect the approach of Technische Universität Braunschweig (Technical University of Brunswick) is insufficient.[21] Aiming at digitized versions of their movable children's books, they merely produced short videos in which the movement can be seen. Interactivity then is limited to starting and stopping the video. From a technical point of view Ellen Rubin presents an only slightly advanced solution:[22] By a simple javascript-based mouse-over effect, the reader is actually capable of interactively controlling the movement with his mouse. This is very basic but takes the right direction. One could obviously think of an extension for the mouse, which takes the reader closer to the original pull-movement.

The present project aims at figuring out a technical solution working on multiple stages. We will have to serve the reader, for whom browser-based consumption is kind of cutting edge technology. But obviously we are aware of Augmented Reality solutions and see in it a huge potential for making our objects accessible, be it a tablet-based implementation as provided by tiger-books[23] or a realization working with head-worn displays. The decisions as to which is the proper execution will have to be made on a case-by-case basis. There are movable books which make a 3D-digitization absolutely necessary and which are begging for a virtual reality environment to approach them, for instance the so called peep-shows, which have been a very popular amuse-ment device in the first half of the 19th century.

Last but not least and coming back to movable books as objects for research: One species of the so called movable books is literally realized as playable picture books. The book itself serves as a kind of stage and added to this one

---

21   See https://publikationsserver.tu-braunschweig.de/content/collections/videos_picture_
       books.xml.
22   See http://popuplady.com/mm-main.shtml.
23   https://www.tigerbooks.de/.

gets a couple of little paper-made figures. This toy asks for ever new settings. On the one hand one can literally imagine types of movable book within a VR-environment. On the other hand the project aims at implementing a decent annotation solution in order to make these changing stills citable, too.

4   Conclusion

Movable (children's) books are – 130 years after they flourished for the first time at the end of the 19th century – still very captivating objects. On the one hand they quite obviously have not lost their fascination being a well-established item of many nowadays children's rooms. On the other hand they help to raise questions about best-practices for digitizing specific media. At this their call for interactivity is mostly inherited:

Now Children, dear, pray come with me
And see some comic sights,
You all will laugh with mirth and glee,
Or should do so by rights.

When you to them your hand apply
These figures dance and caper
"Tis really" hard I hear you cry
"To think them only paper."

The men and creatures here you find
Are lively and amusing,
Your fingers must be slow and kind
And treat them well while using.

But more of them we must not tell,
The pictures would be jealous,
So turn the leaves and use them well
And don't be over zealous.[24]

---

24   Cf. Meggendorfer, Lothar. Comic Actors: A New Movable Toybook. London: H. Grevel & Co., 1895, which is the English translation of the German 1st edition: Meggendorfer, Lothar. Lustiges Automaten-Theater: ein Ziehbilderbuch. Eßlingen: Schreiber, 1890.

Literature

[Ashb56]   Ashby, W. Ross (1956): An introduction to cybernetics, London: Chapman & Hall.

[Bach16]   Bachmann, Christian A., Laura Emans and Monika Schmitz-Emans (2016): Pop-up-Bücher und Movable Books. Vorbemerkungen zu den Gegenständen des vorliegenden Buches. In: Bachmann, Christian A., Laura Emans and Monika Schmitz-Emans (ed.): Bewegungsbücher. Spielformen, Poetiken, Konstellationen. Berlin: Ch. A. Bachmann Verlag, pp. 7–18.

[Goße16]   Goßens, Peter (2016): Kinetik und Bildlichkeit um 1900. In: Bachmann, Christian A., Laura Emans and Monika Schmitz-Emans (ed.): Bewegungsbücher. Spielformen, Poetiken, Konstellationen. Berlin: Ch. A. Bachmann Verlag, pp. 53–84.

[Hick10]   [Hick10] Hicks, Dan (2010): The Material-Cultural Turn: event and effect. In: Dan Hicks and Mary C. Beaudry (ed.): The Oxford Handbook of Material Culture Studies. Oxford: Oxford University Press, pp. 25–29.

[Kass08]   Kassung, Christian, und Albert Kümmel-Schnur (2008): Wissensgeschichte als Malerarbeit? Ein Trialog über das weißeln schwarzer Kisten. In: Georg Kneer, Markus Schroer, und Erhard Schüttpelz (ed.): Bruno Latours Kollektive. Kontroversen zur Entgrenzung des Sozialen. Frankfurt a. M.: Suhrkamp, pp. 155–79.

[Kuem10]   Kümmel-Schnur, Albert (2010): Vom Nutzen und Nachteil der Simulation. CAD-Rekonstruktionen historischer Apparate. In: Albert Kümmel-Schnur and Christian Kassung (ed.): Bildtelegraphie: Eine Mediengeschichte in Patenten (1840-1930). Bielefeld: Transcript, pp. 323–70.

[Math16]   Mathieu, Christian (2016): BeWeB-3D – Bewegungsbücher und dynamische Buchobjekte digital". SBB Aktuell, 9 November 2016. http://blog.sbb.berlin/beweb-3d/.

[Megg87]   Meggendorfer, Lothar (1887): Nah und Fern: ein Tierbilderbuch zum Ziehen. München: Braun & Schneider.

[Megg90]   Meggendorfer, Lothar (1890): Lustiges Automaten-Theater: ein Ziehbilderbuch. Eßlingen: Schreiber.

[Megg95]   Meggendorfer, Lothar (1895): Comic Actors: A New Movable Toybook. London: H. Grevel & Co.

[Pohl00]   Pohlmann, Carola (2000): „Nur Für Brave Kinder". Spiel- und Verwandlungsbücher im 19. Jahrhundert. Online available: http://webdoc.sub.gwdg.de/ebook/aw/2000/sdd_vortrag/Vortrag_pohlmann.pdf.

[Schu15]   Schulz, Christoph Benjamin (2015): Poetiken des Blätterns. Georg Olms Verlag.

Using the Power of the Web in Mixed Reality

Claudia Müller-Birn, Guangtao Zhang

Institute for Computer Science

Freie Universität Berlin

{clmb, zhang@fu-berlin.de}

Abstract

Computers and networks have become increasingly ubiquitous over the past decade, and the distinction between the physical and the digital has become blurred. Mixed reality applications have reached a level of maturity that makes them attractive for many settings in the cultural context. Two further advances have accompanied this development. First, the Web 2.0, the Social Web, has allowed people to actively participate in the creation of web content. Second, the Web 3.0, the Semantic Web, has emerged to make it easier for machines to use and exchange data on the web. A similar development can be found in the museum context. Semantic web technologies and linked data are used increasingly to describe cultural and scientific information. Citizen science projects allow people to contribute to research at a museum actively. By bringing both together, we can imagine applications that evolve from the research practice into the visitor's room of a museum to engage visitors even more. We introduce examples how linked data can be used in mixed reality applications and look into the future regarding how we can use the power of the Web fully by enabling a more coupled relationship between humans and machines.

1   Bringing Mixed Reality in the Web

Mixed reality refers to a blend of physical and digital elements. Milgram and Kishino (1994) define the term in their seminal paper as a continuum extending from real environments – over Augmented Reality and Augmented Virtuality - to virtual environments at the other end of the continuum. Augmented Reality (AR) refers to a live view of the real environment augmented by virtual objects, and it can assume different forms. Tangible AR, for example, combines the enhanced display possibilities of AR with the intuitive manipulation and interaction of physical objects. Each virtual object connects to a physical object. Thus the user interacts with virtual objects by manipulating the corresponding tangible objects (Billinghurst, 2008). In see-through AR, optical head-mounted displays such as Microsoft's HoloLens are used for augmenting the real environment (Toyama et al. 2014). Spatial AR refers to a fixed setting, where virtual objects are integrated directly into a user's environment, not simply in their visual field (Benko et al., 2014). In Augmented Virtuality (AV) real world elements merge into the virtual environment. For example, research shows how users can see and use their hands when interacting with objects in the virtual environment (Tecchia et al., 2014). Thus, various approaches exist to realize mixed reality applications, from head-mounted displays to handheld/desktop displays or projection displays. Especially smart phones and their improved technical capabilities allowed to release mixed reality applications that had previously were confined to research laboratories. It made this technology very attractive for Galleries, Libraries, Archives, and Museums (GLAMS), as seen by Google's "Arts & Culture" project that allows people around the world to explore collections such as the Museum für Naturkundemuseum Berlin in 3D or by using Google's Cardboard. Furthermore, in museum's exhibition information on objects are extended with background information related to the exhibit. Compared to traditional dioramas in museum exhibitions, multimodal mixed reality technology generates a diorama scene, which is constructed a pairing related image or video materials with real exhibits (Tanikawa et al., 2013). However, independently from the used display, current developments mainly focus on individual, highly specialized applications. The question is, how this might change, because of WebVR bringing VR into the browser. The idea is that people can mix traditional web content with augmented or virtual reality content. One of the first projects, the Argon project, developed a Javascript framework to allow developers and designers to create augmented reality applications based on standard web technologies (e.g., HTML, CSS) that can be hosted on any web server. More recently, Mozilla's A-Frame is an open-source framework for allowing web developers to include virtual reality elements within HTML. It allows for desktop- or mobile-based experiences by either head-mounted displays or Google's Cardboard. The next consequent step is to integrate existing mixed reality applications more tightly with the capabilities the web offers today, namely with the social semantic web which is briefly introduced as follows.

2 Augmenting Mixed Reality by the Social Semantic Web

The Web 2.0, the Social Web, has allowed people to experience new forms of interaction, communication, and collaboration (O'Reilly, 2005). People create value by writing articles on Wikipedia, tagging shared photos on Flickr, or providing facts in Wikidata. At the same time, web applications offer APIs and allow that information from different information sources, i.e. web applications, can be combined. Schmalstieg and colleagues refer to the combination of Web 2.0 and Augmented Reality as "Augmented 2.0" (Schmalstieg et al., 2011). They envision mobile AR applications to be deployed on a global scale and used by hundreds of thousands of people at the same time. The Web 3.0, the Semantic Web, provides the meaning to data so that the web's content can be used and exchanged by machines and humans alike (Berners-Lee et al. 2001). The Linked Open Data approach enabled publishing machineunderstandable resources on the Web. Furthermore, using ontologies enables not only the interoperability of data from different information resources but also allows for reasoning over data from various resources in order to derive new information. As stated, mixed reality applications are typically made for one particular area using one predefined data set. The Semantic Web allows accessing various public data sets from different disciplines based on linked data or integrating heterogeneous data using ontologies. Thus, we can imagine that Linked Open Data can augment existing mixed reality applications by additional contextual information. For example, van Aart et al. introduce a mobile cultural heritage guide by providing tourists with location-based information about the current environment (e.g., events, artworks or persons) that are also based on Linked Open Data sources (van Aart et al., 2010). Instead of only relying on GPS data, linked data can be used to extend information provided on points of interest by additional data upon request. Nixon et al. present an application that is capable of displaying additional information, for example about an artist, on posters that advertise concerts and clubs on the street (Nixon et al., 2012). More recently researchers have emphasized that both trends can complement each other, the collective intelligence of the Social Web can augment the machine intelligence provided by semantic technologies. That builds upon Douglas Engelbart's vision of human-machine systems, in which both humans and machines collaborate by each doing what they do best (Engelbart, 1962). In the so-called Social Semantic Web, people are producers and consumers at the same time, and they are the source of knowledge, whereas machines are the enablers, who aggregate and recombine data in a meaningful way (Gruber, 2008). Cultural context are exposed to a similar development. Semantic web technologies and linked data are increasingly used to describe cultural and scientific information. Citizen science projects allow people to contribute to research at a museum actively. By bringing both together, we can imagine applications that evolve from the research practice into the visitor's room of a museum to engage visitors even more.

References

Benko, H., Wilson, A. D., & Zannier, F. (2014). Dyadic projected spatial augmented reality. In Proc. of the ACM Symposium on User Interface Software and Technology, pp. 645–655.

Berners-Lee, T., Hendler, J., & Lassila, O. (2001). The semantic web. Scientific american, 284(5), pp. 28–37.

Billinghurst, M., Kato, H., & Poupyrev, I. (2008). Tangible augmented reality. ACM SIGGRAPH ASIA, 7.

Engelbart, D. C. (2001). Augmenting human intellect: a conceptual framework (1962). PACKER, Randall and JORDAN, Ken. Multimedia. From Wagner to Virtual Reality. New York: WW Norton & Company, pp. 64–90.

Gruber, T. (2008). Collective knowledge systems: Where the Social Web meets the Semantic Web. Web Semantics: Science, Services and Agents on the World Wide Web, 6(1), pp. 4–13.

Milgram, P., & Kishino, F. (1994). A taxonomy of mixed reality visual displays. IEICE Transactions on Information Systems, 77(12), pp. 1321–1329.

Nixon, L. J., Grubert, J., Reitmayr, G., & Scicluna, J. (2012). SmartReality: Integrating the Web into Augmented Reality. In Proc. of I-SEMAN-TICS, pp. 48–54.

O'Reilly, T. What is Web 2.0: Design Patterns and Business Models for the Next Generation of Software. 30 September 2005. Available from: http://www.oreillynet.com/lpt/a/6228 (accessed 10 February 2017).

Schmalstieg, D., Langlotz, T. & Billinghurst, M. (2011). Augmented Reality 2.0. In: Brunnett, G., Coquillart, S., Welch, G. (eds.) Virtual Realities. Springer Vienna, pp. 13–37.

Tanikawa, T., Narumi, T., & Hirose, M. (2013). Mixed reality digital museum project. In International Conference on Human Interface and the Management of Information, pp. 248–257.

Tecchia, F., Avveduto, G., Brondi, R., Carrozzino, M., Bergamasco, M., & Alem, L. (2014). I'm in VR!: using your own hands in a fully immersive MR system. In Proc. of the ACM Symposium on Virtual Reality Software and Technology, pp. 73–76.

Toyama, T., Sonntag, D., Dengel, A., Matsuda, T., Iwamura, M., & Kise, K. (2014). A mixed reality head-mounted text translation system using eye gaze input. In Proc. of International Conference on Intelligent User Interfaces, pp. 329–334.

van Aart, C., Wielinga, B. & van Hage, W.R. (2010). Mobile Cultural Heritage Guide: Location-Aware Semantic Search. In: Cimiano, P., Pinto, H.S. (eds) Knowledge Engineering and Management by the Masses. EKAW 2010. Lecture Notes in Computer Science, vol 6317. Springer, Berlin, Heidelberg.

ColourMirror
Visitors Identifying with Museum Exhibits in a Playful Way

Zsófia Ruttkay

TechLab

Moholy-Nagy University of Art and Design

Budapest, Hungary

ruttkay@mome.hu

Abstract

Museums constitute a new terrain for digital technologies, presenting additional challenges for research and application in computer science. Here follows an account of our ColourMirror, a multi-functional digital installation accompanying a museum exhibition in which objects have been arranged according to their colour. When a visitor stands in front of the mirror, the latter responds by showing that exhibit which matches his/her colours the most closely. Visitors may also explore different data visualizations and share their own mirror image, extended with the object they received. An empirical study of usage and visitor experience reveals that visitors enjoy the interaction, remember well and identify with the object they receive, and feel motivated by installations such as this one to visit an exhibition. We sum up major lessons and potential further applications.

1   Introduction

1.1   Museums in a time of change

Nowadays museums tend to exploit the potentials of digital technologies, both to provide novel ways of interpretation and experience to their visitors at the exhibitions, and to enhance their emanation and presence beyond the walls, both in the virtual and in the physical world. The motivations for giving place to interactive digital installations and facilities in an institution which, traditionally, maintained the image of the "temple" of cultural heritage preservation, are multiple:

   a) Inherently, museums must respond to the changes of society and shift more towards serving the needs of the local, national and international communities [Ande12]. Instead of consumers, they regard their *visitors as participants* [Simo12].

   b) The prevalence of the internet and of mobile phones has drastically changed the learning, socializing and leisure habits of the young generations [Jenk06]. In order not to lose them as potential visitors, museums must adapt both in their objectives and in the means they use to reach them.

   c) The digital technologies offer entirely new ways for the collection, restoration, presentation, study and interpretation of the tangible (and the intangible) heritage conserved in museums [Bény15].

1.2   Challenges in the application of digital technologies

From our point of view, the last of these perspectives is the most significant and challenging. The ongoing development of the enabling technologies (e.g. small and cheap sensors, powerful processors in mobile devices, the scaling of image processing, internet and wireless communication) open up entirely new domains of applications, also in cultural heritage preservation and dissemination. But in such a new field of application, the possible genres, the criteria of good design and success and the methods of evaluation all have to be established. This is especially difficult compared to traditional fields of application of computer science (such as banking or manufacturing) for the following reasons:

   a) The collection, the mission and the audience of museums are significantly different.

b) In the process of creating applications, there has to be a close collaboration and mutual understanding of each other's disciplines, working methods and values between museologists/curators and computer scientists/programmers, and this must be extended to other players (visual designers, museum educators, marketing experts), each with their own objectives.

c) Data collection and evaluation of digital installations is (still) rarely done due to a lack of resources and the short time-span of temporary exhibitions.

In our lab we have been developing a series of museum installations[1]. We have especially aimed at bringing out the most from the digital technologies to support the message of an exhibition, the goals of the museum and the – explicit or implicit – needs of the visitors.

In this article we give an account of one of our recent and most complex works for a museum. We introduce the context and explain the components and the working principle of our ColourMirror. We also report on an empirical study about usage and visitor experience. Finally, we sum up the major findings and sketch out further perspectives of application.

1.3   The context of ColourMiror

The ColourMirror is an interactive digital installation accompanying the exhibition "In the Mood for Colours" at the Museum of Applied Arts in Budapest[2]. This exhibition, based on an unusual curatorial concept, displays almost 400 artefacts (glass, ceramics, textiles, furniture) arranged according to their most dominant colour, in three rooms – Red, Green and Blue. The museum asked the interdisciplinary team of MOME TechLab[3] to create an engaging and playful installation which prepares visitors for the colour-centred exhibition.

After exploring different ideas which would allow visitors to experiment with RGB colours or to explore the linguistic expression and the emotional and symbolic connotations of colours, we settled with a transmedial interactive

---

1   For information and videos on a range of projects see our web site (http://create.mome.hu).
2   http://szintukor.imm.hu/en/
3   http://techlab.mome.hu

application which brings the exhibits into focus in a playful way, as a preparation for entering the exhibition. The ColourMirror is placed in a separate room, which visitors may pass through before entering the exhibition. In the corridor, a short bilingual text explains the installation. (There are no other written instructions, neither printed nor displayed.)

The installation consist of three units, at three sides of the room, serving three functions:
1. the main part is a *mirror-like interactive installation*, where the mirror responds to the visitor by displaying one of the exhibits;
2. on the side wall *animated data visualizations* may be observed on large displays;
3. just next to the exit on a touch-screen visitors may *send off an e-mail with their own "mirror image"* that also shows the object they received.

2   The ColourMirror: how does it work?

2.1   Detecting and scanning the visitor

In the dark room of the installation, there is a unit resembling a full-length dress mirror. Behind this semi-transparent mirror there stands a display of the same size, and at the bottom of the mirror there is a hidden Kinect camera. At first, the mirror shows a dazzling mixture of moving colours. When the visitor stands still in front of the mirror, (s)he is scanned by the camera. The few seconds of this scanning process is indicated visually in the mirror, after which there appears an exhibit in the upper right-hand corner of the mirror next to the silhouette of the visitor, which is filled with stripes representing proportionally the six dominant colours that result from an analysis of his/her captured silhouette image. A one-sentence bilingual explanation identifies the object as the one most similar in colours to those of the visitors (see Figure 1).

When a visitor enters, stands still or leaves, this is perceived by processing the amount of movement (the number of changing pixels) in a dedicated captured area in front of the mirror. The silhouette is extracted by depth analysis of the 3D image taken by the Kinect camera. The colour photo of the visitor is processed in a similar way as the object photos (see below).

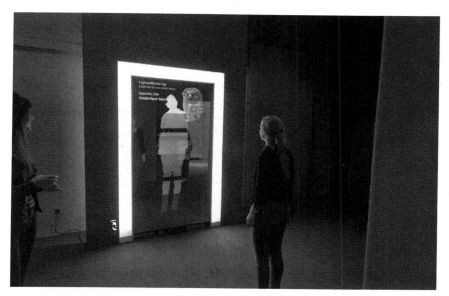

Fig. 1: A visitor in front of the ColourMirror.

2.2   Finding the best matching artefact

The visitor is offered that artefact from the collection of exhibits which matches the best his/her colours. The implicit DB query of the artefacts is based on pre-processed information regarding the colours of each artefact in the DB. For each object, there is also a good-quality photo available, in 3x8 bit colour representation and with removed background. In order to reduce the number of colours for fast query purposes, we reduced the number of colours for each object to six by standard colour quantization [Heck82]. In all computations, we used CIELab representation, which is more suited to model the human perception of colour similarity. For computing the similarity of individual colours, we used the CIE94 measure [Mokr11]. For each object, next to the full colour photo, we also stored the six reduced colours, and the percentage of the presence of each of these in the entire image. Hence a *colour palette*, consisting of six colours and six percentages, was obtained for each artefact, and stored in the DB. From the scanned image of the visitor, a colour palette was obtained each time, in the similar way.

The best match for the visitor's palette was obtained by the following steps:

1. The correspondence of the colour palette of the visitor and that of the
   k-th object was characterised by a number h_k for each of the objects in
   the database:
   a) Using the CIE94 measure, the colour distance c_{ij} of each of the 36
      pairs (6 in the visitor's paired with 6 in the object's palette) was
      taken.
   b) Indicating by p_i and p_j the percentages in the visitors and in the
      object's colour palette, respectively, a representative distance r_{ij} of
      the colour pairs was computed by taking into account the occur-
      rence of the two colours: $r_{ij} = c_{ij} * mint \ (p_i/p_j, \ p_j/p_i)$.
   c) Then, by taking into account the r_{ij} numbers for the 36 pairs of
      colours between the two palettes, we picked the "best match" –
      that is, the best pairing of the 6-6 colours – by using the Hungarian
      Method algorithm [Kuh55], which provided the number h_k.

2. From all the objects, the one with the lowest h_k value was selected as
   the best match and shown in full colour on the display of the mirror.

2.3 Data visualizations

On a large display, slightly animated data visualizations are shown in a loop,
allowing visitors to reflect on past scans in four different views, one after the
other:

1. In the *Catwalk*, the past ten scan results are shown, appearing in a
   2.5D catwalk presentation, where visitors' colour palette silhouettes
   walk alongside their corresponding object (see Figure 2).

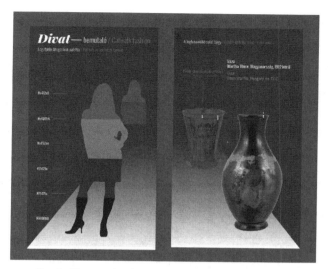

Fig. 2: The result of past scans in the Catwalk view.

2. In the *Calendar*, for the past 30 days all visitors' palettes can be seen in a matrix-like arrangement. This view gives an impression of the dominant colours of the clothes of visitors (see Figure 3).

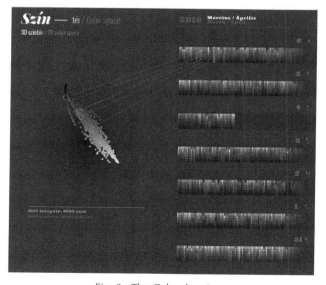

Fig. 3: The Calendar view.

3. In the *Statistics*, a visual impression of statistics of different colours in past periods is given.
4. In the *Extremes* view, the "most colourful" and the "most red/green/ blue" visitor's colour palette is shown in their silhouette, differentiating between adults and children by a guess based on the height of the scanned person (see Figure 4).

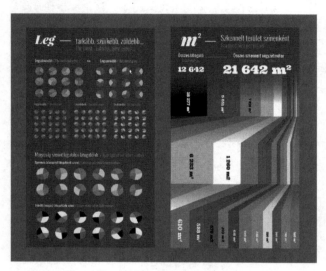

Fig. 4:   The Extremes view.

2.4   Sharing the received artefact

Before leaving the room, visitors pass by an interactive display showing the images taken most recently by the mirror. Here they could select their own mirror image and send it to themselves by email. (For this purpose, we installed wifi in the room.) We wanted to offer a simple and fast means to "take home" the mirror image, also as an alternative to the fashionable selfies that are often shot in museums. Moreover, the email contained more information than had been shown in the mirror, including a more detailed description of the selected object and the codes of the six colours in the visitor's palette. The visitor obtained the content of the email by activating a URL, and could also share the content with others via Facebook, Twitter or email by clicking on a button. About half of the visitors used this option. We found, however, that many of the images were spread further on Facebook.

3 The ColourMirror: How do visitors find it?

With novel – and usually rather expensive – digital installations it is very justified to ask whether the investment was worth the trouble. But how to grasp the "merit": based on feedback in the visitors' book (which is still in use)? In terms of the number of visitors? Or of the time spent with the installation? By the mood of the visitors during the interaction? Through some measure of what visitors really learnt, thanks to the installation? How should these aspects be aggregated? From the designers' perspective, the actual usage is of interest – which may differ from the assumed one. And one should remember that feedback from different people may differ based on static as well as time-based dynamic personal characteristics. We conducted a small-scale research, trying to incorporate several of the above aspects.

3.1 The empirical study

The major body of the research was carried out by means of recording observed behaviour, and through a short interview just after visitors had left the room with the ColourMirror. The data was collected during the winter months, in two-hour recording sessions both during the week and on weekends, by four data recorders who had received some initial training. The observer, sitting in a corner unnoticed like a museum guard, registered data on a tablet in a Google form, considering:

a) *the type and number of scans* (some people modified their dress, pose, formed groups);

b) *the emotions observed* (expressed by the face of the visitors, sometimes by their body language, and very often also verbally);

c) the amount of attention paid to the *data visualizations*;

d) whether they *emailed their mirror image*.

In the interview, the visitors were asked a few questions. The answers were registered by the interviewer in the same form, ticking on choices characteristic of the answers. Spontaneous additional remarks from visitors were typed in. The interview addressed, among others:

a) *recall* of the (first) received object;

b) *liking* for the received object;

c) whether the visitor would *track down* the object in the exhibition;

d) how they thought the *ColourMirror* worked;

e) in what way they *experienced* the ColourMirror installation;

f) what they thought of *digital installations* in museums, in general.

We collected data from 135 visitors. Their age group, nationality. gender and way of visit (single or in a couple, family or group) was also recorded. We also interviewed six museum guards who had been observing and helping visitors for months, by asking open-ended self-completed questions.

3.2 Major findings

Based on the collected empirical data (shown in Tables 1 and 2), we sum up the major conclusions around four general questions.

ASPECT	DISTINCT CATEGORIES with % proportions		
displayed emotion	happy	neutral	other
	72.6	17	10.4
recall of the received object	very good	satisfactory	false or none
	71.5	24.4	4.1
satisfaction with the object	pleased	neutral	unsatisfied
	72.6	20.2	7.3
would track down the object	for sure	perhaps	not
	81	10.7	9.3

Table 1: Summary of visitors' data concerning the Colour Mirror and the object shown.

QUESTION	ANSWERS with % proportions		
How does the Colour Mirror work, in principle?	proper answer	approximate	false/no idea
	33.3	36.7	30
How do you characterise the Colour Mirror?	great, funny	modern	for youngsters
	80.6	27.3	6.5
What do you think of digital installations in museums?	motivates to visit	do not care	dislike the idea
	77.6	18.4	0.4

Table 2: Summary of visitors' opinion concerning the Colour Mirror and digital installations in museums.

How did people use the ColourMirror?

1. About half of the visitors observed did not know what to do in the room, so they asked for assistance from a guard (one was always present in the room). From accounts by the guards, even more people needed some amount of help. Children and young people, on the other hand, had hardly any difficulty and they were the ones to experiment with several scans. Also foreign tourists, who were less hurried and had read the description outside, were more at ease, in general, than Hungarian visitors. It turned out that it was here that many of the subjects met an interactive museum installation for the first time in their life, and some regarded the Mirror as an exhibit to be watched but not to be used. People over 60 complained several times about lack of detailed written instructions on what to do, and about fear of becoming awkward in public with such an installation.

2. As to the technicalities of the usage and enjoyment, children and teenagers were at ease and kept experimenting (e.g. by changing their dress or forming groups), while people above 60 often needed assistance.

3. The data visualization could not compete for attention with the mirror itself: people in general did not look at all the four visualizations and

found some of them (Extremes, Statistics) difficult to interpret. However, foreigners (e.g. tourists) spent a larger amount of time observing and discussing the visualizations.

4. From the point of view of the design and the technical solutions, we (the designers and programmers) spotted some anomalies that visitors usually did not notice. It turned out that certain types of textiles (cord, shiny leather) fooled the detection of a motionless visitor, as their reflection was constantly changing. Due to the lack of light in the windowless room and the low quality of the built-in camera of the Kinect, the scanned colours were not always true to life. The complex selection criteria made sure that the many visitors who wore dark colours also received an object. On the other hand, the colour of the skin was always taken account, which made it difficult at times to interpret the match even if somebody was wearing at least some bright colours.

How did people *experience* the ColourMirror?

1. Visitors enjoyed the experience: they were smiling, laughing (72.6 %), or pleasantly surprised (7.4%) when their object showed up. If they were with someone else, they also made emotionally charged comments about the objects.

2. Children and young adults became especially engaged, made further scans, experimented by changing their dress or altering their pose. Some children spent more than 10 minutes in the room, and several visitors returned later for a second try.

How did people *perceive the object* they were assigned?

1. More than 95% of the visitors could recall the object, over 71% of them very well (describing its details, quoting its textual description).

2. A majority of the people (72%) were happy with the received object. When they were not, the negative linguistic connotations of certain objects as well as gender mismatches (a man receiving a woman's dress) were mentioned as reasons for disliking it. For indifference, aesthetic aspects were sometimes mentioned.

3. 81% of the people planned to track down "their" object – even in cases when they could not find it. Hence the "mirrored object" served as an entry anchor to the near 400 exhibits.

4. People identified with the object – they mostly used terms such as "I am a jar" in spontaneous outbreaks, and in the feedback in the visitors' book.

What did people *think* of the ColourMirror, and of digital installations in museums?

1. Only about one third of the subjects got the right clue about the working of the mirror, one third had no idea or gave very strange answers (assuming for example that it was based on an X-ray scan, or an analysis of their shape). This result really surprised us, as the idea was explained in a text at the entrance outside, as was also mentioned in the mirror whenever an object got displayed. It seemed that many of the people did not read these texts at all (though we did not explicitly check this).

2. A vast majority (above 80%) of the subjects did like the ColourMirror, found it a joyful, funny, enjoyable experience. More than a quarter (also) described it as "modern".

3. For a vast majority of the subjects (more than 77%), digital installations offer an additional motivation to visit a museum.

3.3   Feedback from other sources

Since the opening (April 2016), we have received much positive feedback in the public media (even in TV), and also from museum professionals. The qualitative answers from the guards were in line with the major findings based on empirical data. The museum was very pleased by the free PR due to the mirror images of artefacts that were shared by visitors on Facebook. They are planning to use the ColourMirror in dedicated campaigns and to provide more publicity for e.g. data visualizations on the website of the museum.

We also expected the ColourMirror to confront several people with their – basically dark – clothing habits. We have some clear but anecdotal evidence for this: several people returned in different outfits.

4   Conclusions

The ColourMirror exemplifies how digital technology may be used to enhance museum experience in a novel way, to activate visitors to study the exhibits by a playful and almost magical experience, to create a personal and emotional bond between them and the exhibits, and to offer personal digital take-aways, creating a tap on the visitors' habits of sharing as a free and efficient marketing tool.

The empirical study of the visitors demonstrates that the playful installation motivates people to visit the exhibition, they do pay attention to the embedded "content" not only to the engaging interaction. The study confirms the general belief that young people are more at ease with digital installations, but also pinpoints that the same installations may make elderly people feel uncomfortable. A far-reaching conclusion is that a majority of the visitors considered interactive installations as an additional motivation to go to a museum. The tendency not to read even short texts, but at the same time to require instructions how to use the installation, is a challenge for UX and UI design, especially for non-touch screen installations. Guards playing an active role as hosts rather than "police" may offer a solution that is satisfactory for both parties. The amount of information presented in a single space, even if in appealing visual forms, may be counterproductive, especially if it has to be studied after an interactive experience.

The basic engine of ColurMirror would allow adaptations for different exhibition domains, such as paintings, textiles, fashion or (multi-cultural) ethnography. It would be also interesting to compare colour preferences in the dress of visitors, with respect to their age, gender, culture, or the time of the year, or the daily weather.

5   Acknowledgements

ColourMirror was designed and implemented by an interdisciplinary team: Zoltán Csík-Kovács, Ágoston Nagy, Gáspár Hajdu, Gábor Papp, Bence Samu and Zsófia Ruttkay. We are thankful to Szilvia Silye for her work on the design and execution of the empirical study, and to Katalin Cseh and Krisztina

Heckler for assisting with the data collection. We are also grateful to the staff of the Museum of Applied Arts, especially to the guards, for their support, and to Dániel Kiss for his help with preparing the article.

Literature

[Ande12]   Anderson, G. (Ed): Reinventing the Museum: The Evolving Conversation on the Paradigm Shift 2nd Edition, AltaMiraPress, 2012.

[Bény151]   Bényei, J., Ruttkay, Zs.: A múzeum megújítása a digitális technológiák korában, (Renewal of the Museums in the Age of Digital Technologies) In: A. Tímea, Zs. Pörczi (eds): Határtalan médiakultúra (Mediaculture without Boarders), Wolters Kluwer Complex Kiadó, 2015, pp. 51–80.

[Heck82]   Heckbert, P. S.: Color Image Quantization for Frame Buffer Display Computer Graphics, 16(3), 1982, pp. 297–307.

[Jenk06]   Jenkins, H. (ed.), Confronting the Challenges of Participatory Culture: Media Education for the 21st Century, MacArthur Foundation, The MIT Press Cambridge, Massachusetts London, England, 2006.

[Kuhn55]   Kuhn, H. W.: The Hungarian method for the assignment problem, Naval Research Logistics Quarterly. Volume 2, Issue 1–22, 1955, pp. 83–97.

[Mokr11]   Mokrzycki, W., Tatol, M.: Color difference Delta E – A survey, Machine Graphics and Vision 20(4), April 2011, pp. 383–411.

[Simo12]   Somon, N.: The Participatory Museum. Museum 2.0. Santa Cruz, California, 2010.

Using the Hololens for Mixed Reality Exhibition Design

Robert Meyer
alphaQuest GmbH
Magirus-Deutz-Str. 10
89077 Ulm
r.meyer@alphaquest.de

Martin Steinicke
Creative Media R&D Group
University of Applied Sciences HTW Berlin
12459 Berlin
martin.steinicke@htw-berlin.de

Abstract

This paper describes how the design of exhibition spaces in cultural contexts can be supported by Mixed Reality interaction. Our work builds on the ExpoPlaner3D, a software that enables users to design exhibitions and place exhibits in varied forms of vitrines in a simulated 3D environment. Additionally, the software cross-checks for potential conservatory dangers to the utilised exhibits. To foster the spatial awareness of the exhibition designer and support interdisciplinary interaction of all stakeholders, we evaluated whether and how the ExpoPlaner3D could be enriched with Mixed Reality and especially HoloLens devices. The paper showcases our work on iterating the required key components and testing these prototypes.

1   Introduction

Designing exhibition spaces especially in cultural contexts and museums is a highly complex activity and requires the interdisciplinary cooperation of various highly specialized experts (Haffner, Jeberien & Höpfner, 2013). Generally, these domain experts consider both the exhibit, the design process that forms the showroom as well as the visitor's experience from completely different and oftentimes contradicting points of view. While, for example, the exhibition designer may want to highlight a central piece of the showroom with a strong and focused light source, the conservator may fear for the exhibit's well-being due to its photosensitive properties (Haffner, Jeberien & Höpfner, 2013). In contrast the conservator may propose to organize exhibits in a wall-mounted vitrine that organizes these in tilted position. The latter offers the advantage of a reduced tilting danger without the need of further supports that may interfere both with the exhibit's well-being as well as its aesthetic perception. While this sounds like a win-win situation for designer and conservator, the host institution's representative may disagree – e.g. due to the fact that the chosen presentation scheme discriminates wheelchair users and thus is in contrast to the museum's accessibility guidelines and regulations.

While being potentially less confrontational, the absence of this interdisciplinary cooperation is even worse, but nonetheless a sad reality in many cases that leads to unsatisfactory results and may even severely endanger the well-being of cultural objects (Jeberien & Cernohorsky, 2016).

To counter this, a team of HTW Berlin experts from the conservator faculty as well as from the Creative Media research and development group of the computing faculty joint forces. In a subproject ("Interaktive Medien in Restaurierung und Museumskunde") of the European Regional Development Fund (EFRE) supported project Creative Media the ExpoPlaner3D was developed. The latter is described in the following chapter before the current development of its extension as the ExpoPlaner3D+ is presented in chapter 3.

2   The ExpoPlaner3D

As introduced above, the curation, design and implementation of a given permanent or special exhibition is a multidisciplinary task. Developing a software tool that supports this cooperation, reduces redundancy in subtasks and processes and automates relevant plausibility and security checks is clearly a valuable endeavour. To iterate on this utility proposition and develop a proof of concept an iterative process was started. Following a number of iterations a running minimum viable product (MVP) – the ExpoPlaner3D (Haffner, Jeberien & Höpfner, 2013; Jeberien & Cernohorsky, 2016) – was completed. In the following chapter we will introduce the most important features, which pose relevant requirements and use cases for a Mixed Reality based ExpoPlaner3D+.

2.1 Key Features

The ExpoPlaner3D is a web-based application offering a front-end that supports the curators and museums in inserting data such as venue and exhibit information. Access and permissions are controlled by a user (rights and roles) management component. These components are mainly relevant to ensure the correct administration of the following software components.

The visual centrepiece of the ExpoPlaner3D is the three-dimensional exhibition editor that enables authorised users to place various forms of vitrines and light sources in an exhibition room (see figure 1). The former can subsequently be populated with given exhibits. To model the user interaction as intuitive as possible a drag & drop metaphor is used and further functions such as a grid system can be (de)activated. Whenever an exhibit is selected, a special user interface (UI) element displays relevant information. A further UI component currently on the top-side of the screen automatically displays conservatory information and alerts the user of identified issues and reciprocal effects that should be heeded and ideally be fixed.

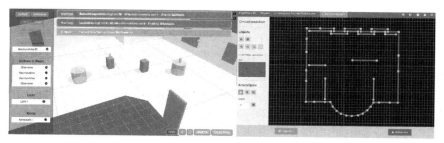

Fig. 1: The ExpoPlaner3D 3D and geometrical projection editor screens
(currently reworked)

Another component that needs to be considered to lay the groundwork for a given exhibition design is the ichnography editor. The latter is vital to create and customize the geometrical projection of the exhibition room and further properties like windows as well as doors (see figure 1). While it would have been possible to integrate the ichnography editor's functionality into the 3D exhibition designer, the separation of concerns has several advantages, e.g. the possibility of restricting access with user rights/roles as well as the reduction of the user interface elements and features.

2.2   Implementation

To reduce the required IT administration workload especially in cultural institutions, the ExpoPlaner3D is designed as a web solution. To nonetheless enable a desktop application-like look and feel, state of the art frameworks such as AngularJS, Laravel and Foundation have been used to create a Single Page Application. A further potential problem with extensive web apps especially in cultural institutions and in mobile contexts is restricted or unreliable connectivity. To counter potential inconsistencies a RESTful (Representational State Transfer) web service was created, which additionally enables reliable scaling of the application. Last but not least, the 3D editor component was developed with WebGL facilitated by three.js.

3   The ExpoPlaner3D+

While the ExpoPlaner3D is a rather promising approach and as a tool that is both web-based as well as optimized for PC it certainly has its merits, the future of designing museum exhibitions is a Mixed Reality and hopefully a cooperative one. In this chapter current work on features of an Expo-Planer3D+ is introduced.

3.1   A note on Mixed Reality

The definition of Mixed Reality especially in contrast to Virtual and Augmented Reality – as well as what is real and virtual in the first place – has long been a contested one [MIL94]. Interestingly, Milgram and Kishino defined MR as anything being located in the virtuality continuum between an absolutely real and a purely virtual environment or (audio/video/...) display thereof. Thus the combined presentation of virtual and real images/objects as

Augmented Reality as well as Augmented Virtuality can be considered Mixed Reality [MIL94]. This stands in contrast to a current view oftentimes expressed at conferences and websites that MR is more/better/newer than AR – see e.g. [FOU17]. This view argues that AR is the augmentation of reality with digital information that in contrast to MR is neither anchored in space nor interactable. Indeed, this distinction may primarily be drawn out of marketing/communication concerns as Milgram and Kishino basically covered this in their Extent of World Knowledge (EWK) dimension of MR [MIL94]. EWK describes the extent in which a (audio/video/...) display is aware of the displayed world and its objects. This is especially relevant in the context of an exhibition planner, due to the fact that the MR display device needs to be context and space aware to display vitrines and other objects at the correct places and scale these correctly in relation to existing ("real") room features and objects. Furthermore, it raises the question of interaction modes with these Mixed Objects [COU06].

3.2 A note on the Microsoft HoloLens

The HoloLens is a new Mixed Reality Head-up-Display (HUD) created by Microsoft that does not require any and especially not cable-bound connection to a PC or smartphone. It differs from VR head mounted displays (HMD) like the Oculus Rift, HTC Vive or Playstation VR in that it does not "simply" fixates two – one for each eye – screens in front of the user, but rather uses a specially treated glass. The glass is transparent with a slight tint comparable to very weak sunglasses. Tiny fiber-optic light guides are integrated into this material. They lead the light from a tiny projector above the glasses to the equivalent "screen" position in front of the user's eyes. This in itself would be enough to realize digital content visualization in the field of vision of the user. To place these at/over beforehand or on-the-fly selected positions – e.g. over QR codes – a simple camera would be sufficient. But the HoloLens combines a number of further sensors: A depth camera, an ambient light sensor as well as four "environment understanding" cameras. These enable the HoloLens via sensor fusion [DAS97, MS17] to scan a given room – i.e. construct a point cloud and through this a mesh thus creating a 3D virtual representation of the spatial environment (see figure 2).

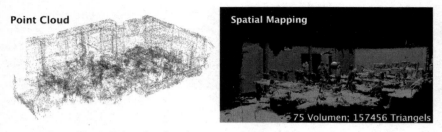

Fig. 2: Point cloud and room mesh created by a HoloLens

3.3   Using the HoloLens in the context of the ExpoPlaner

A central requirement for a MR exhibition design – particularly for Augmented Reality and to a certain degree for an Augmented Virtuality approach, too – is the tracking of the user. This is relevant to e.g. display the correct field of view and to anchor located digital elements so that these are not accidently repositioned when the user moves as well as solve issues like occlusion and transparencies.

To track the user, landmarks are generally required. In case these landmarks are attached to the user and captured by e.g. wall mounted sensors one speaks of outside-in tracking [WEL01 in ORT16]. This would, for example, be the case in a classical motion capture studio, where actors wear a full body suit with special adhesive three-dimensional markers (see e.g. [OPT17]). This can be contrasted with an inside-out approach, in which markers are scattered through the space and the sensor(s) is/are worn by the user [WEL01 in ORT16]. Due to the fact that the HoloLens – in contrast to most VR HMDs – contains a number of marker cognition relevant sensors an inside-out tracking is feasible in the first place. Indeed, the described ability to create a point cloud and mesh enables the HoloLens to use a physical-marker-less inside-out tracking approach, by defining adequate features of the room as tracking relevant landmarks. This is rather important in the exhibition design context due to the fact that one does not need to place obtrusive two- (e.g. QR codes) or even three-dimensional markers all over the place.

The described spatial mapping of the HoloLens provides a further advantage. In contrast to using only the ExpoPlaner3D ichnography editor to create the room layout it is feasible to create the geometrical projection using the created point cloud. Further room properties like windows as well as doors in contrast are way more difficult to define, due to the fact that these are either holes or corridors in the point cloud. A basic automated approach would be able to identify such holes by comparing the average number of points in horizontal and vertical lines of a recognized plane. A further option would be to use pre-defined templates for partial point clouds that are known to be wall plus door combinations and try to match the scanned room point cloud with the templates. Last but not least, genetic algorithms as mentioned in [TAN10] or trained artificial neural networks could be applied for detection. In each case the final decision could be requested from a user, who could be supported with photos created while wearing the HoloLens. In contrast, requiring the HoloLens user to tag doors and windows by using a HoloLens supported drawing tool was found to be comparatively laborious and unfeasible with certain geometries.

Using the HoloLens enables exhibition designers to view the actual room and the placed exhibits and thus evaluate the aesthetic of it by actually standing in it and getting a feeling for perspectives and scales. This is an advantage that is hard to describe in words and even harder to understand without experiencing this sensation.

Furthermore, the HoloLens can be used to actually place vitrines and exhibits in the augmented exhibition design via its gaze, voice and gesture recognition. In accordance to our generally applied iterative design-based research and development approach [BUS16], we tested this without first building a complete connectivity to the ExpoPlaner, but rather with a prototype that enabled the user to move and manipulate simple three-dimensional forms like cubes and pyramids. In contrast to our expectations, gaze- and gesture-wise manipulation worked comparatively well, but in the end were found wanting. The gaze control is primarily oriented on the general field of view, meaning it is more like a "nose control" – once the user had selected a digital object, it snapped to the central cursor. While this had the advantage that object movement is easier to control than with a real gaze-control – i.e. by constantly moving eyes – it nonetheless was comparatively imprecise. Additionally problems arose with the gesture induced (de)activation of the objects movement via the "air tab" gesture that is comparable to a mouse-click. Firstly, it was not always detected, which irritated users, but worse some users tended to subconsciously nod their head when tapping and thus changing the object's position just before it was fixated. We did not test voice control (yet), due to the fact that we believe that this requires quite a lot of implementation work to begin with, combined with doubts about its feasibility and usability in our context of professional exhibition design. In the end, a solution that allows exhibition and exhibit manipulation with an additional tablet computer or even multi-touch table was found to be the best experience for users.

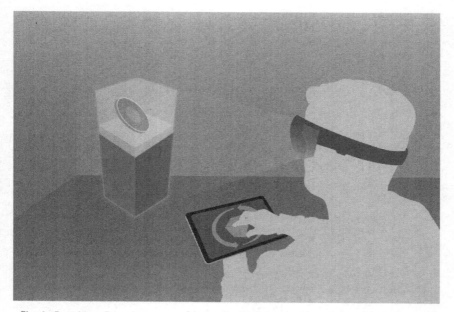

Fig. 3: Best User Experience: combining the HoloLens with mobile tablet computer

Nonetheless, we found that using the HoloLens to change both exhibition layout and exhibit placement to be generally compatible with the current implementation of the ExpoPlaner3D. This is due to the fact that the original REST-API supports these interactions that are primarily driven by the client implementation respectively the prototypes running on the HoloLens. But our interest in supporting the collaborative work of domain experts and exploring the potential of the HoloLens in this context lead us to a point, where the pitfalls of the REST web service API became obvious.

3.4   Multiuser Real Time Interaction

Using Mixed reality Head-up-Displays (MR HUDs) – like the HoloLens – enables designers, conservators and museum staff to move in space, change perspectives, place and manipulate exhibits, and evaluate designs in a coope-rative and interactive way that could result in improved customer experience and increased conservatory protection of (in)valuable cultural and historic exhibits. To enable such a setting the ExpoPlaner3D+ would both need to span a shared "HoloSpace" as well as support concurrent modification of elements in this Mixed Reality exhibition space.

The creation of a shared HoloSpace is more complex than it may appear at first sight, especially in contrast to a Virtual Reality space. This is in part due to a fundamentally different approach to real and virtual space. When producing a VR experience the developer creates the virtual world in the first place. Although these worlds are designed with the preferred interaction mode in mind – e.g. the user being seated, standing or moving in a predefined maximum space – they or at least the play space are nonetheless the same for each user. It does not matter, whether the user's living room is 49 or 10000 square meters wide. It is irrelevant whether the user A has a straight wall, while user B has one with a huge Oriel window – at least as long as neither transcends the boundaries of the play space.

Designers of experiences for the HoloLens in contrast never know the actual play space configuration beforehand, but rather need to create interactions that work with a given spatial environment. Generally spawning a robot 3 meters in front of the player might just not work when the user is sitting in a tiny apartment facing the real wall one meter away. In contrast the application would need to work with the actual architecture, find e.g. a wall or plane object and project a dimensional opening – correctly scaled and with(-out) (un-)intended occlusions – to spawn the robot. To counter this challenge the HoloLens possesses the described spatial exploration features. What has not been covered yet is that each time a given HoloLens completes a scan the resulting point cloud coordinates are very likely not identical to the ones that have been created by another HoloLens or even the same HoloLens previously. This is due to the fact that the HoloLens defines the space it is located in when it starts scanning as the coordinate origin. So the coordinates for the same landmark might differ quite drastically for each scan.

For a shared HoloSpace this could be disastrous. When the designer places a vitrine at a coordinate in one part of the room it may simply appear at another real world space for each user. When using HoloLenses in combination with the Unity game engine this can be countered by using UNET/ "Unity High Level API (HLAPI)" [UNI17] or by using a dedicated HoloLens server software by Microsoft. In both cases the diverging coordinate systems problem is solved with a closed source library that somehow calculates a transformation matrix that enables the transformation of one point cloud into the coordinate system of another point cloud. But due to the fact that this is a closed source solution and using either UNet or a Microsoft dedicated sharing server basically makes all point cloud operation transparent as well as restricts communication primarily to Unity applications, an alternative way needed to be found to guarantee a future development. Using the Point Cloud Library a software module was prototyped that calculates a transformation, too. Additionally it enables inferences about the quality of the model fit as well as enables extraction and sharing of point clouds. Furthermore, an extracted point cloud can thus be used as a general reference model for other point cloud or world/level based devices. Additionally this evades a problem, when using UNet/HLAPI without the dedicated server solution (DSS) from Microsoft. Without using a DSS, the HoloLens basically acts as the server and each new HoloLens would register with the first one as a client. In consequence, when the server HoloLens crashes, is out of power or leaves the scene all clients cease to work, too.

A further problem encountered in creating an ExpoPlaner3D HoloSpace was its REST-API. While using the REST web service approach has – as described in 2.2 – quite a number of advantages it did pose a serious hurdle for real-time multiuser interaction: It does not enable a (distributed) Model View Controller or Observer pattern [GOF94]. Thus when one HoloLens user adds a vitrine or exhibit via the REST-API to the database none of the others would be notified of this change. Sticking with the REST-API, this could be solved by frequently polling the database with each device. In contrast to this and in addition to the goal of evading the proprietary Unity only system, an Actor Model [AGH85] or Agent-based approach using MQTT [MQT17] was prototyped. The latter is a lightweight machine-to-machine "Internet of Things" connectivity protocol that is comparable to the Foundation for Physical Agents (FIPA) Subscribe Interaction Protocol Specification [FIP17], but focuses on a mediating broker server/service and offers further possibilities – e.g. a last will and testament notification in case the connection to the publisher is lost [MQT14]. As can be seen in figure 4 any sensor or agent may subscribe to a given topic, publish information to any topic and receive pushed information referencing a subscribed topic. In case of the shared HoloSpace and the ExpoPlaner3D both clients on the left hand side could be HoloLenses, while the client on the right side would be a client that acts as a wrapper or facade to the REST-API. Thus when the user adds a vitrine, its HoloLens would not directly call the REST-API, but rather publish a message concerning the topic "added exhibit" instead. The REST-API wrapper would now be informed by the broker and then make an API call locally. Just like the API wrapper all other registered subscribers would be notified and thus could update their local data concerning the added exhibit – which could be considered a Mediated Model View Controller pattern.

Conveniently, the described design has two further advantages. First, it works the same way for sharing a reference point cloud so that each connected HoloLens may use it to calculate its transformation matrix. Additionally, due to being implementation agnostic clients-wise, this solution enables the combination of arbitrary devices (tablets, multi-touch tables or even VR headsets) and further software solutions – to a certain degree even on-the-fly.

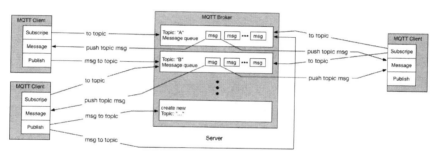

Fig. 4: MQTT example with three clients – e.g. two HoloLenses and the Expo-Planer3D REST-API

4   Conclusion

Using a Mixed Reality Head-up display (MR HUD) – e.g. the HoloLens – enables individual designers to both place and see objects in the future showroom. This enables the team to walk the shared HoloSpace and explore the display of the holographic artefacts from a natural perspective. Nonetheless, we found that while the placement of objects can be done via the HoloLens interface capabilities, this is not optimal due to a number of issues that have been described in this paper. Our working prototype for placing objects in an Augmented Reality session has shown that combining the HoloLens with a touch device such as a tablet or multi-touch table proves to combine the strengths of both modes of interaction. To support the interdisciplinary interaction of stakeholders we prototyped a solution that calculates the coordinate transformation of two disparate HoloLens point clouds and an architecture that enables the sharing of relevant interaction data in a device and software independent manner. Thus we have shown that the ExpoPlaner3D can be enriched with Mixed Reality interaction to bring the fruitful work of exhibition designers, conservators and other stakeholders onto the next level.

Acknowledgements

The ExpoPlaner3D was realized in the subproject "Interaktive Medien in Restaurierung und Museumskunde" of the Creative Media (CM) project. The European Regional Development Fund (ERDF) and the Berlin Senate funded Creative Media. It was lead by Prof. Dr.-Ing. Carsten Busch. The ExpoPlaner3D project was lead by Prof. Dr. phil. Alexandra Jeberien and Prof. Dr. Dorothee Haffner. The technological development was realized by Manuel Banz, Tom Cernohorsky and Christian Höpfner – supported and lead by Henning Müller and André Selmanagic. Concepts and prototyping for the ExpoPlaner3D+ were done by Robert Meyer and Martin Steinicke in the context of the application centres "creative Applied Interactive Technologies (cAPITs)" and "Digital Value", both funded by the ERDF and the Berlin Senate.

Literature

[AGH84]   Agha, G. A. Actors: A model of concurrent computation in distributed systems. Massachusetts Institute of Technology Cambridge Artificial Intelligence Lab, 1985.

[BUS16]   Busch, C., Dohrmann, L., Möhlihs, M., Pasadu, M., Steinicke, M.: Design-based Research on Conceptually Integrated Games to Foster Chemistry Skills in Secondary Education. In: Proceedings of the 10th European Conference on Games-Based Learning ECGBL2016, pp. 89–97, Academic Conferences and Publishing International, Reading, 2016.

[COU06]   Coutrix, C., Laurence N.: "Mixed Reality: A Model of Mixed Interaction." in proceedings of AVI06 Proceedings of the working conference on Advanced visual interfaces, pp. 43–50, 2006.

[DAS97]   Dasarathy, B V.: "Sensor fusion potential exploitation-innovative architectures and illustrative applications." Proceedings of the IEEE 85.1 (1997): pp. 24–38.

[FIP02]   Foundation for Physical Agents. Subscribe Interaction Protocol Specification. Retrieved 10.03.2017 from http://www.fipa.org/specs/fipa00035/index.html.

[FOU17]   Foundry.com Virtual reality VR? AR? MR? Sorry, I'm confused. Retrieved 01.02.2017 from https://www.foundry.com/industries/virtual-reality/vr-mr-ar-confused.

[GOF94]   Gamma, E., Helm, R., Johnson, R., Vlissides, J.: Design Patterns. Elements of Reusable Object-Oriented Software. Addison-Wesley. 1994.

[MIL94]   Milgram, P., Kishino, F.: "A taxonomy of mixed reality visual displays." IEICE TRANSACTIONS on Information and Systems 77.12 (1994): pp. 1321–1329.

[MS17]   Microsoft HoloLens. Retrieved 27.01.2017 from https://www.microsoft.com/microsoft-hololens/de-de/hardware.

[MQT14]   MQTT Version 3.1.1. Edited by Andrew Banks and Rahul Gupta. 29 October 2014. OASIS Standard. http://docs.oasis-open.org/mqtt/mqtt/v3.1.1/os/mqtt-v3.1.1-os.html. Latest version: http://docs.oasis-open.org/mqtt/mqtt/v3.1.1/mqtt-v3.1.1.html.

[MQT17]   MQTT.org. FAQ. Retrieved 10.03.2017 from http://mqtt.org/faq

[OPT17]   OptiTrack Motion Capture Markers. Retrieved 03.02.2017 from http://optitrack.com/products/motion-capture-markers/.

[ORT16]   Ortega, F. R., Abyarjoo, F., Barreto, A., Rishe, N., & Adjouadi, M. Interaction Design for 3D User Interfaces: The World of Modern Input Devices for Research, Applications, and Game Development. CRC Press. 2016. p. 117.

[TAN10]   Tang, P, et al.: "Automatic reconstruction of as-built building information models from laser-scanned point clouds: A review of related techniques." Automation in construction 19.7 (2010): pp. 829–843.

[UNI17]   Unity Documentation – The High Level API. Retrieved 03.02.2017 from https://docs.unity3d.com/Manual/UNetUsingHLAPI.html.

[WEL01]   Welch, G., Vicci, L., Brumback, S., Keller, K., Colucci, D.: Heigh Performance Wide-Area Optical Tracking: The HiBall Tracking System. Presence: Teleoperators and Virtual Environments 10(1), pp. 1–21.

An Interactive Gameboard for Categorization and Examination of Engraved Gems for the Winckelmann Museum

Franziska Juraske, Till Oefler, Karina Sommermeier,
Stefanie Vogel, Dominik Schumacher, Michael A. Herzog
Institute of Industrial Design
Magdeburg-Stendal University
Breitscheidstraße 2, 39114 Magdeburg
{dominik.schumacher,michael.herzog}@hs-magdeburg.de

Abstract

The GemmTable, a prototyped concept of an interactive game board for a collaborative learning scenario for museum visitors, is presented in this paper. The main goal was to demonstrate a simplified touch table access to a huge collection of very small artwork. Gemstones could be categorized and examined by the visitor according to the principle of Johann Joachim Winckelmann in the 18th century. With haptic elements and access via playing cards the usually complex gestures of touch tables are simplified to engage every visitor and allow interactive learning about artwork. To keep the suggested solution technically as simple and economically as affordable as possible, a QR-Code and HD-camera based card detection was combined with a touch display. Completed with realistic tangible gems this offers access also for visually impaired people.

1   Motivation and Context

Earlier, engraved jewelry stones or gemstones were often used as seals (fig. 1). The oldest examples date back to the fifth millennium BC. Motifs on the gems are, in most cases, religious, but might also depict everyday scenes. Baron Phillipp von Stosch and Katharina the Great are well-known collectors of these engraved gems. Johann Joachim Winckelmann, considered the intellectual founder of classicism in Germany, described and catalogued these filigree art objects. The Stosch collection contains more than 3,000 gems [Rich71].
Beside of electronic catalogs (for example, in Museum-Digital.de), gems as specific pieces of art of diminutive size have not yet been a subject of interactive exploration by visitors in museums.

Fig. 1: Engraved gems shown in relation to a one euro coin

To improve visitor experience, many museums rely on multimedia stations. These provide additional information on the exhibits, e.g. by showing videos or providing a touch screen interaction. Recent studies have shown [Hak16] that many museums increasingly use unobtrusive techniques such as NFC (near field communication) and RFID (radio-frequency identification) compatible with mobile devices. As many people are familiar with smartphones and tablets, their usage will work more smoothly. In addition, many users are often not aware of what a media table can do and how it should be used. The complexity of the interaction prevents the expected usage.
However, interactive media stations can still be the first choice if an attractive museum experience is to be offered to the user in the exhibition. For this purpose, it is very helpful to make the interaction inviting and transparent using modern design methods [Bur07]. These methods aim to achieve the

highest possible usability. Depending on prior user experiences sometimes it is useful to limit the scope for interaction to a minimum. Eventually, museums are able to create appealing, easy accessible media stations that use a game-based approach allowing people to acquire more knowledge on a certain topic.

This approach was chosen for the new permanent exhibition in the Winckel-mann Museum Stendal, Germany. Therefore, the visitor should get a more in-depth view of the exhibited gem collection and at the same time, learn about Winckelmann's way of categorizing these objects.

The medial treatment of engraved gems, as described in this paper, is a field of research and development that is little considered until now. The following section provides an overview of related work in the field of engraved gem description and interactive tables.

2 Related Work

The first medial usage of gems already took place in the age of enlightenment (17th/18th century). At that time, gems were brought home after long journeys by representatives of the upper class who met to showcase and discuss their collections. In order to use these ancient stones as a means of learning "for the education of youth, the formation of artists and the improvement of taste and antiquarian knowledge of the educated classes" [Han14, p. 3] dactyliothecas were developed. A dactyliotheca describes a collection of casts of engraved stones, which were arranged in flat drawers or piles. With the *Dactyliotheca Universalis* Philipp Daniel Lippert (1702–1785) created his life's work and one of the standard works for describing gems. He presented over 3000 casts, divided into the two main groups, historical and mythological gems.

For the conceptual development, an examination of the technical possibilities is necessary. After a comprehensive implementation phase (see section 4), the choice was to develop an interaction concept for a touchscreen solution. In [SBM 15], Sulaiman et al describe the different types of multi-touch systems in detail. Capacitive displays or multi-touch tabletop displays mounted with a Digital Light Processing (DLP) projector over the surface are some examples. Tabletop displays use infrared LEDs in conjunction with an IR camera for gesture detection [Han05]. This technique is particularly suitable for large installations.

A good example of the use of multi-touch tables can be found in the "DDR Museum" in Berlin [DDR17]. The exhibition table "Multi-Touch Parteikonferenz" introduces the visitor to the structure and functioning of the SED (East German Communist Party). On the table the visitor will find nine objects symbolizing different topics. By placing cards on the table, texts, pictures, and videos will open and give information e.g. about the party's apparatus and the relationship between SED and State Security (Stasi). This offers the user "almost infinite possibilities" of interaction and information.

Investigations by Hornecker and Fischer [HF14] at the Naturkundemuseum in Berlin showed, that multi-touch tables sometimes have problems with usability. For instance, a change of language through unintentional pointing to a field with the text "German" or "English" was detected. In addition, only a few users read more than one piece of information or exchanged what they had read. Furthermore, a few of the visitors complained about a missing link between the presented content and the immediate environment. Multi-touch tables provide a lot of information in a small space. Therefore, many visitors often experience their disposal as incoherent and random in the museum rooms. Finally, the researchers found out that installations with a small selection of content directly related to the environment are better received by visitors.

These criticisms were crucial for the development of a concept that is limited to the essential content and integrated well into the environment. The concept is described in the next section.

3   Approach and Design Concept

The project presented was created to develop an interactive board game approach. This research was conducted on the basis of the Design Science paradigm based on Hevner [HMPR04] and the DSRM process model of Pfeffer et al. [PTRC07] (fig. 2).

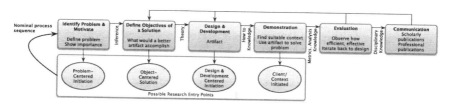

Fig. 2: Design science research methodology (DSRM) process model [PTRC07]

Problem centered entry point was defined by the demand to provide access to lots of similar miniaturist art exhibits to the visitor. The same setting provided an understanding of the artwork and more importantly, an understanding of how these artworks may be categorized. Improving the reception of small and very small three-dimensional art objects within the complex museum redesign was the target and starting point of this process. Therefore, the design and development of the underlying artefact has been realized after the principles of a User-Centered Design process [ISO9241].

The interactive table should allow game-based exploration of a classification for the Stosch collection in the Winckelmann Museum of Stendal. The gem catalog of Johann Joachim Winckelmann, who created a principle of order for the Stosch collection during his lifetime [Win13], served as a model for this classification. For the development of the game board four categories from Winckelmann's gem catalog were used, namely Romans, Gods, Hieroglyphs/ Engravings, and Animals. By using a printed gem card deck (GemmTable) the gems can be categorized and investigated.

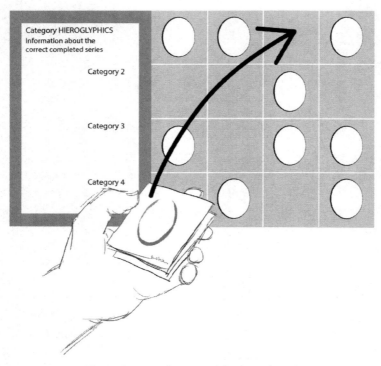

Fig. 3: Concept drawing of the game board

The game board is set up with several fixed engraved gem replicas that are not removable. These prearrangements make it easier for the user to assign the respective gem card to the correct category. The gem cards also give haptic feedback. To bring various types of production closer to the visitor, the surfaces are designed differently. For example, relief printing can illustrate the technique of stone cutting.

The cards are distributed in different places all over the exhibition of the Winckelmann Museum and may be collected by the visitor during his or her visit on interest. However, it is also possible to find them in the room, where the interactive Gem Table is located, in order to use it as a game board.

The next step for the visitor is to place the collected cards on the available spaces of the game board. Employing the card to an incorrect category results in an appropriate optical feedback via an integrated touch screen on the GemmTable. If the visitor assigns the gem card to the right category, he or she receives further information on the gem, as well as on the category itself.

After completing the game, the information will be displayed and the user can learn more about the Stosch collection as well as Winckelmann's gem catalog.

Therefore, the newly designed interactive media table offers a game based learning opportunity for gem categorization according to Winkelmann 's principle of engraved gem classification.

The described interactions are designed to aim at higher dimensions of learning according to Bloom's taxonomy (Anderson, Krathwohl & Bloom 2001). Related to this taxonomy, the visitor undergoes the phases of "Understanding", "Applying", "Analyzing" and "Evaluating". The gem card notebook also addresses the dimension of "Creating", in which the visitor takes the ownership of a categorized section of the gem collection.

4   Implementation

After a comprehensive research on the life and work of Winckelmann, ideas were developed to give a closer understanding of the collection and categorization of gems. The idea of a sorting process at the game table originated from an initial gem case, an interactive showcase, a drawer system, through an interactive gem catalog in connection with Winkelmann's categorization. Important criteria for the development were the immediate and simple visitor operation by the visitor as well as a pleasant haptic feedback. By combing modern tools with traditional content and an optically adapted wood and glass design, the GemmTable could be well integrated in to the museum's context.

The technical implementation was deliberately simplified (figure 4) to keep the product affordable and easy to design. A QR code is printed on the back of the gem card. This code is read by a HD webcam placed under the game board and then evaluated by the CPU module. We used an Intel NUC, which has been adapted to our needs.

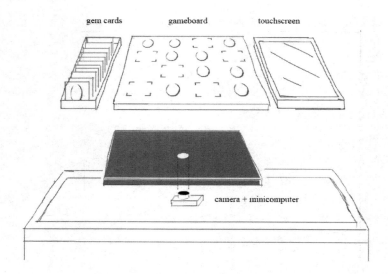

Fig. 4: Draft of technical implementation

A processing sketch runs on the PC on a software environment specifically designed for interaction design.

The integrated processing video library is used to control the camera. The ZXING4PROCESSING Library evaluates the recognized QR code and converts it into a string, which is then compared to the respective category by an algorithm. If a gem fits to the category, the information is shown on the display. In addition, the software sends over serial connection a command to an Arduino forcing the connected multicolor LED to illuminate the game board with green light. In case the gem does not fit to the category, the user receives an error message and the multicolor LED signals red.

5   Evaluation

For the evaluation of the GemmTable eight persons were surveyed about its usability. Therefore, the users completed a questionnaire according to the Likert scale method (table 1). Additional information was obtained by using methods of observation, direct survey, and loud thinking.

The evaluation came to the following results:

- The usage of the gem cards was usually clear.

- For the majority of the test persons, it was not obvious that the gem cards could be collected and taken home.
- The touchscreen was identified for knowledge transfer. Besides the class affiliation of the screen design was not clearly evident.
- The conceived finger swipe interaction was not often used. Many test persons thought they had to use finger tipping.
- Without a short introduction, some users were not able to use the GemmTable.

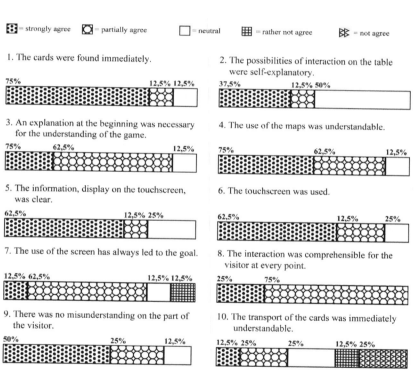

Table 1: Evaluation results of GemmTable prototype

6 Findings

The following solutions were developed from the results of the evaluation:

- A visual guide is under development.
- The graphical design of the gem cards will be revised, so that the meaning of the collection is more obvious for the user. In addition, more motifs are provided for a larger game variation.
- The arrangement of the elements is changed on the table top in order to achieve a more understandable order.
- The existing touch gestures are reduced in favor of intuitive use. A finger-tip interaction simplifies the application significantly.
- A reset card or a restart button is easy to implement.
- A design medium – a panel or a starting image – is also developed and tested so that less technology-conscious user will find the function more attractive.

Fig. 5: GemmTable prototype in the exhibition

Some conceptual limitations were identified in the implementation. Providing all 3,000 gems of the Stosch collection to the museum visitors in a limited time window is unrealistic. Moreover, only a small number of the engraved gems can be plastically imitated, otherwise a stimulus overflow would occur. The advantage of a targeted selection is that the visitor can deepen according to topics of interest, like topics of "Eroticism in Antiquity" or "Sports in Herculaneum", which enhances cognitive learning. The GemmTable makes the engraved gems more tangible to the user, while at the same time providing playful insights about the Stosch collection. This allows individuals and groups, but also people with a visual impairment, to interact directly with the table.

Compared to other multi-touch installations described in the literature (see chapter 2), the principle underlying the GemmTable prototype with haptic elements and access via playing cards already offers a way to simplify the interactions for the user. Furthermore, a more direct reference to the immense diversity of a kind of exhibition objects is given.

7 Outlook

The GemmTable represents a cross-generational learning table, explaining the historical background of engraved gems in a playful manner and motivates users to experience something new. Other small items such as coins, stamps, small sculptures, pewter figures, or biological models are also well suited for the implementation in such a game table.

The motivation principle of playful learning can be applied in kindergartens, schools, or in senior citizen institutions. These interactive stations, enriched with concrete haptic elements, offer diverse and memorable possibilities for collecting, playing, adding, categorizing and learning. Especially the haptic feedback combined with sound output offers an extension possibility for the target group of visually impaired or blind people. For these people, comparatively fewer opportunities for interaction are available for learning support.

Literature

[AKB01]   Anderson, L. W., Krathwohl, D. R., & Bloom, B. S. A taxonomy for learning, teaching, and assessing: A revision of Bloom's taxonomy of educational objectives. Allyn & Bacon 2001

[BBW09]   Benko, H., Morris, M. R., Brush, A. B., & Wilson, A. D. Insights on interactive tabletops: A survey of researchers and developers. research. microsoft. com., 2009

[Bur07]   Burmester, Michael. Usability und Design. Kompendium Medieninformatik. Springer Berlin Heidelberg, 2007, pp. 245–302

[DDR17]   Multitouch-Parteikonferenz, DDR-Museum in Berlin, http://www.
           ddr-museum.de/de/ausstellung/highlights/multitouch.html, Aufruf
           am 15.03.17
[Hak16]   Hakvoort, Gido Albert. Multi-touch and mobile technologies for
           galleries, libraries, archives and museums. Diss. University of
           Birmingham, 2016.
[Han05]   Han, Jefferson Y. Low-cost multi-touch sensing through frustrated
           total internal reflection. Proceedings of the 18th annual ACM
           symposium on User interface software and technology. ACM,
           2005.
[Han14]   Hansson, Ulf R. Die Quelle des guten Geschmacks ist nun
           geöffnet: Philipp Daniel Lipperts Dactyliotheca Universalis, in F.
           Faegersten, J. Wallensten & I. Östenberg (Hrsg.), Tankemönster: en
           festskrift till Eva Rystedt, Lund 2010, pp. 92–101, Translated by
           Jorun R. Ruppel 2014 in Göttingen
[HF14]   Hornecker, Eva, and Patrick Tobias Fischer. Interaktion in öffentli-
           chen Räumen. Informatik-Spektrum 37.5, 2014: pp. 440–444.
[HMP04]   Hevner, A. R., March, S. T., Park, J., & Ram, S. Design science
           in information systems research. MIS quarterly, 28(1), 2014,
           pp. 75–105
[ISO9241] ISO 9241-110:2006 Ergonomics of human-system interac-
           tion – Part 110: Dialogue principles. https://www.iso.org/stan-
           dard/38009.html (2017-03-16)
[PTRC07]   Peffers, K., Tuunanen, T., Rothenberger, M. A., & Chatterjee,
           S. (2007). A design science research methodology for infor-
           mation systems research. Journal of management information
           systems, 24(3), pp. 45–77.
[Rich71]   Richter, G. M. A. (1971). Engraved Gems of the Greeks, Etruscans,
           and Romans: Engraved gems of the Romans; a supplement to the
           history of Roman art (Vol. 1). Phaidon.
[SBM15]   Sulaiman, S., Bin Mahmood, A. K., Khan, M., & Madni, M. (2015).
           Applications of multi-touch tabletop displays and their challen-
           ging issues: an overview. International Journal on Smart Sensing &
           Intelligent Systems, 8(2), 2015
[Win13]   Winckelmann, J.J. (1760): Description des pierres gravées du feu
           Baron de Stosch, In: Schriften und Nachlaß, Bd. 7,1, Hrsg. Max
           Kunze, Adolf H. Borbein, Axel Rügler. Verlag Philipp von Zabern,
           Mainz 2013.

Researching the Behaviour of Visitors with a Game – the Exhibition Game "game (+ultra)"

Thomas Lilge

Cluster of Excellence Image, Knowledge, Gestaltung

The Interdisciplinary Laboratory

Humboldt-University Berlin

Unter den Linden 6

10099 Berlin

thomas.lilge@hu-berlin.de

The development was realized in cooperation with Nolgong, a South Korean Gamestudio headed by Peter Lee, Frauke Stuhl from the exhibition department of the Interdisciplinary Laboratory and the gamelab.berlin, a base project of the Interdisiplinary Laboratory headed by Thomas Lilge.

Abstract

The location-based mobile browser game "game (+ultra)" was tested as a replenishment of established formats like audio guides, guided tours and catalogues during a science exhibition in the Martin-Gropius-Bau in Berlin. During a three month period of time 5.000 players participated. In a questionnaire 92% replied with "yes" or "yes, very much" to the question *"Is the format of a game appropriate to enhance the experience of other exhibitions, too?"*. In regard to this success the paper points out the possibilities of games as a new format for museums and exhibitions with a focus on games as research instruments.

Fig. 1: Copyright Thomas Lilge/gamelab.berlin

1   Games and Knowledge

One of the first things children learn is where it is allowed to play and where not to. Not surprisingly museums and exhibitions are places where mostly invisible codes strictly rule the visitor´s behaviour. Above all it is clear to everyone that especially playing violates these behavioural rules. As adults we have internalized these rules to the extent, that these prohibitions seem natural to us. We think it is normal that we are not allowed to talk at these places, that we may not take pictures or use our smart phone at all. There is this sacred atmosphere – please do not touch – and the degree of participation, interactivity and playfulness is reduced close to zero. One reason for this might be, that the majority of people still believe that playing games conflicts sharply with the task of museums and exhibitions to impart the cultural heritage to their audiences. But the distinction between seriousness and play is a misunderstanding, as e.g. Gadamer points out: "Play and seriousness (...) are profoundly interwoven. They interact with one another, and those who have looked deeply into human nature have recognized that our capacity for play is an expression of the highest seriousness."[1] This quote leads to the important

---

1   Hans-Georg Gadamer. The Relevance of the Beautiful and other Essays. Cambridge. 1987. P. 130.

findings the cultural historian Johan Huizinga has presented in his famous book "Homo Ludens" where he delivers proof that knowledge is profoundly connected with the culture of play. The origin of science is play, "Philosophy springs up in the shape of a game".[2] In view of this fact it is small wonder that nearly all theories about learning from Montessori to Piaget indicate the importance of play. The connection between learning and playing has nowadays been implemented impressively by the Institute of Play which runs a School in New York City showing the potential of game-based learning.[3] Against this background, the central questions that motivate this paper are: How can we use the potential of play to impart our cultural heritage in a way that visiting a museum or an exhibition turn into a playful, interactive, partici-pative experience for a broad audience, including all ages and all levels of education? How could a game look like that offers personalized and playful access to knowledge, that produces a cooperative player behaviour on a global scale, that enhances communication-, critical thinking-, and problem-solving skills and ensures long-term motivation? It might look like this is too much to ask for, but the results of our first experiment are promising.

2 game (+ultra): Design Goals

The idea was to design a game that could work as a supplement for esta-blished formats like audio guides, exhibition catalogues or guided tours to help visitors to engage with the exhibition "+ ultra. Knowledge & Gestaltung" which took place during a three month period of time in the Martin-Gropius-Bau in Berlin from September 2016 to January 2017. An important source for the content of the exhibition was the work of the Interdiciplinary Laboratory, a Cluster of Excellence at Humboldt-University Berlin, which, at this moment in time, had already been established since 2012. In this quite unusual ecosy-stem 150 scientists and designers from over 40 disciplines work together to tackle complex problems. From this background derived six design goals for the game.

1. Fun

Most importantly we wanted the game to be fun. This might be regarded as a matter of course, but unfortunately a lot of so called *serious games* suffer from

---

2   Johan Huizinga. Homo Ludens. Hamburg. 1956. P. 108. (Translated by the author)
3   http://www.instituteofplay.org/work/projects/quest-schools/quest-to-learn/

the desire to deliver a certain message or to gain interest for their content, but while doing so, forget to prioritize the fun factor. But if playing a game is not a fun experience, players won´t play it. However important the content might be, our main goal was clear: Fun first.

2. Interdisciplinarity

To give a glimpse behind the scenes of current research taking place at the Interdisciplinary Laboratory we used the categories *natural science, humanities* and *design* and let the players choose, which category they would like to start with. Designers e.g. could choose design, biologists natural science and so on. After playing for a while in their category, further progress in the game was possible only by switching to another category. To win the game, all categories had to be completed. Furthermore, each category discussed different perspectives. In the category *design* players faced challenges from the fields of physics, behavioural research and material science.

3. Nonlinear Gameplay

The freedom of research is a guiding principle for universities. This well-known fact lead to the decision to provide the player with the maximum amount of freedom in the game. Instead of guiding him through the game, we gave him the opportunity to decide, from a certain point of progress on, where he wants to go next by himself. This nonlinear gameplay also seemed to resemble more accurate the research conditions in the Laboratory.

4. All Ages

The game should be interesting for all ages. As nowadays gamers are at an age around 35 years our aim was to test, if playing could also be an attractive and appropriate way of experiencing an exhibition for all ages.

5. Intensify the occupation

The challenge was to use the smart phone as a gaming tool, but to avoid at the same time, the players staring at the screen all the time. A location-based game should take the architecture of the venue into account and intensify the occupation with the exhibits, instead of distract from the content.

6. No gamemaster

The order required the game, being playable during the opening times of the exhibition (8 hours a day during 4 months). Employing staff especially for the game would have exceeded the budget. We therefore had to design the game without any personell support.

3   Player Journey

Onboarding

A visitor, lets call him Peter, arrives at first room of the exhibition. After curiously looking around, his gaze remains fixed at a huge slogan written at the wall, informing him about a game. Underneath this slogan he then discovers four pedestals, each quipped with a tablet on top. The illuminated screen is tempting him to come closer. He arrives at the tablet and reads the request "push the button". As he pushes the button the small printer besides the tablet ejects a slip of paper, showing a room plan and further instructions. With his smart phone he logs into the local wifi, browses the game website and types in his Game ID he found on the paper.

Gameplay

First of all Peter has to decide which category he would like to start playing with. He decides to play humanities and the mission „Discover the rules". He then receives a first riddle, which is the room description. In order to understand where his mission takes place, he has to analyze the riddle and look closely at the room plan. Once he reached the room he submits his solution and, depending on wether he is right or wrong, receives a confirmation or a helping note. Each mission starts with a personal letter by a famous scientist. We called them science heroes, asking Peter to help him with urgent problems. The science heroe will only reveal his identity after Peter has proven his expertise. Now the core game mechanic comes into play. Peter receives orders from the science hero, telling him to find certain objects in the exhibition. Each mission consists of three exhibits. But, that is where the challenge begins, the description of the exhibits are also riddles. To identify the desired objects, Peter has to examine the exhibits and compare the possible solutions. Therefore many details have to be taken into account. Once he believes he has identified the right object, he types in the object ID into his mobile phone and gets the result, wether he has accomplished the challenge or not. Once an object is identified correctly, Peter gets additional information about the artefact, deepening his understanding. If all three objects were found, the science heroe reveals his identity and presents his recommendation. The number of recommendation at the end of the game is crucial, for wether Peter will become a member of the club of science heroes or not. Together with the recommendation Peter will receive more additional information about the science heroe, in this case hewill learn something about Wilhelm von Humboldt.

End of the game

Peter can stop playing at any stage. Whenever he decides to end the game, we ask him to move back to the starting point, because there we provide the opportunity to print out his game results. On the printout he will find: All missions he accomplished. All information concerning the objects. Pictures from and information about the science heroes he succesfully has helped out. The number of helping notes he applied. The longest duration per mission. The shortest duration per mission. His overall playing time. The level he has accomplished.

For an average player this printout had a length of approximately 1,5 meters, which was welcomed by the players as a great analog give-away at the end of the game.

4 Technical Implementation

We created game (+ultra) as a browsergame for iOS and Android. The preferred browser was Google Chrome. This decision was based both on the most common operating systems for mobile devices and on the fact, that we had to develop the game content parallel to the curating process of the exhibition. Therefore we wanted to be able to easily change or correct the game content, even after the opening of the exhibition. By doing this we hoped to avoid any complication, which could otherwise have occurred from the need of updating an application. A browser game also simplified the onboarding process, as the players did not have to download anything, but instead could simply browse our website. We installed a local WiFi to ensure connectivity and sufficient bandwith in all rooms of the venue.

5 Evaluation and Statistics

Once the player decided to end the game, he was asked to fill in a questionnaire. 175 players completed the questionnaire, but not all of them answered all questions. In average 160 players answered the multiple-choice questions. In the questionnaire we additionally asked three questions which could be answered in a blank text field. We also tracked the players path through the game, by registering his in-game decisions and actions.

The first interesting finding resulting from the questionnaire is that, gender-wise, the structure of players was well balanced: 53% were male, 43% were female. This is also the case for the age structure: 21% were between 25 and 35 years old, 14% were between 7 and 14 years, between 36 and 45 years and also between 46 and 55. There were also 5% over the age of 66 years! Very convincing is also the result that while 53 % played the game alone, 40% chose to play it together with a peer or in a group out of three.

41% had an academic degree, including bachelor and master, 20% had a highschool degree, 12% visited secondary school and 7 % had an PhD. As mentioned before, one of our design goals was to discuss interdisciplinarity, so we asked wether the players would categorize themselves as natural scientists (45%), in the category humanities (37%) and design (27%). Concerning the question, *if the game lead to a more intensive interaction with each exhibit and the exhibition generally*, 70% answered "yes" or "yes, very much". 20% chose "not really" and 9% marked with a cross "The game was rather distracting". With regard to the question *"Did the game enhance your experience of the exhibition"* 82% stated "yes", or "yes, very much", while 10% answered "it was ok". 87% would recommend the game to others and, very important for the last chapter of this paper, 92% answered the question *"Is the format of a game appropriate to enhance the experience of other exhibitions too?"* with "yes" or "yes, very much".

Some statements from the players responding to the question „How would the game format enhance the experience of other exhibitions" might throw light on the question, why the results of the questionnaire are in general so positive: "Learning in a playful way is fantastic". "The game widens your interest and intensifies the ocupation with the exhibits". "Because of the activity you remember more". "Interactivity!" "It´s fun.".

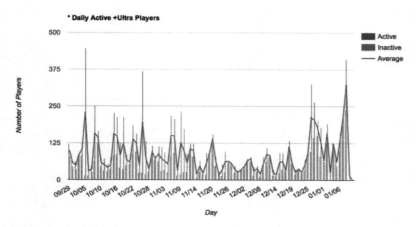

Fig. 2: Copyright Peter Lee/Nolgong

This chart shows the number of active and inactive players during the entire period of time the exhibition took place. Inactive players are players, who printed out the game ID but did not start playing any mission. Once a player started playing a mission, we call him active player. This differentiation allows us to monitor how many visitors were attracted by the tablets and pushed the button, but afterwards did not login to start the game. The comparison between nearly 15.000 inactive players to the number of 5,100 active players provides us with the conversion rate of about 34%. Compared to the average landing page conversion rate in online marketing (about 2,35 % and 5% are considered as a remarkable rate[4]), the conversion rate of game (+ultra) seems to be satisfying. This holds even truer, if one takes into consideration that playing a game in an exhibition is an innovative offer and the traditional visitor is not at all used to take profit of it. Also because there was no personal support, an unknown amount of inactive players might have dropped out, as they struggled with either choosing the right Wifi, opening the browser, typing in the website or with any other technical issue. game (+ultra) had 166 average players per day and 57 average active players per day.

---

4   http://www.wordstream.com/blog/ws/2014/03/17/what-is-a-good-conversion-rate

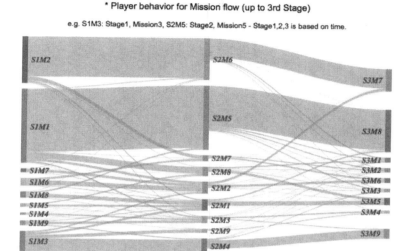

Fig. 3: Copyright Peter Lee/ Nolgong

This chart shall serve as an example, what data can be monitored. It shows the player's behaviour over three stages, so that we can understand the mission flow. Where did the players start and how did they move through the gameplay? This could serve as a basis for further investigation: What are the most popular missions? How does this popularity correlate with gender, age or educational status? How does the gameplay differ, depending on these factors? Combined with the answers from the questionnaire this delivers a powerful set of data. Curators and directors of museums and exhibitions get thus the opportunity to significantly enhance their understanding of their audience as well as of their venue. From the designer's perspective but also from the perspective of the curator it also enables to modify the experience and to monitor the effects resulting from these modifications. Given that the curator realizes, that a very important exhibit draws too less attention, it is then easy to spotlight it by simply changing the game dramaturgy.

Back to the data of game (+ultra): Out of the 5.100 active players, 1.748 have at least completed one mission or more. On average each person spent 29 minutes per mission and played 2.7 missions.

6   The Future of Museums as common Playgrounds

On the evidence of recent success stories like e.g. Ingress, an Augmented Reality game based on the Google maps technology, which is still being played by millions around the world, motivating them to explore the outside world guided by their smart phone or the great success of FoldIt, where 240.000 registered players contribute to the science of protein structure prediction by solving puzzles, the idea to transform museums into playgrounds may no longer seem utopian.

Todays technology makes it imaginable to offer a personalized, easy-to-use access for everyone to our cultural heritage. The smartphone could work as a digital assistant, using the intrinsic motivation of its owner to raise interest for the exhibits, intensifying the occupation with the complexity of our traditions, offering a playful and participative experience for everyone, no matter what age or what educational background the players have. Why not use topics from the popular culture to tempt audiences spending their time in museums? Why not using a Spiderman-Game which shows the children that this popular figure has so much in common with ancient heroes? And while the children play the Spiderman-Game, their parents enjoy the Buckminster Fuller Game, both, children and parents look at the same content at the same time at the same location, but it is the game dramaturgy which makes the difference, because the needs and interests of the specific user group is perfectly matched which the experience. The playful experience using popular topics could work as a bridge between the communicative memory and the cultural memory Jan Assman has written about.[5] The communicative memory is what we share within our community on an everyday basis. With the communicative memory we, as a society, can memorize a timespan of no longer than three generations. The cultural memory is where we store everything that goes beyond three generations. A game-based experience could in this way connect the communicative with the cultural memory. Since the individual character[6] as well as the society "creates" itself within the process of memorizing, this could be a major contribution for society building.

---

5   Jan Assmann. Religion und kulturelles Gedächtnis. München. 2000.
6   Thomas S. Henricks, taking into account the contributions of researchers like Jean Piaget, Roger Callois and others, comes to the conclusion: „Play is not a trivial endeavour. It is necessary for comprehending what we can be and what we can do." Thomas S. Henricks. Play as Self-Realization. Toward a General Theorie of Play. American Journal of Play. Volume 6. 2014. S. 211.

Just by playing the game, a second archive comes into life. Based on the fact, that the actions of the players deliver data about their interests, this would also allow to actively influence the process of memorizing. The Gamedesign could highlight or also hide certain aspects. In a large scale scenario this would mean, that we, to a certain extent, would be aware of what we have in our memory and what is currently forgotten. It is important to emphasize that these possibilities would have serious political and ethical implications: Who decides about what is important to memorize? Ideally a second step therefore should result in softening the boundaries between player and game designer creating a new figure which could be named "playsigner", a combination of a player with a game designer, because only then, the "drama of memory"[7] would truly be transformed into a participative, engaging "game of memory".

Literature

Assmann, Jan: Religion und kulturelles Gedächtnis. München 2000.
Gadamer, Hans-Georg: The Relevance of the Beautiful and other Essays. Cambridge 1987.
Henricks, Thomas S.: Play as Self-Realization. Toward a General Theorie of Play. American Journal of Play. Volume 6. 2014.
Huizinga, Johan: Homo Ludens. Hamburg 1956.
http://www.instituteofplay.org/work/projects/quest-schools/quest-to-learn/
http://www.wordstream.com/blog/ws/2014/03/17/what-is-a-good-conversion-rate

---

7   Jan Assmann. Religion und kulturelles Gedächtnis. München. 2000. S. 123.

Game Co-design with and for Refugees

An Intercultural Approach

Güven Çatak

Bahcesehir University Game Lab (BUG)

guven.catak@comm.bau.edu.tr

Jesse Himmelstein

Centre for Research and Interdisciplinarity

jesse@cri-paris.org

Carolina Islas Sedano

Ubium

carolina.islas@ubium.net

Daniel K. Schneider, Nicolas Szilas

University of Geneva

{daniel.schneider,nicolas.szilas}@unige.ch

Jouni Smed, Erkki Sutinen

University of Turku

{jouni.smed,erkki.sutinen}@utu.fi

Abstract

Mobile games have a potential to assist in the acculturation of immigrants and refugees. We propose how to design such games collaboratively based on co-design approach. We also review relevant game mechanics and technologies such as multiplaying, interactive storytelling, gamification, and virtual reality.

1   Introduction

Recent years have seen a growth of games designed to raise awareness of social issues. These "Games for Change" have brought attention to a variety of problems such as climate change, violence against women, homophobia, and clinical depression. There are also games aiming at raising awareness amongst host societies about the plight of refugees seeking asylum. Most of these games put the player in the position of a refugee forced to flee (e.g. *My Life as a Refugee, Darfur is Dying*) and who travels (e.g. *Passages, Cloud Chasers, Against All Odds*) to arrive at a border (e.g. *Papers Please, The Migrant Trail, Frontiers*). However, none are created to help refugees to integrate into their new communities. This shortcoming might be related to a somewhat alienated attitude to the newcomers: they are mostly a target for the host society's paternalistic care and caretakers. Whatever the reason for omitting refugees as gamers may be, this paper explores ways that bring immigrants as subjective users and co-designers of the games, interacting with players of the host society, rather than being sources of inspiration for games.

Based on a European research consortium's members' joint expertise and experiences from diverse encounters with newcomers, our intention is to devise an approach for developing games that help immigrants to adjust to their new surroundings and help people from the host culture to interact with refugees and to learn from them (e.g. their culture and traditions) while they re-discover their own. More precisely, the scheme calls for co-designing games and tools that allow both locals and immigrants to develop their intercultural competence to that brings them together (i.e. facilitate an effective acculturation process) [Hamm15]. Acquiring intercultural competence includes developing cultural awareness, knowledge about other cultures, intercultural sensitivity, and competence to act and to communicate in a cross-cultural context.

In the context of integration, both the host and refugee populations have much to learn about, from and with, the other. Hence, we want to merge a game design principle with a co-design approach that takes place in the physical environment where newcomers meet with the locals. First, the game mechanics used in the game will be designed to motivate players from both groups to learn and appreciate the other's culture, both the similarities and differences, and to become able to communicate effectively and to establish interpersonal relationships. Built upon an equal encounter, our scheme complements the traditional approach that separates between the domestic, intended users' culture and a foreign, observed culture. Secondly, on a more practical level, refugees who find themselves in an unfamiliar land are confronted with the demand to learn a new language, understand important elements of a new culture, and figure out how to conduct everyday matters and administrative procedures. Our design supports the refugees in developing strategies and skills to navigate and cope with their new reality, often by pulling the willing help of the host population who are well placed to assist. Following the co-design principles, games that our approach will help to create also should allow locals to develop new attitudes, skills and behaviors allowing them to interact in a more meaningful way with various groups of immigrants, with the ultimate goal of sharing life so that no one remains excluded or marginalized. Thus, the co-design principle complements the traditional approach that is based upon the exclusively assumed needs of the observed or cared newcomers.

2   Background

Europe is facing a crisis as the largest group of refugees in decades flees war and insecurity in their home countries and attempts to gain entry into Europe. This influx of refugees comes at a time when Europe is still struggling to escape from economic recession. Eternal fears of immigrants "stealing jobs", increasing crime, and bankrupting the welfare systems are accentuated by fears of terrorism. Some political groups are calling on the European Union to reject the refugees altogether, or to form new barriers to immigration between EU countries.

Integration is a complex and dynamic process. Figure 1 illustrates Ager's and Strang's conceptual framework that defines ten core domains of integration [AS08]. Most refugee support organizations focus on primary needs such as rights, housing, and health. However, two-way integration requires a long-term commitment and major cultural, financial and political investments. Some refugee support organizations do provide services beyond the basic needs (e.g. legal advice regarding various administrative procedures, language tuition and professional mentoring). Too little is done to enhance the process of building bridges between refugees and locals, maybe because too little is known on pathways and processes facilitating and driving integration [Loso15]. As a result, refugees are rarely considered and valued for the skills and experience they bring from abroad.

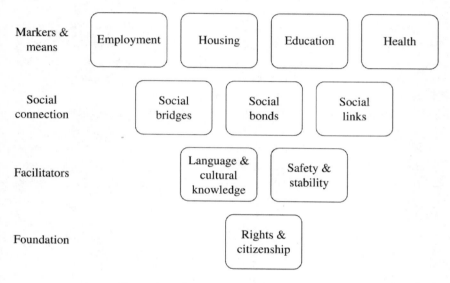

Fig. 1: Core domains of integration [AS08].

We perceive an opportunity to improve intercultural communication and social connections, two pillars for successful integration. It is important to attempt to facilitate acculturation of the newcomers and host societies through improving the cultural competence of its individual members, which is connected to identity, belonging, recognition and self-respect [CKVV02]. With respect to the Ager's and Strang's model, we aim to work on the language and cultural knowledge "facilitator" and the social connections "layer", within an intercultural competency perspective or put more simply: help people talk to each other and understand each other.

3 Game mechanics and technology

Mobile gaming technology is a natural platform for accomplishing our goal, for several reasons. First, mobile games are an excellent way to reach refugees, who for a large part have smartphones but not necessarily computers or game consoles. Owning a €100 Android smartphone or €30 second-hand iPhone is not a luxury but a matter of survival for refugees, and they are likely to be ready to pay for necessary services. Moreover, smartphones work well in a variety of settings, including within social events and when the player is on the move. Finally, the cameras and microphones embedded in mobile devices can empower games that stress personal communication, such as between players from different communities. Last but not least, to take into consideration for the design of certain games that central locations in particular countries (e.g. down town, touristic points) provide free-wifi allowing the players to diminish costs and enhance different game possibilities.

Given that integration is a relatively unexplored subject in games, there is a need to investigate a number of techniques and technologies that can be useful (see Figure 2). To provide a glimpse of what directions our game projects will likely take, we will discuss a number of promising approaches that we have already identified. Each is supported by one or many technologies that, in our view, are particularly appropriate.

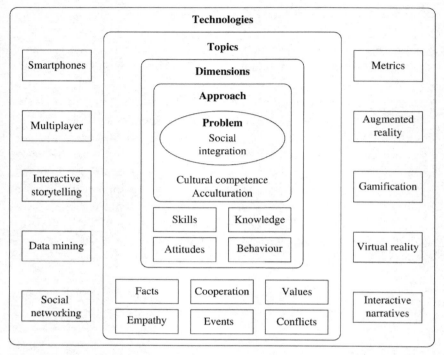

Fig. 2: Gaming technology supports the game topics that in turn target the dimensions of cultural competency and acculturation.

3.1 Basic knowledge and skills

It is only human to fear the unknown. Immigration can easily summon sentiments of "us versus them", by drawing stark contrasts between the host population and the immigrant group based on anything from religion to diet to wealth. Conversely, learning about the other culture leads to a better understanding of what the differences really are, and how they will affect exchanges between people of different backgrounds.

Perhaps the simplest type of game for education involves quizzes, in which the player must guess about another person's culture or history. Although quizzes are considered a type of game, and often are used in learning and lately as an important tool in gamified applications, they can be also considered as game components upon which to build more elaborated game mechanics.

Moreover, they can form the basis for more interesting dynamics when placed within a group context, such as a *multiplayer games using smartphones.*

Another type of game that is well adapted to education is *interactive story-telling,* in which a player makes choices that will generate dramatically compelling stories based on the input [Smed14]. In our context, the story-scape could reflect the realities of the refugee's travel from her home to the new host country as well as the realities of the new host country. Here, the player – whether a refugee or a local person – will learn to see a broader picture as the story unfolds during the gameplay. The refugee will encounter the worries of the local people (e.g. fear of losing a job, rising rents and reducing social security) as well as the local people will encounter the traumas and worries of the refugees and maybe their own as well (e.g. anxiety of what has happened to the loved ones, starting a new life and finding an identity in the new society). Storytelling games can also foster collaboration and cooperation among the players of different backgrounds while they immerse into visualizing a brilliant future together.

3.2   Empathy, respect, curiosity and openness

If integration is about the fusion of two or more cultures to create a new and richer culture while maintaining their identities, then it stands to reason that interacting with another culture may require a change in various attitudes. A starting point is empathy (i.e. to be able to put oneself in "other's shoes"). This could be formed through social contact with the other group as mediated by the game technology. Empathy is not foreign to games especially *role-playing games* where the player has to assume the role of a character and stay true to it. Another example would be a smartphone game that allows a refugee and non-refugee to exchange photos of their daily activities, therefore removing language as a barrier for communication. Such a game could also benefit from social networking so that players spread their own discoveries to their friends, family, and associates.

Alternatively, a game could make teams out of refugees and non-refugees in which they have to work together to accomplish their shared goal, as a way to build community and contacts. By cooperating with someone from a different background, a player learns to accept, and perhaps even value, what that person has to offer.

A more radical way to create empathy is through *virtual reality* (VR). In the recent project *The Machine to be Another* [BeAn17], two users are given VR headgear that simultaneously films one person's view and shows them what the other person sees. As the users move in a synchronized fashion, the system provides the powerful illusion of inhabiting another person's body. This project provides an intriguing jumping-off point for similar projects to create empathy via VR that could be performed between refugees and non-refugees.

Two other powerful motivators in games and learning, are curiosity and fantasy. These motivators engage the players to immerse themselves into the game mechanics and the game theme. While co-design games with the diverse audience will allow us to understand how to stimulate the player's curiosity and fantasy [ILVSE13].

3.3   Cooperation and behavioral change

Networked multiplayer games have brought large groups of players together. However, the usual stance is to put the players opposing and competing against one another or to collaborate in small groups against a common enemy. Competition between groups can widen and deepen the gap that divides the communities. Collaborative game mechanics can naturally high-light the advantages of working together in mixed groups, instead of perceiving other groups as threats. Cooperative gameplay, which allows players to work together, has gained popularity in the recent years. It is present in many games genres and can take forms such as having the human to play against a common AI-controlled opponent, sharing resources or information among allies, or assisting and guiding other human players.

In the development of digital collaborative and cooperative games, it aids us to understand better their mechanics, when analyzing cooperative and collaborative board games such as *Pandemic* or *Ghost Stories*. The combi-nation of competition and cooperation found in team sports can also be exploited here, by forming diverse teams that compete against each other. Teams could be formed on criteria that are common to all people, such as birth month, or simply in a random fashion.

In collaborative and cooperative games, the actions of all the players are relevant to achieve jointly the game's goal. The story of the game might be changed and at the moment might not be so explicitly related to the reality they are leaving behind, but to the reality they want to achieve, for example, the narrative to develop a new international business. While visualizing the future, players will learn the basic skills, grounded in the present, to reach the game's goal.

Extraordinary examples of cooperation occurs in crisis or disaster situations, when distant strangers brought together by the realities of the same dangerous situation can suddenly become communicative and helpful of one another. This phenomenon could be exploited by games that put people into situations in which they must work together. Through the process, it becomes evident to players that teamwork is their only way toward success. This concept could take a number of forms, including that of a role-playing game as is done in crisis management trainings.

3.4   Value of diversity and immigration

Another approach is to promote the value of diversity and immigration in itself. This could be done in an abstract way such as by creating a simulation game in which the user can control and see the valuable effects of immigration on the economy of a society. It also could be accomplished in a more concrete fashion, by providing stories of successful immigrants, and of relationships between people of diverse backgrounds that lead to valuable life changes.

This approach can be powered through a combination of theory, evidence, and anecdotes. For example, despite the popular belief that immigrants (and thus refugees) hurt the host economy, economists generally agree that both low-skilled and high-skilled workers improve the economy that they are moving to.

Indeed, recent economics research finds that immigration actually improves wages for unskilled workers in the host country [FP15] as well as the country the immigrants are leaving [Clem11]. As the economist and author Philippe Legrain points out:

> *"... Many of the arguments that are framed in the economic way actually are xenophobic in origin. ... When migrants are working they're*

accused of stealing our jobs, and when they're out of work, they're
accused of sponging off welfare. When they're rich, they're accused
of driving prices up and when they're poor, they're accused of driving
standards down." [Frea15]

The relation between crime and immigration is harder to quantify, due to the
complicating factors of police practices, judicial discrimination, unemployment, and uneven crime reporting. However a recent study on immigration
into Europe during the 2000s found "that an increase in immigration does not
affect crime victimization, but it is associated with an increase in the fear of
crime, the latter being consistently and positively correlated with the natives'
unfavorable attitude toward immigrants. Our results reveal a misconception of
the link between immigration and crime among European natives." [Nunz15]

A further approach of this type is to use metaphor to discuss immigration and
diversity in a fictional context such as animals or space exploration.

3.5   Current events

Newsgames are a type of game that focuses on current events. Often they
involve casting the player in the role of a journalist in order to discover the
gritty reality of a situation in the form of *personal narratives*. Since the refugee
crisis regularly makes the headlines, and is tied to a number of ongoing
conflicts, it makes an ideal context for this kind of game.

For example, one could imagine a game in which the player investigates
(perhaps using virtual reality to heighten perceptions) the shocking and scary
realities that Syrian refugees are fleeing. By putting the player in the active
role of investigating these events, they are more likely to take them to heart
then they would in a more passive role by watching TV news or reading
newspaper headlines.

Another approach often used by newsgames is that of *interactive data visualization*. Players are provided with an interactive environment that empowers
them to explore and comprehend publicly available data through which they
come to their own conclusions on what the data reveals. Taking data visualization an additional step forward, *augmented reality* could be used to effectively insert an additional viewpoint (that of the other culture) into current

events, in order to glimpse how another group perceives the same news. For example, UNITAR works already in this direction.

3.6   Motivation

A central premise of *gamification* and game design alike is that players can be motivated by game mechanics to adopt certain behaviors in order to win a game. Such motivators may be extrinsic, such as point and leaderboard systems that play on a player's desire to outcompete their peers or simply overcome the challenge held before them. Or they can be intrinsic, when playing the game in itself provides enough pleasure or satisfaction to motivate the player to continue.

We can use gamification techniques based on analyzing and utilizing the eight core drives behind the games and players [Chou15]:

1. "Epic meaning and calling" taps into the players' believe that they are something greater than they are or that they are chosen to do something.
2. "Development and accomplishment" uses the internal drive to make progress, develop skills and overcome challenges (e.g. points, badges and leaderboards).
3. "Empowerment of creativity and feedback" keeps the players engaged in a creative process where they continuously have to figure out things and try different combinations (e.g. Lego bricks and *Minecraft*).
4. "Ownership and possession" recognizes that when players feel ownership, they want to make what they own better and own even more.
5. "Social influence and relatedness" focuses on the social elements driving people (e.g. social acceptance, companionship and competition).
6. "Scarcity and impatience" uses the players' fear of losing an opportunity or missing a chance (i.e. so-called "appointment dynamics")
7. "Unpredictability and curiosity" taps into finding out what happens next (e.g. stories and gambling).
8. "Loss and avoidance" recognizes the players' wish to avoid something negative to happen.

These core drives can be combined in gamification. For example, a recent refugee could be motivated to navigate the local administration by making it a mission (Accomplishment, Meaning), learn the local language and culture together with locals (Social influence, Empowerment), or attend trainings that will allow them to advance their position in society (Ownership, Avoidance). Similarly, a local could be motivated to reach out to refugees, provide them with useful guidance (Social Influence, Accomplishment), or learn about skills and training that refugees could contribute to the local community (Meaning, Empowerment).

Finally, gamification techniques could speed data gathering efforts that in turn empower *data mining* to better track the fate of refugees and the effect of social programs meant to encourage their integration.

4   Conclusion

There are possibilities to develop games using co-design to include refugees and local people to work together in the same project that will benefit both of them, in particular when games themselves include collaboration mechanics between locals and refugees. The ideas that we presented in this paper use different game mechanics. These mechanics are not the only ones available but they seem to be the best candidates for creating such applications. The implementation of these ideas is still underway and the first prototypes are currently under development. Although the results of their usability and effects still need to be evaluated, the co-design process alone has turned out to be a fruitful one and it has allowed us to see its potential.

The Co-design approach has a potential to address difficult topics in game design. Games are normally designed by specialized game designers. Even in projects dealing with gamification or serious games, the end-users are often seen as a customer that is kept out from the actual design process; they can give initial input on the design and possibly feedback during the development phase but they are not seen as designers themselves. We want to challenge this view, not only for the current setup, but also more broadly. We envision a new type of a game designer who can share their work, share their know-ledge and also learn from their co-designers.

Literature

[AS08]   Ager, A., & Strang, A. (2008). Understanding Integration: A Conceptual Framework. Journal of Refugee Studies, 21(2), pp. 166–191.

[BeAn17]   BeAnotherLab, http://www.themachinetobeanother.org/. Accessed Mar. 6, 2017.

[CKVV02]   Castles, S., Korac, M., Vasta, E., & Vertovec, S. (2002). Integration: Mapping the field. Home Office Online Report, 29(03), pp. 115–118.

[Chou15]   Chou, Y. (2015). Actionable Gamification: Beyond Points, Badges, and Leaderboards. Octalysis Media.

[Clem11]   Clemens, M. (2011). Economics and Emigration: Trillion-Dollar Bills on the Sidewalk? Journal of Economic Perspectives, 25(3), pp. 83–106.

[FP15]   Foged, M. & Peri, G. (2015). Immigrants' Effect on Native Workers: New Analysis on Longitudinal Data. CReAM Discussion Paper Series. Centre for Research and Analysis of Migration (CReAM), Department of Economics, University College London. http://ideas.repec.org/p/crm/wpaper/1507.html. Accessed Feb. 28, 2017

[Frea15]   Freakanomics podcast, "Is Migration a Basic Human Right?". Dec 17 2015. http://freakonomics.com/2015/12/17/is-migration-a-basic-human-right-a-new-freakonomics-radio-podcast/.

[Hamm15] Hammer, M. (2015). The Developmental Paradigm for Intercultural Competence Research. International Journal of Intercultural Relations, 48, pp. 12–13.

[ILVSE13] Islas Sedano, C., Leendertz, V., Vinni, M., Sutinen, E., Ellis, S. (2013). Hypercontextualized Learning Games: Fantasy, Motivation and Engagement in Reality. Journal of Simulations and Games.

[Loso15]   Losoncz, I. (2015). Goals without Means: A Mertonian Critique of Australia's Resettlement Policy for South Sudanese Refugees. Journal of Refugee Studies. doi:10.1093/jrs/fev017

[Nunz15]   Nunziate, L. (2015). Immigration and crime: evidence from victimization data. Journal of Population Economics, 28(3), pp. 697–736.

[Smed14]   Smed, J. (2014). Interactive Storytelling: Approaches, Applications and Aspirations. International Journal of Virtual Communities and Social Networking, 6(1), pp. 22–34.

Simple Baseline Models for Multimodal Question Answering in the Cultural Heritage Domain

Shurong Sheng, Marie-Francine Moens
Department of Computer Science
KU Leuven
Celestijnenlaan 200A, 3001 Leuven, Belgium
{shurong.sheng, sien.moens}@cs.kuleuven.be

Abstract

With the increasing use of mobile devices, taking pictures becomes an easy and natural way for people to interact with cultural objects. In such circumstances, we propose multimodal question answering (MQA) to offer personalized answers to users' questions. In this research, a query from an end user consists of an image of an artwork and a textual question referring to this image. For this purpose, we built a dataset especially for MQA in the cultural heritage domain (Sheng et al., 2016). In the present study, we give a detailed introduction about this multimodal question answering system and its advances. Three baseline models are implemented for retrieving answers from the documentation in the dataset, including a text-matching model, an image-matching model and a multimodal intersection model. These three models use different methods to perform the matching. The text-matching model ranks the candidate passages purely by their similarity with the textual part of a multimodal query. The image-matching model ranks the candidate passages purely by the similarity between the images around these passages that match the visual query. The intersection model performs the ranking task by comparing both the textual and visual part of a multimodal query with the content in documentation and taking the shared passages that were found relevant. The mean average precision (MAP) score is adopted as main evaluation criterion for these three baseline models and it reaches a highest value of 0.2079 when using the intersection model. NIL recall and precision will be reported instead if no answer exists in the document collection for a particular multimodal query.

1   Introduction

With new emerging technologies like smartphones, augmented reality, high-resolution digital imaging and many more, the visitors' experience inside a museum has been entirely redefined. Yet, to the best of our knowledge, there is still no mobile-friendly application which dives deeper into very engaged guidance by answering detailed and personalized questions from visitors. We hereby propose multimodal question answering (MQA) research in the cultural heritage domain in which personalized and flexible questions of visitors are expressed as a multimodal query. i.e., a query composed of a photo of a whole artwork (or detail of it) taken by a visitor augmented by a natural language phrased query as shown in Fig.1. Questions in the left column of Fig.1 are labeled full-image-level (FIL) questions and questions in the right column are labeled part-of-image-level (POIL) questions, which are concerned about details of the artwork in the bounding boxes. With this multimodal question answering system, visitors will receive personalized answers to their questions.

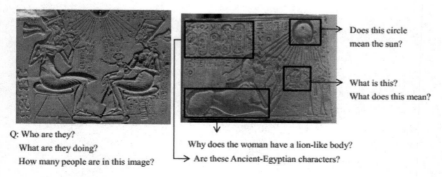

Fig.1: Exemplary questions.

The MQA system proposed in this study serves as a digital tool in the cultural heritage domain. State-of-the-art research on digital tools in the area of cultural heritage mainly focuses on augmented reality. Some of them are unimodal such as showing a 3D model of an artwork image (Alsadik et al, 2014; Tait et al, 2016) and some concern multiple aspects including story telling and topic searching by designing a game (Chang et al, 2015; Coenen et al, 2013). However, to the best of our knowledge, none of these studies give fine-grained information which is exactly what users desire. Therefore, MQA in the cultural heritage domain constitutes a more personalized and intuitive way which does not exist yet for people to learn about cultural information. Moreover, interest in MQA has increased rapidly in recent years. Compared to other application areas of MQA, e.g., in-door scenes and wild-life animals, MQA tasks in the cultural heritage domain are more challenging. Due to the uniqueness of ancient artworks and historical factors, it is tough to obtain a large amount of data for each artwork and thus MQA has to deal with few training data. Therefore, MQA research in other applications can not directly be transplanted to the cultural heritage domain.

Our contributions in this paper are three-fold: (1) We propose MQA in the cultural heritage domain to further improve the experience of users; (2) We implement three baseline models retrieving answers from the documentation in our dataset to users' full-image-level questions; and (3) We verify the efficacy of these three proposed models on the collected full-image-level multimodal questions.

The remainder of this paper is organized as follows: section 2 introduces existing related research in the cultural heritage domain, section 3 provides a short description of the dataset we use, section 4 details the three baseline models, section 5 describes the results of the baseline models and gives some analysis, and section 6 concludes this paper and points out future research.

2   Related Work

There are few studies that concern MQA in the cultural heritage domain. The pre-dominant method in the MQA task when performed in other fields regards employing a deep neural network which is trained on a large amount of question-answer pairs. After training, the model then can be used to predict or classify the answer to a new question (Malinowski et al, 2015; Yang et al, 2016). It is difficult to collect training data in the cultural heritage domain that contains sufficient question-answer pairs due to uniqueness of each artwork as mentioned in the introduction section. This is why we perform the MQA task from the viewpoint of information retrieval without the need for a large amount of training data, i.e., retrieval of relevant images and passages from the documentation with regard to a multimodal query.

The mature indoor positioning and data (metadata) linking technologies saves our time to do image retrieval in this MQA task. On one hand, indoor positioning for mobile devices is a very popular commercial technology based on techniques including magnetic positioning, Bluetooth, Wi-Fi positioning, etc[1]. Such techniques also enable mobile software pushing notifications to mobile users based on their location as mentioned in (https://en.wikipedia.org/wiki/IBeacon). Therefore, we assume that for a given multimodal query concerning an artwork from an end user, we know the metadata e.g., title, description of the artwork according to the indoor position of the visitor. On the other hand, there are extensive studies on data (metadata) linking in the cultural heritage domain (Isaac et al, 2013; De et al, 2013). And most digital archives of cultural heritage such as Europeana[2], Google Arts & Culture[3], Museum of Fine Arts, Boston[4] allow searching by the metadata of an artwork and returns its related documents afterwards. Hence, for each artwork in a museum room, its related documents can be regarded as prior knowledge. Related images regarding an artwork can then be figured out beforehand by simple annotation of the images as related or not in the related documentation as also done for our small-sized dataset that represents the artworks in a museum room.

As for text retrieval in the cultural heritage domain, (Marijn Koolen et al, 2009) give an overview about how information retrieval techniques can be used to provide information access to cultural heritage and provide a case study of applying a vector space model for information retrieval in practice within a museum. (Markantonatou et al, 2017) perform the retrieval of structured information from unstructured documentation of the Europeana collection. We follow (Markantonatou et al, 2017) storing the data from the unstructured web documents as structured items into MongoDB and utilize a vector space model which computes the distance of passages and questions as the retrieval model.

---

1   https://en.wikipedia.org/wiki/Indoor_positioning_system
2   http://www.europeana.eu/portal/en
3   https://www.google.com/culturalinstitute/beta/u/0/
4   http://www.mfa.org/

3   Dataset

3.1   Statistics

As mentioned in (Sheng et al., 2016), the dataset we use in this paper includes typical artworks of the old Egyptian Amarna period. This dataset also contains multimodal documentation obtained from the Web and multimodal questions with regard to the collected artworks, which are drafted by many different users. The documents in the dataset serve as target source where the answers are retrieved from, and each passage in the documentation is a candidate answer. The statistics of the documentation are shown below in Table 1.

Number of passages	Number of images	Vocabulary size
19587	414	17074

Table 1: Statistics of the documentation in the dataset.

As mentioned in the introduction section, there are two coarse-grained types of multimodal questions in our MQA research: full-image-level (FIL) questions whose textual part refers to a full image, and part-of-image-level (POIL) questions whose textual part refers to part of a query image marked by a bounding box. We focus on methods regarding FIL questions in this paper.

As questions in the dataset are realistic samples from users, not all FIL questions have corresponding answers in the documentation. For example, for the question "why is the woman so ugly?", we call its response "NIL" following the TREC 2003 question answering shared task (Voorhees et al, 2003) and the statistics of such questions are shown in Table 2.

Number of FIL questions	Number of non-NIL questions	Number of NIL questions
423	290	133

Table 2: Statistics of the FIL questions in the dataset.

3.2   Database scheme

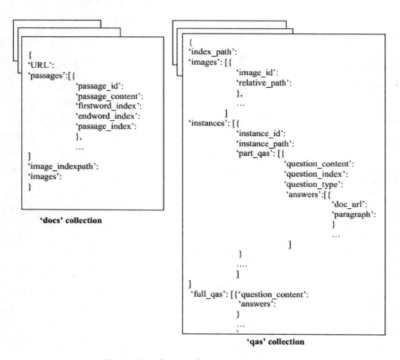

Fig. 2: Database scheme in the dataset.

As shown in Fig. 2, the documentation information and question-answer pairs are stored into two collections "docs" and "qas" in "Bason" (Binary Jason) format in MongoDB. In the "docs" collection, each document is a record containing all its relative visual and textual information as structured items. A document is identified by its "URL" and each passage is identified by a starting-word index and ending-word index within the document. Passage_index is the index for a passage in the whole documentation. Similarly, question_index in the "qas" collection is used to identify each question in the whole question collection. Answers for each question are identified by both their originating documents ("doc_url" in Fig. 2) and passages.

4 Approaches

In this section, we give a detailed explanation of the three baseline models to retrieve answers for full-image-level questions in the dataset including the retrieval methods, the parameter set-up methods and evaluation methods for each model.

4.1 Representation of textual questions and documents

For each full-image-level multimodal question q_i in the dataset, we have built a corpus of the textual question t_{qi} and a candidate passage set $P_{candidate} = \{p_1, p_2, ..., p_t\}$ in the "docs" collection. The question and all passages in $P_{candidate}$ are projected into a common vector space based on the corpus after tokenization and removal of stop words, with each element in the vector being the term frequency of the corresponding question or passage (number of word occurrences) in the corpus, i.e., $t_{qi} = [tf_{1i}, tf_{2i}, ..., tf_{ni}]$ and $p_j = [tf_{1j}, tf_{2j}, ..., tf_{nj}]$, where n is the vocabulary size.

4.2 Text-matching model

In this model, for each textual query t_{qi} in the textual question set $T_q = \{t_{q1}, t_{q2}, ..., t_{qm}\}$, the passage set is $P = \{p_1, p_2, ..., p_t\}$ from the whole documentation. The similarity between a passage p_j in P and a question t_{qi} is computed by the semantic gap between them using cosine similarity.

$$\text{sim}(p_j, t_{qi}) = cosine(p_j, t_{qi}) = \frac{p_j \cdot t_{qi}}{|p_j| * |t_{qi}|}$$

The result of this model is a similarity vector $s_i = [s_{i1}, s_{i2}, ..., s_{it}]$ which leads to a ranking list of the passages corresponding to t_{qi}.

4.3 Image-matching model

As introduced in section 2, for each visual query v_{qi} in the query image set $V_q = \{v_{q1}, v_{q2}, ..., v_{qm}\}$, its related documents are known as prior knowledge. The corresponding related image set $V_{di} = \{v_{di1}, v_{di2}, ..., v_{dih}\}$ (images referring to the same artwork with the query v_{qi}) is composed of all images which are manually annotated as related for our small-scaled dataset. The answer candidate passage set $P_i = \{p_{i1}, p_{i2}, ..., p_{in}\}$ for a query v_{qi} contains all the passages around the relevant images in V_{di}. The similarity between a candidate answer p_{ij} in P_i and a visual query v_{qi} denotes the similarity between the image v_{dij} in V_{di}

around the passage p_{ij} and the visual query v_{qi}. The passages in P_i are ranked based on their relative position to the relevant images, details about the ranking method are introduced in section 4.5. The result of this model is a similarity vector $s_i = [s_{i1}, s_{i2}, ..., s_{in}]$ with regards to a query v_{qi}.

4.4   Intersection model
In this model, the candidate answer set $P_i = \{p_{i1}, p_{i2}, ..., p_{in}\}$ for each visual query v_{qi} is obtained in the same way as the image-matching model. However, the ranking method in this model is based on the matching between a textual question t_{qi} (corresponding to v_{qi}) with a passage p_{ij} in P_i performed using cosine similarity. All experimental settings for this model are the same as for the image-matching model.

4.5   Parameters set-up
In the text-matching model and the intersection model, a similarity threshold m_s is set up for the similarity vector s_i to check whether a query q_i has NIL as its answer. That is,

$$\text{if } \begin{cases} max(s_i) > m_s, & not\ NIL\ answer \\ otherwise, & NIL\ answer \end{cases}$$

With the above formula, the full-image-level questions are classified into two sets: set $Q_g = \{q_1, q_2, ..., q_x\}$ where questions have ground-truth answers and set $Q_{nil} = \{q_1, q_2, ..., q_y\}$ where questions have NIL answers (We call this procedure "NIL classification" further in this paper).

In the image-matching and the intersection model, different number of passages n_p around each relevant image yields different results since these passages compose the candidate answer set for a query. Thus, n_p is a parameter needed to set up in these two models. Here we assume that a fixed number of passages before and after a relevant image are of the same importance.

In the image-matching model, when the number of passages around each relevant image equals 2 ($n_p = 2$), i.e., only the passages before and after each relevant image, all the passages in the candidate answer set are the nearest passages as for the relevant images with regard to a query. Hence all of them receive a same score (1.0 in our case). When the number of passages around each relevant image exceeds 2 ($n_p > 2$), the nearest two passages within the whole candidate answer set, i.e., the passages before and after all relevant images, still receive a same score of 1.0. This score is then discounted by a fixed number (0.2 in our case) which is the same for all documents for further away passages. The passages are then ranked by the score they receive.

4.6 Evaluation metrics

We focus on full-image-level (FIL) questions when evaluating the three baseline models. Mean average precision (MAP) is adopted as the main evaluation method to evaluate each model. Details about parameter adjusting are introduced in section 4.7.

For the question set $Q_g = \{q_1, q_2, ..., q_x\}$, where x is the number of queries with ground truth answers, we use MAP to perform evaluation. Let $\{p_{1j}, p_{2j}, ..., p_{tj}\}$ be the set of t_j relevant passage, i.e., ground truth answers for a question $q_j \in Q_g$, and let R_{jk} be the set of ranked retrieved results ordered from the highest scored passage till the found relevant paragraph. The MAP score for the set Q_g is given as:

$$\text{MAP} = \frac{1}{x} \sum_{j=1}^{x} \frac{1}{tj} \sum_{k=1}^{tj} P\text{recision} \quad R_{jk}$$

where precision is the fraction of the passages retrieved that are relevant to the query. When a relevant passage is not retrieved, the precision value in the above equation is zero. MAP score ranges from 0 to 1.

For question set $Q_{nil} = \{q_1, q_2, ..., q_y\}$, where y is the number of queries with NIL answers, we use NIL precision and NIL recall to perform evaluation following the TREC QA 2003 guidelines (Voorhees et al, 2003). NIL precision is the fraction of correctly retrieved NIL answers, and NIL recall is the ratio of the number of times NIL was correctly returned versus the number of ground truth NIL questions.

4.7 Experimental set up

1) For the text-matching model, the similarity threshold m_s is obtained by a 4-fold cross validation method. The full-image-level question set is divided into three sets, i.e., training set (60% data), validation set (20% data) and test set (20% data). We empirically pick up some maximum values from the similarity vectors in the training set as candidate thresholds $T = \{t_1, t_2, ..., t_q\}$ and compute the corresponding MAP score for each threshold with the validation set in each fold. The t_i in T yielding best average MAP score in the cross validation method is adopted as m_s. For the image-matching model, the parameter needed to set up is the number of passages around each relevant

image n_p, which is obtained also by a 4-fold cross validation method. And for the intersection model, both the number of passages around each relevant image n_p and the similarity threshold m_s are parameters needed to set up. The combination of these two parameters is obtained similarly as in the text-matching model using a 4-fold cross validation method. We assume that n_p should be even, i.e., 2, 4, 6 respectively for the image-matching and intersection models.

2) We construct pipeline experiments evaluating the text-matching model and the intersection model with only MAP (without performing NIL classification). By comparing different MAP results of experiments with and without NIL classification, we can qualitatively study its influence on the system's ability of retrieving correct answers measured by MAP.

5   Results and Analysis

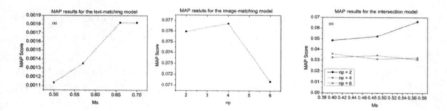

Fig. 3: (a) MAP results when changing the similarity threshold m_s in the text-matching model. (b) MAP results when changing the passage number n_p around each relevant image for the image-matching model. (c) MAP results when changing both m_s and n_p for the intersection model.

From Fig. 3, we can figure out the parameters yielding the best MAP in each model. For the text-matching model, the similarity threshold m_s should be 0.7; for the image-matching model, the number of passages n_p around each relevant image should be 4, and for the intersection models, the combination of m_s and n_p should be 0.57/2. The best results for each model with these values are shown in following sections.

5.1 Text-matching model

	MAP	NIL recall	NIL precision
Without NIL classification (T1)	0.038	N/A	N/A
With NIL classification (T2)	0.0006	0.2089	0.1052

Table 3: Evaluation results for the text-matching model with and without NIL classification. Note: NIL recall and NIL precision are not applicable in T1.

	What	When	Who	Why	Where	Which	How	Yes or no	Selective
T1	0.026	0.003	0.12	0.08	**0.13**	0.004	0.0005	0.009	0.031
T2	0.0003	0.0004	0.0015	**0.0036**	0.0004	0.0013	0.0003	0.0029	0.0001

Table 4: MAP for different types of questions using the text-matching model.

5.2 Image-matching model

	MAP	NIL recall	NIL precision
Without NIL classification (T1)	0.0762	N/A	N/A

Table 5: Evaluation results for the image-matching model without NIL classification.

	What	When	Who	Why	Where	Which	How	Yes or no	Selective
T1	0.0667	0.0	0.1121	0.0255	0.0221	0.0952	0.0513	0.1170	**0.2019**

Table 6: MAP for different types of questions using the image-matching model.

5.3   Intersection model

	MAP	NIL recall	NIL precision
Without question classification (T1)	0.2079	N/A	N/A
With question classification (T2)	0.083	1.0	0.4268

Table 7: Evaluation results for the intersection model with and without NIL classification.

	What	When	Who	Why	Where	Which	How	Yes or no	Selec-tive
T1	0.202	0.0178	**0.3130**	0.1122	0.1999	0.0571	0.1662	0.2482	0.1776
T2	–	–	0.083	–	–	–	–	–	–

Table 8: MAP for different types of questions using the intersection model.

5.4   Results analysis

In the above sections, we compared the MAP scores of the three models with different similarity threshold m_s and number of passages around each relevant image n_p, details of the best results for each model are listed. MAP results without NIL classification are also reported to study the impact of NIL classification on the system's capability of retrieving correct answers. The results that are obtained even with the best parameter setting are very low, showing the difficulty of the task.

When applying the NIL classification, the intersection model performs best among the three models both in recognizing correct answers measured by MAP and in recognizing NIL questions measured by NIL precision and recall. Therefore, it is optimal to combine the two modalities, i.e., text and image in our multimodal question answering task. The processing time for each question of the baseline models is under 10 milliseconds.

Overall, after performing NIL classification, the system is weak in retrieving correct answers from the documentation measured by MAP because of the propagated errors of the NIL classification. Moreover, the image-matching model and intersection model filter out many passages based on their mechanisms. These passages may contain answers to quite a few questions. Finally, the cosine similarity in the text-matching and the intersection-models heavily relies on matching words between question and answer passages, resulting in an insufficient ability to find out accurate answers.

As for MAP, the models may perform better for certain types of questions as shown in Tables 4, 6 and 8. These question types are consistent with (Sheng et al, 2016): "what" questions are about the features of an object (e.g., "What does this picture want to express?") , "When" questions are related to time with regard to the subject (e.g., "When does this person die?"), "Who" questions are about the identity of a person (e.g., "Who is this?"), "Why"questions are about the reason of some phenomenon (e.g., "Why does she look so abstract?"), "Where" questions are about the location of an object (e.g., "Where do they live in their period?"), "Which" questions typically need reasoning about the object (e.g., "Which country does the person come from"), "How" questions are about the methods related to an object (e.g., "How was this statue made smooth?"), "Yes or No" questions are the ones that you can answer with Yes or No (e.g., "Is this person a queen?"), and "Selective" questions (e.g., "Is this person a man or a woman?"). Considering different types of questions, the type of "Who" questions yield the best MAP of 0.3130 using the intersection model when there is no NIL classification.

6   Conclusion and Future Work

In this paper, we have introduced three simple baseline models and have used several methods including MAP, NIL recall and precision, to evaluate all models with full-image-level questions. We conclude that a combination of two modalities, i.e., text and image, yield the best results.

Since the overall MAP value after NIL classification is quite low in this paper, in a next step, we will seek methods to improve the question-answering performance according to the result analysis in section 5.4. Meanwhile, we will study computer vision methods which can deal with part-of-image-level questions in the dataset.

Literature

[Alsa14]   Alsadik, Bashar, et al. "Minimal camera networks for 3D image based modeling of cultural heritage objects." Sensors 14.4 (2014): pp. 5785–5804.

[Coen13]   Coenen, Tanguy, Lien Mostmans, and Kris Naessens. "MuseUs: Case study of a pervasive cultural heritage serious game." Journal on Computing and Cultural Heritage (JOCCH) 6.2 (2013): p. 8.

[De13]   De Boer, Victor, et al. "Amsterdam museum linked open data." Semantic Web 4.3 (2013): pp. 237–243.

[Isaa13]   Isaac, Antoine, and Bernhard Haslhofer. "Europeana linked open data–data. europeana. eu." Semantic Web 4.3 (2013): pp. 291–297.

[Karo15]   Karoui, Aous, Iza Marfisi-Schottman, and Sébastien George. "Towards an efficient mobile learning games design model." Proceedings of the European Conference on Games Based Learning. Academic Conferences International Limited, 2015.

[Kool09]   Koolen, Marijn, Jaap Kamps, and Vincent de Keijzer. "Information retrieval in cultural heritage." Interdisciplinary Science Reviews 34.2-3 (2009): pp. 268–284.

[Mark17]   Markantonatou, Stella, Panagiotis Minos, and George Pavlidis. "Retrieving Structured Information from (Semi-)/(Un-) Structured Cultural Object Documentation." International Journal of Computational Methods in Heritage Science (IJCMHS) 1.1 (2017): pp. 89–99.

[Mate5]   Malinowski, Mateusz, Marcus Rohrbach, and Mario Fritz. "Ask your neurons: A neural-based approach to answering questions about images." Proceedings of the IEEE International Conference on Computer Vision. 2015.

[Shen16]   Sheng, Shurong, Luc Van Gool, and Marie-Francine Moens. "A dataset for multimodal question answering in the cultural heritage domain." Proceedings of the COLING 2016 Workshop on Language Technology Resources and Tools for Digital Humanities (LT4DH). ACL, 2016.

[Tait16]   Tait, Elizabeth, et al. "(Re) presenting heritage: Laser scanning and 3D visualisations for cultural resilience and community engagement." Journal of Information Science 42.3 (2016): pp. 420–433.

[Voor03]   Voorhees, Ellen M., and L. Buckland. "Overview of the TREC 2003 Question Answering Track." TREC. Vol. 2003.

[Yang16]   Yang, Zichao, et al. "Stacked attention networks for image question answering." Proceedings of the IEEE Conference on Computer Vision and Pattern Recognition. 2016.

Disrupting Screen-based Interaction

Design Principles of Mixed Reality Displays

Moritz Queisner

Image Knowledge Gestaltung. An Interdisciplinary Laboratory
Cluster of Excellence Humboldt-Universität zu Berlin
Unter den Linden 6, 10099 Berlin
moritz.queisner@hu-berlin.de
www.moritzqueisner.de

Abstract

Transparent display technology fundamentally challenges the concept of the screen: it turns viewing first and foremost into using. Transparent media presents users with a complex ensemble of imaging techniques and visual information that is embedded into their action routines, viewing habits and working processes. It shifts the focus from the analysis of visual elements on screen to the iterative interplay of structures and processes in front of and behind the screen. In order to show the associated transformation of design and interaction principles, the paper suggests three elementary conditions to be taken into account when designing transparent media technology: a) the position of the screen, b) the point of view of the user and c) the augmentation of objects.

1   Rethinking Opacity

Screens form a fundamental part of daily routines and practices, from professional environments to entertainment and everyday life. Their function as a
static monitor to display images has increasingly turned into a tool that is
integrated into visual practice. While computer monitors or cinema screens
assign the viewer a comparatively passive and immobile role as a consumer,
new display technology has made interacting with screens increasingly
responsive to the user's surroundings. Today's screen users are confronted
with a multiplicity of imaging processes and visual representations that
present them with the challenge to integrate a complex ensemble of image
techniques and information into their action routines, viewing habits and
working processes. Mobile games, navigation systems or augmented reality
applications are embedded into the user's action and perception; they turn
viewing first and foremost into using.

With evolving display technology, screens have become mobile, curved or
touchable and, most recently, transparent. Transparent display technology
usually projects light on a semi-transparent screen, a so-called combiner, that
redirects the light while at the same time letting light through from beyond
the screen – think for instance of the popular pepper's ghost illusion (fig. 1).
More current display technology is based on organic light-emitting diodes
(OLEDs) in which the emissive electroluminescent layer is a transparent film.
As OLED is an emissive technology it does not require a backlight which
implies that brightness and color reproduction are significantly better. Despite
the hype around so called mixed-reality applications popularly featured in
head-mounted displays or smart window technology it remains unclear what
problem transparent displays are actually trying to solve.

Fig. 1: Pepper's Ghost. Adolphe Ganot/Edmund Atkinson, Natural Philosophy for General Readers and Young Persons, 1876.

In order to define hardware and software requirements and the underlying design and interaction principles of transparent media, it is necessary to look beyond the omnipresent marketing game of augmenting everything and investigate what transparent display can and should actually do. This paper suggests three elementary propositions that need to be taken into account when designing transparent media technology: a) the position of the screen, b) the point of view of the user and c) the augmentation of objects.

2   Situating the Screen

The first proposition is that transparent screens establish types of images that only "work" when they are situated. Design concepts for transparent displays will need to position the screen in front of a scene or object. Screens are certainly always situated – embedded in the context of a situation – for instance when a mapping app on a smartphone will display the current location and orientation or when a surgeon positions a mobile monitor arm in the operating room in order to have a computer tomography closer to the patient. Even a standard television screen on a living room shelf creates a specific viewing situation. Transparent displays however, do not only address the field of vision in front of the display but also reveal an object or a scene behind it. Accordingly they need to allow users to see an image on the display and a scene or object behind the display at the same time. While the observation of a scene or object and their representation on screen are generally considered distinct processes, the position of transparent displays implies a structurally different architecture than opaque screens. This can for instance simply imply to take into account light or colours behind the display. But the inherent potential of transparent screens is that they allow for the linking of image and space: objects behind the display can be annotated, augmented, diminished or transformed by superimposing them with a visual layer on screen.

Ivan Sutherland's experiments with transparent displays in the late 1960s mark the first attempt to correlate image and space in real-time. Together with his student Bob Sproull, Sutherland constructed a head-mounted display that projects a simple wireframe model on a binocular display: an optical system consisting of two cathode ray tubes placed in front of each of the user's eyes. As the display is made of half-silvered mirrors, users can simultaneously see images coming from the cathode ray tubes as well as their surroundings. The perspective of the wireframe model adapts to the position of the user's head. Accordingly, "as the observer moves his head, his point of view moves and rotates with respect to the room coordinates system." (Sutherland 1968: 758) According to Sutherland, images for this type of display could be made "either to hang disembodied in space or to coincide with maps, desk tops, walls, or the keys of a typewriter."(ibid.: 759) In The Ultimate Display from 1968, remarkably predating the invention of the personal computer, Sutherland claims that the "user [...] of today's visual displays can easily make solid objects transparent – he can see through matter! The kinesthetic display [...] will lead not only to new methods of controlling machines but also to interesting understandings of the mechanisms of vision." (Sutherland 1965: 508)

Sutherlands experiments identified fundamental design principles of transparent displays. Sutherland emphasised that their strength is the ability to coincide with the structures they superimpose. This may sound obvious but the majority of contemporary use cases does actually not consider the materiality of the screen: why should I display the temperature or a tweet on my kitchen window at the cost of image quality? In his concept study "The

Future of Search", Mac Funamizu strengthens the concept of superimposition by arguing that the interaction with transparent displays in mobile interfaces will become integrated with the position of the screen (Funamizu 2008). According to Funamizu, users will navigate through space by superimposing transparent screens on a scene or object in order to search for spatially related information (fig. 2).

Fig. 2: The Future of Search. Mac Funamizu, 2008.

While the technical feasibility of Funamizu's concept is certainly challenging, a similar configuration is applied in augmented reality applications, such as in location-based games like Pokémon Go. The game is based on performing operations through and with images – and those images do not only represent or visualise, but they actively affect the user's position in space as well as their disposition towards the screen. Pokémon Go matches three dimensional objects with video images on the basis of geo data. As most augmented reality applications it links different image layers based on the perspective of a sensor, such as a smartphone camera which is often mistakenly referred to as representing the "the real world". The challenge for transparent display technology on the contrary is to link a computer generated object with an actual real world object or scene while taking into account the point of view of the user, which is a significantly more complex undertaking – not only from a technical point of view.

3 Situating the User

The second proposition is that design concepts for transparent displays will need to adjust the point of view of the user. Besides the correlation of screen and object, transparent displays need to align with the perspective of an individual user. Conceptualising a screen-based practice that correlates the positions of user, screen and object in real-time elucidates the technological and practical complexity of transparent media. But knowledge in designing this kind of screen architecture has become an issue long before the rise of transparent display technology in the early 19th century.

A variety of popular screen-based practices have been developed for central perspective construction. One of them is illustrated in Robert Fludd's drawing of a transparent screen in an encyclopaedia entry from 1618 (fig. 3). In the figure, the screen functions as a surface and an aperture at the same time – a constellation that gave rise to the ever-present notion of the image as a window. A transparent screen (tabula) moves in position between a building and the beholder's eye (oculus), which is fixed on the upper end of a pencil (stilus). By transferring each section of the grid on the screen to the paper (carta) users were able to systematically project their point of view onto an image plane (cf. Belting 2009). Contemporary transparent display concepts are still based on this scheme of alignment between user, screen and object. They often feature the same rigid relation between the eye and the screen as for instance with head-mounted displays where the synchronisation of the screen and the user's head movement facilitates the matching of an object with the user's point of view.

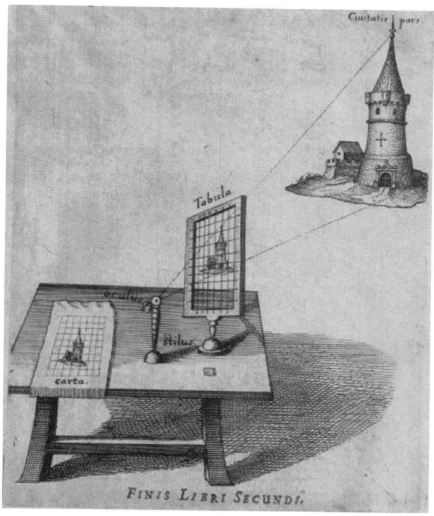

Fig. 3: Apparatus for central perspective construction. Robert Fludd, 1618.

The significant difference compared with contemporary transparent display technology is that Fludd's construction required tools and techniques that inhibited the simultaneous production and presentation of images. Observation and representation remained spatially and temporally separated from each other. This separation has been suspended by contemporary transmission, sensor, and display technologies that enable image production, processing, and transmission in real-time. The cockpit of the fighter aircraft of the type Eurofighter Typhoon contains three liquid crystal displays (LCD) as well as a transparent head-up display that allows pilots to display additional flight information (fig. 4). The LCD displays necessitate a mode of interaction in which the pilot's attention must switch back and forth between air space and screens. This is a complex operation, namely, bridging the cognitive gap between observation and representation, for instance when applying carto-graphic information from display to air space.

Fig. 4: Eurofighter Typhoon, cockpit with transparent head-up display.
Royal Air Force, 2010.

Superimposing the air space with visual information through the head-up display on the contrary allows for an image guided navigation of the aircraft without looking downwards on the cockpit's displays. While a juxtaposition of image and airspace requires the constant comparison of forms of observation and representation, the head-up display combines image and airspace in a joint perceptual space. As seeing and acting become intertwined, transparent display concepts need to situate the user in front of the screen so that they are able to perform operations through and with images.

4   Situating the Object

The third proposition is that images for transparent displays need to inform and not overlay a scene or an object behind the display. Transparent displays have disrupted the concept of the screen: they do not only visualise or represent a scene or object on screen but superimpose a "real" scene or object with visual information. The consequence is a dissolution of the conventional distinction between image and (so-called) reality towards a hybrid and synthetic form of visuality. Images no longer function as second order observation but intervene into the user's field of vision in such a way that the order of the visible becomes uncertain.

However the missing offset between image and object is hardly ever seen as an advantage considering that the majority of transparent display concepts on the market aim for the annotation of scenes or objects. Most products currently focus on helping people "getting a job done" by visually informing tasks next to a scene or object instead of obscuring it with visual elements. This corresponds to a type of applied or operational images, that focus on the situation instead of on the result of imaging. They do not only show, but also prompt the viewer to carry out an action. Surgical practice for instance significantly relies on the synchronisation of image and action: In order to translate medical images into practice, surgeons need to be able to relate visual information to the patient's body. When using an image in the operating room, surgeons must cope with the architecture of image display. A monitor may not necessarily be mobile and can require a surgeon to switch between the visualisation of the body on-screen and the actual patient's body. Spatially, these images may not correspond to the surgeon's perspective or to the proportions, alignment and dimensions of the patient's body.

Sauer et al. have superimposed the surgeon's field of vision in visceral surgery with a three dimensional liver model displayed on a transparent display using Microsoft's Hololens (fig. 5). The pre-operative images are aligned with the surgeon's field of vision by registering with the head's position in real-time. In this way the surgeon is able to integrate the position and orientation of preoperative images more effectively into the workflow being able to move, scale, or rotate the image during the intervention. This display concept is not conceptualised to superimpose the actual liver, as this would obscure access to the operating field. It rather annotates the field of vision alongside the surgical intervention in order to integrate images more directly into the work-flow without the need to turn attention towards a remote display which may not be aligned with the surgeon's own position and the spatial orientation of the patient. The concept demonstrates that user experiences for transparent display concepts need to be designed for a particular role of images that guide and inform the user's action and perception.

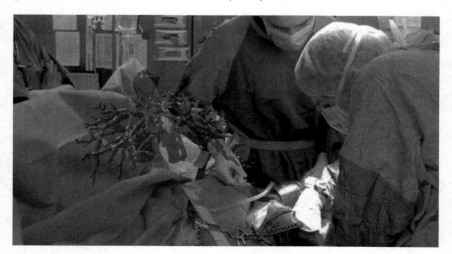

Fig. 5: Transparent display in visceral surgery. Igor M. Sauer, Department of Surgery, Charité – Universitaetsmedizin Berlin, 2017.

5 Rethinking Transparency

Reconsidering the level of opacity within screens has fundamentally challenged the way we interact with them. The design of transparent display concepts does not only need to address the internal relations of the image, or respectively what we see on a screen but requires to investigate the iterative interplay of structures and processes in front of and behind the screen.

Understanding transparent displays, therefore, does not only comprise the analysis of their technical functionality but also includes the operative conditions of transparent images. Even though cultural and media theory has ever since dealt with the hybrid status of the image, transparency has hardly been addressed from the perspective of operation. According to Emmanuel Alloa the debate about the transparent images is divided into two categories: the order of signs and the order of things. As signs, images either reveal the view to an underlying meaning—what Alloa calls the transparency paradigm – or, as things or opaque media, images reflect their view back to the observer – what Alloa calls the opacity paradigm. (Alloa 2011)

But as transparent images dissolve the conventional distinction between image and object they do not correspond to those conventional classifications insofar as they can neither be genuinely related to the concept of the image nor do they reveal an underlying meaning solely in a symbolic sense. Instead transparent images shift focus onto the situation rather than to the outcome(s) of an imaging process. Accordingly, the conventional classifications of image and media theory do not seem to provide a suitable approach to deal with this type of visual practice yet. Though cultural and media theory has recently emphasised the connection between image and operation (Farocki 2004; Hinterwaldner 2013; Hoel & Lindseth 2014; Krämer 2009) focusing on practices through which images become media of control and instruction, a perspective on acting with and through transparent media is still to be established.

Literature

Alloa, Emmanuel 2001, Das durchscheinende Bild. Konturen einer medialen Phanomenologie, Diaphanes Verlag, Berlin.

Farocki, H. 2004, "Phantom Images", Public, vol. 29, pp. 12–24.

Funamizu, M 2008, "The Future of Search", Available at: https://petitinvention.wordpress.com/2008/02/10/future-of-internet-search-mobile-version/ [Accessed 1 March 2017].

Hinterwaldner, I. 2013, „Programmierte Operativität und operative Bildlichkeit", in R Mikulá, S Moser & KS Wozonig (red.), Die Kunst der Systemik, Lit Verlag, Berlin.

Hoel, A.S. & L. Frank 2014, "Differential Interventions: Images as Operative Tools", in I Hoelzl (red.), The Operative Image–an Approximation. Available at: http://mediacommons.futureofthebook.org/tne/pieces/differential-interventions-images-operative-tools-2. [Accessed 1 March 2017].

Krämer, S. 2009, „Operative Bildlichkeit: Von der ‚Grammatologie' zu einer ‚Diagrammatologie'? Reflexionen über erkennendes ‚Sehen'", in M Hessler & D Mersch (red.), Logik des Bildlichen: Zur Kritik der ikonischen Vernunft, Transcript, Bielefeld.

Sutherland, I. 1968, "A Head-mounted Three Dimensional Display", in Proceedings of the AFIPS Fall Joint Computer Conference December 9–11, 1968, New York: Association for Computing Machinery.

Sutherland, I. 1965, "The Ultimate Display", in Information Processing: Proceedings of International Federation for Information Processing Congress, London: Macmillan and Co.

3D Modelling of Large and Narrow Indoor Spaces using Stereo Vision Aided Inertial Navigation and Semi-Global Matching

Jürgen Wohlfeil, Denis Grießbach, Dirk Baumbach,
Eugen Funk, Ines Ernst, Anko Börner
German Aerospace Center (DLR) · Institute of Optical Sensor Systems,
Department Information Processing of Optical Systems
Rutherfordstr. 2 · 12489 Berlin
{juergen.wohlfeil, denis.griessbach, dirk.baumbach,
eugen.funk, ines.ernst, anko.boerner}@dlr.de

Abstract

Digital modeling of cultural heritage is usually performed using expensive and heavy equipment (e.g. laser scanners) to achieve 3D models that are accurate and true to scale. In indoor environments the process of measurement can be very time consuming, especially when the objects to be examined are large, narrow and labyrinthine, like caves, historical mines, and other underground structures, but also narrow buildings and town centers, ships, deep excavation, etc. In such cases it is almost impossible to generate a 3D model with laser scanners with justifiable effort. This is because of the huge number of scans that is necessary to resolve most of the occlusions and to achieve the measurement overlap that is necessary for the adjustment of the single measurements. An alternative approach is to take many photos and use the so called Structure from Motion (SfM) approach to generate the 3D model directly from the images, using a photogrammetric approach. As a first step towards 3D modelling from photos, the poses where the photos have been taken from have to be determined. Usually this is performed using the image information itself, as shown [Woh13]. But in narrow environments this essential step of the approach becomes critical because the image mosaic becomes unstable due to the few and loose connections between the images. Another problem is that the computational complexity of this step becomes insurmountably high for large objects.

In this paper it is shown that IPS (Integrated Positioning System), developed at the German Aerospace Center (DLR), provides a solution for this problem. Coming along without any absolute positioning systems (e.g. GPS or pseudolites) IPS can navigate through unknown and unstructured places, providing the poses of each image taken. This enables to create 3D models using SGM stereo matching. Several examples of different sensor configurations are illustrated.

1   Introduction

For the 3D modelling of large, narrow and labyrinthine objects, like caves, historical mines, and other underground structures, but also narrow buildings and town centers, ships, deep excavation, etc. classical methods like laser scanning are not usable in practice. But also the novel photogrammetric approaches that use images for the reconstruction (SfM, structure from motion) have their limitations. An essential step of the approach is the reconstruction of the camera poses of all images by using the images' contents. One problem is the huge computational complexity needed to compare every image with every other image in order to find homologous points (points that are visible in two or more images, belonging to the same object point). Another problem is the limited accuracy of the reconstruction. In long scenes the unavoidable, small errors being made when calculating the camera poses quickly sum up to large errors. These errors drastically influence the dimensional accuracy of the reconstruction.

As already proposed in [Woh13] there is a solution for these problems. If the poses of the images can somehow be measured, then the photogrammetric approach can be used with all of its advantages. For the measurement of the poses the DLR's Integrated Positioning System (IPS) is used [Gri15, Wil15]. IPS (Fig. 1) is a system for ego motion estimation that comes along without any prior knowledge of the environment or absolute positioning information, e.g. GPS. Therefore it is capable of operating in outdoor spaces, but also in buildings, underground and other GPS-denied environments. The system is based on a multi-sensor approach with a basic configuration including a low-cost inertial measurement unit (IMU) combined with a stereo camera system for optical navigation. The main concept is to compensate the disadvantage of each sensor component by another. This way, the navigation error growth is significantly reduced in comparison with the achievable accuracy of each single sensor.

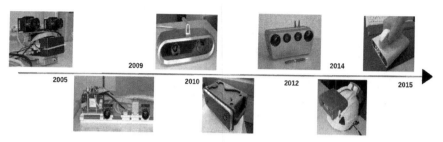

Fig. 1: Evolution of DLR's IPS. It always contained at least an IMU and a stereo camera pair with accurate timestamping. But its design is open for any other sensor, as needed.

2   3D Modeling via IPS

2.1   IPS only

One way to create 3D Models is to use the stereo cameras of the IPS. They are the main navigation sensor of the system but they can also be used as a 3D sensor. The synchronously exposed stereo image pairs can directly be processed by Semi-Global Matching (SGM) [Hir08] to generate a 3D point cloud, similar to a laser scanner. Using an FPGA or GPU implementation [Ern08] this step can even be performed in real time. Mandatory for SGM is the well calibrated stereo geometry, which already exists as it is essential for the navigation.

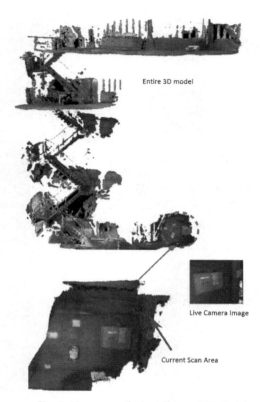

Entire 3D model

Live Camera Image

Current Scan Area

Fig. 2: Live scan of a headframe (IPS-Only)

Thanks to the known position and orientation of the cameras at every exposure the point cloud from each image pair can easily be transformed from the camera coordinate system to the navigation coordinate system. Doing this for all image pairs, a point cloud of the whole object can be created, also in real time [Fun16].

Scanning is rather easy and fast. The system is switched on and carried by hand or on a helmet through the object that needs to be scanned. Long and narrow corridors, can be scanned as quick as wide open rooms.

A slight disadvantage of scanning with IPS directly is the resolution of the IPS' stereo cameras. In history, all systems had a resolution of about 1 megapixel because this turned out to be an optimum compromise between different factors, including processing time, navigation accuracy, size and light sensitivity. Due to similar reasons the cameras are panchromatic and so the resulting point clouds have only intensity values and no color information.

If the application requires high resolution and/or color, this can be achieved with the following approach.

2.2   Additional High-Resolution Camera(s)

As IPS is open for additional sensors, one or more high resolution RGB cameras can easily be combined with it. The exposures of the high resolution camera(s) are synchronized by IPS. This way the high resolution images can later be assigned to the navigation trajectory and the camera poses can be extracted for photogrammetric processing. It has been shown that 3D reconstruction can be performed in two different ways. One way is the usage of an internal processing chain, involving VisualSFM, a customized bundle adjustment tool (DLR) and SGM for 3D matching [Wohl13]. Another way is to use Agisoft Photoscan for the whole process. This software offers a way to input the preliminary camera poses to speed up the initial SFM step. Experience has shown that for large scenes with many images this is the only way to reduce the computation time needed for this step to a feasible time. The very impressive results have been published in [Spr17].

Fig. 3: Scan of a mine shaft (Nikon DSLR camera as main imaging sensor)

3 Conclusion and Outlook

In this paper it was shown that IPS can be used for 3D modeling in different applications. One very interesting application is the 3D modeling of cultural heritage. Mainly qualitative results have been presented in this paper. The positioning accuracy of IPS is currently reevaluated. Up to now it can be said that it is clearly below 1% of the travelled length. In the coming months IPS positioning accuracy is evaluated more in detail and will be published in a separate paper.

Currently IPS is about to be produced in a small series by the company DMT GmbH & Co. KG. This way it will soon be possible to use IPS by qualified land surveyors and research institutions.

Literature

[Ern08]   Ernst, I. and Hirschmüller, H.; Mutual Information based Semi-Global Stereo Matching on the GPU. International Symposium on Visual Computing, Las Vegas. 2008.

[Fun16]   Funk Eugen and Börner Anko (2016). Infinite 3D Modelling Volumes. In Proceedings of the 11th Joint Conference on Computer Vision, Imaging and Computer Graphics Theory and Applications - Volume 3: VISAPP, ISBN 978-989-758-175-5, pages 246–253. DOI: 10.5220/0005722002460253

[Gri13]   Grießbach, Denis und Baumbach, Dirk und Börner, Anko und Zuev, Sergey (2013) Accuracy Evaluation of Stereo Vision Aided Inertial Navigation for Indoor Environments. ISPRS Acquisition and Modelling of Indoor and Enclosed Environments 2013, 11.–13. Dez. 2013, Kapstadt, Südafrika.

[Gri14]   Grießbach, Denis und Baumbach, Dirk und Zuev, Sergey (2014) Stereo-Vision-Aided Inertial Navigation for Unknown Indoor and Outdoor Environments. International Conference on Indoor Positioning and Indoor Navigation (IPIN 2014), 27.–30. Okt. 2014, Busan, Korea.

[Hir08]   Hirschmüller, H., Stereo Processing by Semiglobal Matching and Mutual Information. IEEE Transactions on Pattern Analysis and Machine Intelligence 30 pp. 328–341, 2 2008.

[Spr17]   Spreckels, Volker und Schlienkamp, Andreas (2017): Erfassung untertägiger Hohlräume mit dem IPS-System bei der RAG Aktiengesellschaft. In proceedings of Oldenburger 3D-Tage, At Oldenburg, Germany, Volume: 16

[Wil15]   Wilken, Mark und Cabos, Christian und Baumbach, Dirk und Buder, Maximilian und Choinowski, André und Grießbach, Denis und Zuev, Sergey (2015) IRIS - An Innovative Inspection System for Maritime Hull Structures. International Conference on Computer Applications in Shipbuilding, ICCAS 2015, 29. Sept.–2.Oct 2015, Bremen, Germany. ISBN 978-1-909024-43-4.

[Woh13]   Wohlfeil, J.; Strackenbrock, B.; Kossyk, I: Automated high reso-lution 3D reconstruction of cultural heritage using multi-scale sensor systems and semi-global matching, International Archives of the Photogrammetry, Remote Sensing and Spatial Information Sciences, Volume XL-4/W4, 2013, pp.37–43

Virtualization of the Cultural Heritage of the Solovetsky Monastery

Nikolay Borisov, Artem Smolin, Valentina Zakharkina, Pavel Tserbakov, Denis Stolyarov, Sergei Shvemberger, Elena Logdacheva, Ludmila Nikitina, Vasiliy Trushin, Arseniy Nikolaev
ITMO University
197101, Kronverksky Pr. 49, St. Petersburg, Russia
Saint Petersburg State University
199034, Universitetskaya Emb., 7-9, St. Petersburg, Russia
{nikborisov, artsmolin77, zakharkina, paul.tscherbakov, shvemberger,
e_logdacheva, vasilii.trushin}@gmail.com
denis1900@mail.ru, kinoprofil@mail.ru, nikars@bk.ru

Oleg Volkov
Solovetsky National Historic and Architectural Museum and Natural Reserve
164070, Settlement Solovetsky, Primorsky district,
Arkhangelsk region, Russia
volkov@solovky.ru

Abstract

The article details the experience of designing an information-cum-multimedia resource that presents a unique historical site, the architectural ensemble of the Solovetsky Monastery. The final product is a complex entity, consisting of an information and research internet portal, a 3D virtual reconstruction Ensemble of the Solovetsky Monastery in the Period of Its Highest Prosperity (XVI-XVII Centuries), as well as an interactive 4D tour of the Solovetsky Monastery based on Video 360 technology.

The project is being realized by an interdisciplinary team, joining the efforts of research staff of Solovetsky National Historic and Architectural Museum and Natural Reserve, ITMO University and Saint Petersburg State University.

1   Introduction

There is a large number of unique historic religious sacred sites within the Russian Federation, that are still being used for the initial purpose and attract special attention of pilgrims, tourists, researchers etc. One of such sacred sites is definitely the Solovetsky Monastery, listed as a Highly Valuable Object of Cultural Heritage of the Peoples of the Russian Federation [Solovky].

The Solovetsky Monastery (Fig. 1) is a vast architectural entity, it is on the UNESCO World Heritage list. It has always played a prominent part in the Russian history and culture, for it was highly instrumental in the advancement of the Russians into the White Sea region, the subsequent exploration of the Arctic Ocean by the Russian mariners and the emergence of Russia as a great Arctic power.

Fig. 1: Solovetsky monastery

The Solovetsky Monastery was founded in the first half of the XVth century, in 1436, when St. Zosima of Solovki had arrived to the archipelago.

Solovetsky Islands are a unique historic, cultural and natural site, since their preserved ecclesiastic structures, residential buildings, household structures, fortifications, waterworks, roads etc. are unparalleled. The architectural complex took shape between early XVIIth and early XXth century. The highlight of the Solovetsky Monastery as a historic and cultural site is the main ensemble that includes the fort, the church complex, residential and household structures, waterworks, operational buildings and units.

An impressive number of unique historic relics and artifacts has been preserved on the grounds of the Solovetsky Monastery (Fig. 2): a collection of icons, cult objects, pieces of applied arts, manuscript books and incunabula, Mediaeval manuscripts etc.

Fig. 2: The Stone Cross of St. Zosima of Solovki

1.1   Using Information Technologies in Cultural Heritage Preservation and Tourism

Virtualization of the objects of non-material cultural heritage pursues the following goals:

1. Virtual reconstruction of the object, to show what it looked like in the past. For this purpose, it is essential to have the adequate amount of content, i.e. blueprints, archival images, engravings etc.
2. Virtual conservation of the object in its current state, in order to preserve its digital image for the future generations. The principal technologies used for the purpose are 3D scanning and photogrammetry.
3. Introduction of various interactive products, using various virtual and augmented reality technologies.

The three abovementioned approaches can be combined in various modifications, in order to meet the goal of actualization of a certain cultural heritage site.

The obtained results can be used in a number of ways, depending on the goal; one of the options is to design an information source that features structured site-specific historic and research information. With the use of GIS and the augmented reality technologies for smart phones, tour applications can be designed that would enhance the visit to the cultural heritage site in question, offering a more comprehensive educational experience.

One of the successful examples of virtualization of a cultural heritage site with the use of 3D scanning technologies and the technologies of augmented reality is the digitalization of a whaling station in the Kerguelen Islands.

In December 2010, Eurl Pérazio team performed the 3D scanning of a whaling station in the Kerguelen Islands; they did over 46 hours on a site across 6 hectares with the help of 3 laser scanners: 2 HDS 6000 and 1 C 10 by Leica® (Fig. 3) on a tripod [Boris16].

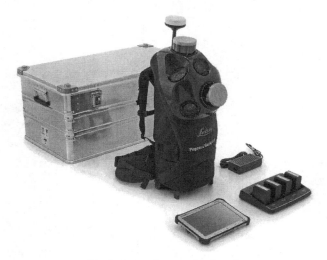

Fig. 3: Leica Pegasus Backpack

The result is a textured model. The simulation of the site as a whole was carried out with Blender program. After that, ITMO University team, in collaboration with Eurl Pérazio team, have designed a virtual interactive walk through a recreated site in Oculus Rift DK2 virtual reality helmet (Fig. 4).

Fig. 4: 4D reconstruction of the whaling station in the Kerguelen Islands

1.2   Multimedia information system "Architectural ensemble of the Solovetsky monastery in the period of its highest prosperity (XVI–XVII centuries)"

With the support of Grant 16-01-12022 (2016–2017) of the Russian Humanitarian Research Foundation, ITMO University and Saint Petersburg State University, in cooperation with Solovetsky National Historic and Architectural Museum and Natural Reserve, designed a multimedia information system Architectural Ensemble of Solovetsky Monastery in the Period of its Highest Prosperity (XVI–XVII centuries) [Solovky.IFMO] that encompass the following features:

1. Authentic virtual 3D reconstruction of the Solovetsky Monastery (XVI-XVII centuries) with the option of viewing it through the virtual reality headsets;

2. Quality information base featuring various data on the history of the site;

3. Virtual interactive 4D tour of the Solovetsky Monastery in various multimedia formats.

What adds urgency to the creation of this particular information system is the major renovation and reconstruction program that is currently under way in the church complex, which will definitely affect its authenticity. There's a multimedia exhibition on the grounds of the Solovetsky Monastery, that can use new multimedia products. Besides, there's a web site of Solovetsky National Historic and Architectural Museum [Solovky]; it seems essential to enhance it with a complementary interactive internet resource.

Using a vast number of sources (iconography of the Solovetsky Monastery, photographs, archeological records, restoration projects, historic descriptions, inventory lists of the Monastery, accounting and donation books etc.) we managed to create the authentic virtual 3D reconstruction of the Solovetsky Monastery (Fig. 5).

Fig. 5: An old engraving featuring the Solovetsky Monastery

Autodesk 3D Studio Max program was used for designing the virtual 3D reconstruction of the Solovetsky Fortress.

One of the main challenges was to render the unique masonry work of the structures. The stonework of each curtain wall in unique, featuring boulders of a different size; in each case it depends on the type of the structure and the technological preferences of the period.

To ensure the authentic rendition of these objects, we resorted to photogrammetry and generation of bump maps and normal maps, based on the photographs.

Using the photogrammetry technology, we created 3D maps of high verisimilitude, both as far as the geometry and texture maps go, to obtain the information on the shape of the real objects and to transfer it on the reference models (Fig. 6).

Fig. 6: Korozhnaya Tower, photogrammetry results

For some of the objects, high-resolution texture maps (ca. 35,000 pixels for the long sides of the curtain walls) were assembled manually, to be used as the textures for the models. To optimize the process, we created reduced copies of the textures (16K, 8K, 4K) to be used at the distances that do not require very high resolution. To prevent the objects made of the boulders from looking flat, customized software was used to generate, on the basis of the resulting images, the height map and the normal map; they were superimposed on the reference models that were based on the blueprints.

Fig. 7 presents the result of the virtual 3D reconstruction of the architectural ensemble of the Solovetsky Monastery.

The virtual interactive 4D tour is structured as a map of the Solovetsky Monastery, that is divided into sections. In each section the user can select one of the following viewing formats:

1. A tour in 360 format – our times;
2. A tour in 3D 360 format --16–17th centuries;
3. Textual illustrated information at each sector.

This virtual interactive tour gives the user a chance to experience an in-depth personified immersion into the virtual space of the Solovetsky Monastery.
The video tour in Video 360 format was filmed in cooperation with Video-360production [Video360] project, using a custom-designed two-camera system and Entaniya Fisheye lenses.

Fig. 7: Virtual reconstruction of the architectural Ensemble of Solovetsky Monastery

Fig. 8: Selection menu for the interactive map of the Solovki

The result of this project is the information and multimedia portal that incorporates a number of multimedia elements (3D reconstruction, Video 360, interactive map etc.), as well as educational content on the history of the emergence and evolution of the Solovetsky Monastery.
Multimedia information system Architectural Ensemble of Solovetsky Monastery in the Period of its Highest Prosperity (XVI–XVII Centuries) is available online at: http://solovky.ifmo.ru/.

This work was supported by the project "Multimedia information system 'Architectural ensemble of the Solovetsky monastery in the period of its highest prosperity (XVI–XVII centuries)'" (Grant No. 16-01-12022, Russian Foundation for Humanities).

Literature

[Boris16]   Borisov N., Smolin A., Chambaud L., Couesnon P., Jacquot E., Mielcarek F., Peral J., Perazio G., Rebiere J., Trushin V., Valcke S. Digitalisation of a whaling station in the Kerguelen islands (southern french and antarctic lands)/EVA 2016 Saint Petersburg. Electronic Imaging & the Visual Arts International Conference, St. Petersburg, June 23th–24th, 2016 Conference Proceedings. – SPb ITMO University, 2016. – pp. 79–84

[Solovky]   URL: http://www.solovky.ru/

[Solovky.IFMO] URL: http://solovky.ifmo.ru/

[Video360]   URL: http://www.video360production.com/

The Automatic Generation of Movie Trailers As Semantics-based Video Abstracting

Till von Wenzlawowicz[1], Otthein Herzog[1,2]

[1]TZI – Technologie-Zentrum Informatik und Informationstechnik
Universität Bremen
Am Fallturm 1, 28359 Bremen, Germany

[2]CIUC – China Intelligent Urbanization Co-creation Center
Tongji University
1239 Siping Road, Shanghai, PR China

Abstract

An abstract like this one has the purpose of summarizing the most important aspects of a larger text. Similarly, a video abstract should exhibit the important pieces of the source video. In the literature, video abstracts are mostly composed out of sets of key frames or come as video skims [Truo07]. With the arrival of billions of videos in the public domain it is becoming even more important that video abstracts are available in order to select, e.g., interesting videos with a reasonable overhead. However, the additional (and expensive) effort for an additional video abstract precludes its creation. Therefore, it appears to be worth the effort to explore the automatic generation of video abstracts. The actual results of this research are presented in this paper: a semantics-based approach for an automatic resp. interactive video abstracting system. For demonstration purposes, this system automatically creates movie trailers as special video abstracts for the genres action, horror, and comedy movies that compare favorably to contemporary Hollywood movie trailers. The presented approach is based on four major steps:
1. The semantic concepts deemed essential for a video genre must be defined up-front (interactively), e.g., through combinations of syntactic image, video and sound features that constitute them. In addition, some of these semantic concepts with broad instance

variations, e.g., screams, need to be learned through supervised Machine Learning with sufficiently large numbers of examples. In addition, the formal structure model of the dramaturgy of a trailer or video abstract must be defined including the positions of the instantiations of the semantic concepts on the timeline of the final trailer.

2. The video is segmented into its shots, and the syntactic low-level mage, video, and sound features are extracted from the video source by running the appropriate image, video and sound feature detectors in an unsupervised "batch run".

3. The subsequent step determines which semantic concepts are contained in the video, stores them in a knowledge base, and notes their location in the video.

4. In the last step, the system constructs a non-deterministic chain of video clips of the segmented video footage according to the prede-fined formal dramaturgic trailer model, enhances the transitions, and adds textual animations, sound effects, and musical excerpts.

Automatically generated trailers for the three different genres were evaluated focusing on their semantical structures. Each trailer was compared to the corresponding original Hollywood trailer by manu-ally segmenting it into dialogue-based scenes containing semantical information, filler shots, and textual animations. It could be shown that a) the automatically generated trailers share a similar, although less complex structure with the original ones, b) they satisfy the purpose of summarizing the story of the movie, c) they show interesting pieces, and d) give rise to some curiosity for the viewer to watch the correspon-ding complete movie.

1　　Video Abstracting – Related Work

The automatic generation of video abstracts is a rather small research area, especially when it comes to the special case of automatic trailer generation with its artistic implications. Video abstracting can be achieved by two main categories of abstracts which are more or less based on syntactic features: key frame-based systems, which represent the source video by at least one still image, and video skimming systems that result in a shortened version of the source video [Truo07]. Among common forms of video abstracts are sports summaries containing the highlights, e.g., for a soccer or basketball game, and trailers for movie and TV programs.

In contrast, movie trailers are a prominent example of video abstracts, and carry specific purposes by advertising the movie. Contemporary movie trailers follow a dramaturgic structure similar to the narrative structure used in typical Hollywood movies [Hedi01, p.44]. This observation was confirmed in the course of the project through the manual analysis of 60 Hollywood movies and their trailers. It allowed for a generic formal definition of trailer structures and a formal description of these structures as abstract models: this generic trailer structure is broken down into four consecutive phases serving different narrative purposes: the intro, story, action, and outro phase. Each phase has a different narrative purpose and features distinctive arrangement patterns as well as a different musical background.

The intro phase establishes the characters and the setting of the movie. Their relationships and conflicts are deepened and problems and obstacles are introduced in the story phase. The action phase consists of shorter shots and shows spectacular and fast sequences, which reach a climax towards the end of the action phase. In the outro phase, the built-up tension is calmed down, and the title and credits are shown. Some trailers also feature a final impressive scene, the so-called button.

Xu and Zhang [Xu13] created an assisting system, which automatically selects and recommends video clips from the original movie while the arrangement of the clips in a trailer is left to the user. Smeaton et al. [Smea06] built a system for action movies that employs machine learning on low level features. The approach by Ionescu et al. [Ione06] is specifically designed for animated movies and employs specific features of such films. Among projects close to ours is the work of Lienhart et al [Lien97]. They segment and analyze a movie based on feature extraction, chose clips for the trailer and determine temporal arrangement and transitions in the MoCA system. Another trailer generation system is Vid2Trailer developed by Irie et al. [Irie68] that focuses on symbols, e.g., impressive scenes, musical themes and the title.

The approach presented here has been started by the digital media student project SVP [Brac09, Wenz12]. In this project, the feasibility to automatically generate trailers was demonstrated by an experimental software system including some semantic features of the trailer structure for action movies after the manual analysis of 15 Hollywood trailers, which included also the level of single shots and transitions. The selected shots and transitions form a pair, and a trailer is automatically constructed out of a chain of such clip/transition pairs according to the pre-defined trailer structure. In order to generate trailers in a non-deterministic way, the SVP system uses a hierarchical trailer model, which allows inferring different alternative clip/transition pair chains.

2   Analysis of Movies for Automatic Trailer Generation

In addition to the action movie genre developed in the previously described SVP system two more dialogue- and less action-based genres were contemplated: the Hollywood movie genres horror and comedy were selected in addition to the action movie genre. In order to determine the corresponding trailer structures, at first, a manual shot-by-shot analysis was performed of two horror and two comedy trailers, and, not surprisingly, the same generic structure was identified as it applies for action trailers. However, there were semantic differences in the shots for the new genres, which are detailed in the next section.

2.1   The Structure of Horror and Comedy Trailers

In the manual analysis of horror and comedy trailers, basically the same structure of four phases as in the action trailers could be identified. These phases are prominent in horror trailers, but less distinct in comedy trailers.

Horror trailers introduce the setting and characters in the intro phase. The story phase establishes the basic storyline of the movie. The climax of the analyzed trailer in the action phase consists of frightening and spectacular scenes supplemented with text inserts showing the names of the main actors. The outro phase is bringing down the tension by means of calmer and slower sequences. An optional button scene is sometimes placed between the movie title and the concluding credits. A stylistic element found in horror trailers is the use of black sequences between the shots and the use of mysterious and frightening music.

The first two phases in comedy trailers serve similar purposes by first introducing settings and characters and then the conflict or the problems. A change in the world of the protagonist marks the transition from the intro to the story phase. In the action phase, the story telling is loosely continued, but this phase also emphasizes slapstick and humorous scenes. Towards the end of the action phase, the name of the main actor is shown and/or announced by a text insert or voice-over narration. A humorous button scene is used in all analyzed comedy trailers, which is finally followed by the closing credits. Comedy trailers often feature pop songs as soundtrack and less prominent background music during conversation scenes.

Compared to action and horror trailers, comedy trailers consist mainly of several speech-based scenes surrounded by short and fast-paced filler shots, e.g., setting shots showing a city. Additionally, they often rely on a voice-over narrator to connect the individual scenes in order to summarize the story of the movie.

Therefore, the footage categories had to be extended compared to action trailers to better suit the new genres and for horror and comedy trailers an adapted formal trailer model was defined.

In order to allow for an easy definition of formal trailer models, the implemented software contains a model editing widget. In this widget, formal abstracting models can be visualized and edited as well. It presents a hierarchical view of the model tree structure as well as a list of the nodes grouped by their hierarchical level. Each node allows for the definition of alternative sets of child nodes in order to enable the automatic generation of non-deterministic trailers. The bottom layer containing the clips and transitions also allows specifying the semantic category from which a clip should be selected and setting the desired duration.

2.2 Semantic Categories for Action, Horror, and Comedy Trailers

A trailer consists of chains of shots that are adapted to the intended effects in each of the four trailer phases intro, story, action, and outro.

A category is defined by a set of category parameters. Each category parameter sets a minimum and maximum threshold for a specific syntactic feature, and only if all category parameter constraints are satisfied, the corresponding footage excerpt is added as a clip to the category. In Table 1, a survey on semantic categories is given which are used for the trailer generation.

Character1CloseUp-Silent	Character1CloseUp-Speaking	Characer1Silent
Character1Speaking	PersonCloseUpSilent	PersonCloseUpSpeaking
PersonSilent	PersonSpeaking	FaceRecognition
Quote	QuoteLong	Explosion
Crash	Gunshot	Fire
SpectacularEvent	FastAction	SlowAction
Setting	Dialogue	Crowd
Volume-basedSound-Segment	SoundEvent	Scream
Shout	SpeechPresent	SpeechRecognition
MusicPresent	SuddenVolumeChange	Text

Table 1: Footage categories

These categories can be interactively defined by a second widget in the implemented software system through the constituting syntactic features and the corresponding filter parameters. This widget also offers a video player for viewing the footage clips grouped in a category. This enables a user to easily alter and improve the definition of the semantic categories, and also to adapt the system for new genres.

2.3   Syntactic Analyzer Modules

A set of detector modules is used which extracts those syntactic features from the source movie, which are needed to constitute the semantic categories. The following describes briefly some of these modules, which are described in more detail in [Brac09].

Shot Detection: This module segments the movie into shots and is based on changes in the gray-level histogram. Additionally, basic color information of the shot is computed, e.g., average brightness and color intensities.

Movement Detection: Motion intensity and direction are calculated based on the optical flow, and the footage is grouped in sections of similar movement intensity.

Face Detection and Face Recognition: The Haarcascade classifier [Lien02] and PCA combined with k-means clustering are used to locate sequences containing faces. The clustering also allows to identify the characters and to count their appearances in the movie.

Text Detection: Since the automatically generated trailers are enhanced with custom textual animations, footage containing text has to be avoided. The text detection module filters sections containing text, i.e., the movie, actor names and the credits.

Sound Volume Segmentation: This module divides the movie into segments of similar volume in order to indicate loud sequences, e.g., action sequences and explosions, or calmer parts, e.g., dialogues.

Sudden Volume Change Detection: Spectacular events in the movie are often accompanied by a sudden change of loudness. This detector module monitors the volume and marks parts with a sudden in- or decrease.

Speech Detection and Speech Recognition: As speech often contains semantic information, the presence of audible expressions is important to rate a shot containing faces according to its semantic value. Furthermore, the speech recognition module is able to spot quotes in the soundtrack, which are retrieved from the Internet Movie Database to provide the corresponding shots with proven or at least famous semantic content.

Shout Detection: Special cases of speech are screams. The shout detection module filters the output of the speech detection module for a certain minimal volume threshold.

Music detection: The music detection looks for stable power spectrum peaks in the soundtrack to identify pieces of music. This allows the system to mute sequences containing music to avoid an undesired mix between the existing film music and the trailer music, which will be added in the generation process later on.

Sound Event Detection: Especially action movies contain a range of distinct sound events, e.g., gunshots, explosions, crashes and screams. By utilizing Machine Learning for the classification, this module is able to identify those characteristic sound events.

3   The Automatic Generation of Trailers

The workflow for creating trailers and also video abstracts in general consists of the following steps:

1. Extraction of syntactic features from the movie by the detector modules
2. Categorization of footage by means of the extracted features (and possibly also the definition and change of categories)
3. Generation of a chain of clips and transitions out of the trailer/abstracting model
4. Selection of footage, animations and sound clips and rendering into a video file

Since the feature extraction of step 1 is a non-interactive process this step can be carried out as a "batch-run" independently of the subsequent trailer generation steps. By separating out this step, it is always possible to define new semantic categories later on without being forced to re-analyze a movie for the syntactic features. The output of the detector modules is merged into an XML file.

There are two modes for the automatic trailer or video abstract generation:

1. Automatic generation of a raw trailer with a subsequent opportunity to change it interactively and completing it automatically in a second step.
2. Fully automatic generation of the trailer or video abstract in one process without any further manual intervention.

The third implemented widget, the abstract viewer, implements those two modes together with the Generation module. After the user has chosen the appropriate parameters for the trailer or video abstract (source movie, formal abstracting model, sound archive, animation style), the system generates a sample clip/transition chain and visualizes it. For each clip/transition pair a screenshot and metadata (semantical category, duration, start, and end frame) are displayed. This automatically generated video draft can now be played, saved into a video file, or be altered by a user if an interactive process is wanted. The system also allows changing categories and/or the chosen footage clip if the user wishes so.

In the next step, the Generation module selects the matching clips from the categorized footage based on the description of the clip/transition pair chain, places them in the right order, and associates the suitable transitions. In addition, requests for animation clips can be rendered here. It also selects suitable audio excerpts and generates a cut list for rendering. In a third step, an external video processing tool is started and renders the media files according to the cut list into a final video file. The following animation categories are rendered for the final trailer: Greenscreen, Title, ActorName, Tagline, CompanyName, DirectorProducer and Credits.

4   The Horror and Comedy Trailer Models

To evaluate the video abstracting application, two abstracting models were created, one for horror and one for comedy trailers. These abstracting models are based on the generic structure that was extracted from the manual annotation of horror and comedy trailers. Additionally, the set of semantic categories was extended to suit the requirements of the horror and comedy genres: A new detector module for dialogue-based sequences, the speech part detection, was implemented which looks for a pattern of speech, a short break and speech again. The speech part detection allows us to find those sequences which are especially well suited for comedy trailers. By combining the output of the speech part detection with a temporal filter the system was enabled to extract dialogues and other speech-based footage from interesting events in movies.

Horror Trailers: The new abstracting model for horror trailers uses a similar concept as the one for action trailers, however a different set of music files was provided, and black frames were added between the video clips.

In the intro phase, the abstracting model is defined to start with the production company logo and uses character shots, setting shots and speech-based sequences from the beginning of the movie. In the story phase, two different modes can be used: one focuses on repeated slow action and black frame combinations, the other one uses an animation of the movie tagline with speech-based scenes from the first half of the movie. The action phase is started by a repeated pattern of actor name animations and fast action sequences. It is followed by the director name and spectacular shots, and is completed by a close-up face shot and a scream sequence. The outro phase is started with a speech part sequence taken from the climax of the movie, a quote from the last part of the movie and a slow action filler sequence. The trailer is completed by the movie title, a spectacular scene acting as button and the credits.

Comedy Trailers: As described before, comedy trailers mainly consist of speech-based or slapstick scenes surrounded by filler shots from categories like slow action or setting. Consequently, the abstracting model for comedy trailers uses these categories extensively.

The intro phase is opened by a typical green screen animation and the company logo. The following clips first introduce the character and then focus on speech-based and humorous scenes from the beginning of the movie. In the story phase, this pattern is continued with excerpts from within the movie's middle, framed by transitional setting shots. The change between story and action phase is marked by the inclusion of the tagline. The action phase continues the pattern of transitional shots and speech part sequences. Towards the end of this phase, the names of the main actor and the director are shown. The outro phase of comedy trailers is rather short and simple. It contains the movie title, a humorous button scene and the credits.

5   Evaluation

In order to evaluate the automatic trailer resp. video abstracting application, two horror and two comedy trailers were created automatically using the respective video abstracting models described above. Then we compared the automatically generated trailers to the corresponding original Hollywood trailers in a descriptive evaluation of semantical and technical aspects.

The semantical structure of the automatically generated trailers turned out to be similar but less complex compared to the Hollywood trailers. The story line is less clearly visible in the automatically generated ones, which is due to the lack of narration, e.g., an external voice-over narration or the use of explaining speech excerpts from the movie. However, the automatic trailers are able to exhibit the mood of the movie, e.g., anxiety and mystery in horror trailers, as well as humor and a positive atmosphere in comedy trailers.

Regarding the technical aspects such as matching cuts, clearly audible speech, and footage selection, the automatically generated trailers still have some deficits, which are mostly caused by the quality aspects of the features extracted by the detector modules. Some additional effort in this area would definitely be of advantage to improve the overall quality of the semantic categories, and thus the resulting trailer.

6 Conclusion and Outlook

In this paper, a video abstracting system was introduced by applying it to the domain of movie trailers. It is remarkable that Hollywood trailers have a rather uniform dramaturgy that can be mapped into a formal abstracting model. Based on a manual analysis of horror and comedy trailers, the appropriate semantic categories were defined which served as a basis for the automatic arrangement of the components of trailers according to the rules for the automatic composition in the abstracting model. A software system was implemented for the interactive creation of the abstracting model with the semantic categories, for the generation of the trailer and the final rendering of the video including animations. Horror and comedy trailers were generated automatically which showed very satisfactory results in a qualitative evaluation.

The current quality of the automatically generated trailers could be improved by the inclusion of further detector modules. This would add more syntactic features for the categorization of footage, and thus would allow more detailed abstracting models. The system can be extended easily to other movie genres or video abstracting areas just by interactively defining the proper formal abstracting models, the appropriate semantic categories, and the inclusion of the suited syntactic detectors.

Literature

[Brac09]   Christoph Brachmann; Hashim Iqbal Chunpir; Silke Gennies. Benjamin Haller; Philipp Kehl.   Astrid Paramita Mochtarram; Daniel Möhlmann; Christian Schrumpf; Christopher Schultz; Björn Stolper; Benjamin Walther-Franks; Arne Jacobs; Thorsten Hermes; Otthein Herzog. Automatic Movie Trailer Generation Based on Semantic Video Patterns. In: Michael Ross, Manfred Grauer and Bernd Freisleben (eds.). Digital Tools in Media Studies (2009). transcript Verlag: Bielefeld, pp. 145–158.

[Hedi01]   Vinzenz Hediger. Verführung zum Film: der amerikanische Kinotrailer seit 1912. PhD thesis, Marburg, 2001.

[Ione06]   Bogdan Ionescu, Patrick Lambert, Didier Coquin, Laurent Ott, and Vasile Buzuloiu. Animation movies trailer computation. In: Proceedings of the 14th Annual ACM International Conference on Multimedia, MULTIMEDIA '06, New

York, NY, USA, 2006. ACM: New York, pp. 631–634. DOI: 10.1145/1180639.1180770.

[Irie68]   Go Irie, Takashi Satou, Akira Kojima, Toshihiko Yamasaki, and Kiyoharu Aizawa. Automatic trailer generation. In: Proceedings of the International Conference on Multimedia, MM '10, New York, NY, USA, 2010. ACM: New York, pp. 839–842. DOI: 10.1145/1873951.1874092.

[Lien97]   Rainer Lienhart, Silvia Pfeiffer, and Wolfgang Effelsberg. Video abstracting. Commun. ACM, 40(12):54–62, December 1997. DOI: 10.1145/265563.265572.

[Lien02]   Lienhart, R., Maydt, J.: An extended set of haar-like features for rapid object detection. In: IEEE ICIP, Vol. 1:900–903 (September 2002).

[Smea06]   Alan F. Smeaton, Bart Lehane, Noel E. O'Connor, Conor Brady, and Gary Craig. Automatically selecting shots for action movie trailers. In: Proceedings of the 8th ACM International Workshop on Multimedia Information Retrieval, MIR '06, New York, NY, USA, 2006. ACM: New York, pp. 231–238. DOI: 10.1145/1178677.1178709.

[Truo07]   Ba Tu Truong and Svetha Venkatesh. Video abstraction: A systematic review and classification. ACM Trans. Multimedia Computing, Communications and Applications 3(1), Article 3 (February 2007).

[Wenz12]   Till von Wenzlawowicz and Otthein Herzog. Semantic video abstracting: automatic generation of movie trailers based on video patterns. In: Ilias Maglogiannis, Vassilis Plagianakos, and Ioannis Vlahavas (Eds.). Proceedings of the 7th Hellenic Conference on Artificial Intelligence, 2012: Theories and Applications (SETN'12). Springer: Berlin, Heidelberg, pp. 345–352.

[Xu13]   Zhe Xu and Ya Zhang. Automatic generated recommendation for movie trailers. In: Broadband Multimedia Systems and Broadcasting (BMSB), 2013 IEEE International Symposium, pp. 1–6. DOI: 10.1109/BMSB.2013 6621738.

Augmented Reality to Evoke a Site at the Origin of the Information Technology Age

Case study on the Guglielmo Marconi's Radio Station in Coltano, Pisa

Giorgio Verdiani, Carlo Gira, Andrea Pisani

Dipartimento di Architettura,

Florence University, Italia

Via della Mattonaia, 8, 50100 Firenze

giorgio.verdiani@unifi.it, {carlo.gira, andreapisani83}@gmail.com

Abstract

Guglielmo Marconi brought on his experiments obtaining the first radio transmissions in Coltano, near Pisa, in a radio station opened in 1911. Nowadays in that place it is possible to see only some ruins and the traces of various large antennas. To face this poor condition and to discover back the site, a specific research has been started, focusing the efforts in the try to give back a sense of place and proposing a system of interventions integrating real/digital elements into a possible plan of restoration. After a first digital survey of the area, this research started to develop reconstructed 3D digital models, giving large importance to an augmented reality experience, capable to bring back in place the colossal antennas and guiding the visitors to the value of this place.

1　Introduction

Wishing to find one of the starting points of the age of information technology it is possible to identify one of its beginning in the early XXth century,
with the first attempts of wireless communication. In the first "traditional"
radio communication it is possible to see the very first start of the ongoing
revolution in information technologies: a sequence of steps, made here and
there in the world brought little by little to our multimedia and "real time"
system of communication. Technology is something ever-changing, all that
is left behind easily becomes old and decay. In a certain way this was the
destiny of the settlement former directed by Guglielmo Marconi in Coltano
near Pisa (just two kilometers from the Airport of Pisa). Thus, even after World
War II destroyed the high antennas built there and the architectures entered
a long period of decay, this area remained on the borderline between being
a total lost and a fascinating presence. The structures were left to themselves
and used for improper activities, depot, social activities and when the decay
began to compromise the safety of the building: completely abandoned.
None of the intentions about some recovering never succeeded in neither
a minimal part. Thus the potential strength of this place is present but barely
perceived in the proposal of restoration appeared in time. The importance of
the place will be nothing without an approach putting the technologies at the
first point in the renovation of this area, or there will be the risk of betraying
the real sense of the innovative and scientific genius once moving between
these walls.

1.1　The story so far

Guglielmo Marconi (1874–1937), inventor, scientist, politician, a pioneer
man and pillar of wireless technology, Nobel Prize for physics in 1909, identified in Coltano, which was a real estate at the beginning of the XXth century,
the ideal place for the realization of one of the first ultra-powerful radiotelegraph for colonial and transoceanic communication, potentially capable of
communicating with Argentina [Ciabat1995].
The estate of Coltano, at the beginning of the XXth century, resulted marshy,
with altitude near to the sea level, and its landscape was in contrast with
the two next cities of Livorno and Pisa [RuMa1997]. The radio-towers were
located in the so-called *Padule Maggiore* and *Padule del Porcile*, and both
were near to the main historical architecture of this area: the *Villa Medicea,*

built in the XIth century, developed in the XVIth century and expanded and transformed in the XVIIIth century [Simoni1911].

About the importance of this experience, the words from Marquis Luigi Solari, a trusted man and collaborator of Marconi, sound very significant: "The most important part of the history of radio in Italy with all its technical, economic and political vicissitudes, took place virtually in Coltano" [Solari1939].

In 1903, Vittorio Emanuele III, King of Italy, receives Marconi in San Rossore, Pisa, to grant him, free of charge, with the site of Coltano to build structures for the radiotelegraph scientific research; such a marshy zone was ideal for the purpose of long-wave transmission because the dispersion was minimized [Valluri1924].

Gradually the main building began to rise on the site, the original site received several changes during this phase, the erection of the first transmissions towers, radio-reception houses, as well as depots and housing for the officers and streets. At the end of the first decade of 1900 there was the realization of a second station; in November 1911, the station began to be connected to Massawa in Eritrea and Glace Bay in Canada. The whole set of electric machinery was supported by two groups of 200 kilowatt alternators, transformers carrying the tension from 2000 to 10000 volts [Solari1928].

Throughout the years some important communications have been found and they deserve to be mentioned: the first messages to the colonies of Africa and in November 19, 1911, during the inauguration at the presence of King Vittorio Emanuele III,, Marconi wrote to the director of the New York Times: „My sincere greetings transmitted by wireless telegraph from Italy to America. Coltano, Pisa hours 5:47 pm"; It is also worthy of mention that in October 1931 with a push of a button from there he turned on the radio signal that enlights the statue of Christ the Redeemer in Rio de Janeiro. The "Marconi" Radio Telegraphy Station, one of the first in the world, was located on *Poggio di Corniolo*, it was designed by the scientist himself; the realization of the first project began in 1904 and the physical realization has been modified during construction through various steps based on the requests of the Marconi's Company. Changes which were made mostly apart from the original project; Civil Engineers inspections in 1907 and later on, were then rectifying situations of fact that in other cases would have been considered irregular [Lions2004].

The main changes to the initial plot concern increases in the central compartment heights, in the sizing of the walls, in the coverage that became terraced with a continuous parapet enriched by a balustrade of concrete columns and later again changed into a pavilion roof. Other alterations were the addition and later the removal of a large plate in cast iron with the Savoy emblem (nowadays completely disappeared) and the replacement of the large windows in the central hall and the substitution of the ceramic tiles on the floor with concrete ones.[ArchSPI]

From the architectural point of view the building has a typical neoclassical style, recognizable by the statements with smooth ashlars, a common element for the eclectic language in use at that time, with fine moldings all along the arched windows and cornices. The general plot is "T"-shaped, with the central square building housing the main rotating disc generators machines, and the rectangular shaped area leading to the building with the offices; the fronts of the building bring the signs of Annibale Biglierie, a civil engineer in Pisa. The approval from the Superior Council of Public Works is dated 1907. [ArchSPI]

The development of the towers, a group of eight called "Eritrea" and the second equivalent group called "Canada", were growing according to an axis one kilometer long. They had the shape of iron trellis recalling the well known Eiffel Tower, and culminating with a long wooden pole of Weymouth Pine. The total height of each tower was about 75 meters.

They all could communicate with each other by means of a large aircraft wire, the electrical energy was transmitted to them by the electro-generator machinery placed inside the station; the project of the towers shows the basic dimensions of 8.00 x 6.90 meters placed 2 meters above sea level, grounded on concrete foundations of crushed and hydraulic stones [ArchSPI] *(See Fig. 1)*.

Fig. 1: 1911, Coltano landscape and skyline with towers, radio station and marshy area

1.2   A long period of decay

Stazione Marconi is currently in a state of advanced decay, abandoned and damaged by the vagaries of time, vandalism and carelessness; however, its static integrity is acceptable, except for many elements of the roofs that are broken and unstable.

In the last years the area has been surrounded by an one-meter-high metallic netting, fixed on wooden poles, a try by the municipality to prevent trespassing, vandalism and abusive settlement, and to prevent imprudent visitors from possible injuries.

The decay of the building is strongly ongoing, amplified by the growth of vegetation: the walls are vastly covered by ivy and other climbing plants, with resulting damages to plasters and decorative features; some fig trees grew inside the building itself, reaching and damaging the roof structures. As a consequence of the uncontrollable vegetation growth, some areas are almost inaccessible.

The outside and inside of the building show various degradation forms: erosion caused by weather conditions, breaking and loss of stone and brick elements are common and evident.

Roof structures presents some cave in and deformations, due to loss of wooden structures integrity and breakings due to the aforementioned fig trees. Metal gutters are heavily eroded or missing, as for the windows fixtures, damaged both from vagary of times and vandalism.

In many rooms the floor is covered with debris from the collapses, earth and bird's guan, this favours the growth of vegetation; Tractor tires, threshing machine components, rusty and abandoned, decayed toys, broken bottles and every kind of waste spread on the floor, as a sign of abusive dump function found for some insane reason in the *Stazione Marconi*.

In the last 15 years the local community tried to focus the attention on this area, and some of the damage could have been prevented with a preventive action by the proprietor itself (the area belonged to the National Demanio for a long time, then, in recent time, it has been passed to the local municipality), avoiding to reach the current state of decay. Thus no real intervention was done until now. It is worth to say that in its current condition the building is highly dangerous, with many parts, mostly from the roofs, at risk of falling or collapsing. [Paglia2000]

2 The Survey Campaign

The Survey campaign answers the need to produce a reasonable and reliable graphic representation of the building, over a century after the planning and construction of the building. No accurate survey was available previously. The state of decay of the building creates some obstacles to the direct survey methodologies, impossible where the growth of plants prevents access. The instrument used for the survey was leased from the Laboratory System of the "Dipartimento di Architettura" (DiDALabs), from the Florence University. It is a Z+F (Zoller+Fröhlich) imager 5006h, a phase shift 3D laser scanner, a fast and reliable measuring machine, capable to get points up to a distance of 80 meters and with an accuracy of around 2 millimeters at a distance of ten meters. Mounted on a topographical tripod it was in the correct condition to operate inside a difficult subject like the heavily damaged station.

Most of the scanning stations were operated using the "high mode" setting of the scanner, to achieve a good detail level, required for the decorative features of the buildings, to keep a reasonable distance from certain dangerous parts and resolve the need to correctly take the measurements of temporary targets and small details around the ruins as a system of reference in between a real invasion of trees, ivy, grass and other vegetation.

The survey with the 3D laser scanner took a whole day, totalling 76 scansions from the outside of the western façade, to the northern facade, through which the central hall was reached. The southern and eastern façades closed the data collecting process; North and East facades were heavily covered by vegetation, so the survey of these parts was incomplete, even though a recent operation of cutting off the plants laid open a certain sector of previously infested walls, so it is now possible to plan a partial new survey, to integrate the first one.

The alignment of all the scans (originally in ZFS format) was done with Autodesk Recap 360 pro, which processed all the scans in a single session, almost automatically (just a few sets of scans were in need of manual intervention, most of the time because of some differences caused by the wind between the generous vegetation), giving back a global pointcloud of the Stazione Marconi in RCP (Recap) format.

Using Autodesk AutoCad 2016 and its possibility to connect and operate directly on the RCP format the pointcloud was imported to obtain plan views, sections and elevations of the actual condition of the Stazione Marconi, to obtain a first reliable base, after a century of perfunctory drawings. For some specific needs (like an easier reading of the section lines between foliage, ruins and trash) a version of the pointcloud was imported inside Bentley Pointools, a software offering some very interesting features for better managing the pointclouds and extracting in a very practical way images and animated sequences from the pointcloud data *(See Fig. 2)*.

Fig. 2: 3D Laser scanner survey and Point Cloud inside Bentley Pointools:
Section of the destroyed structure

3   3D Reconstruction

Every digital reconstruction starts with a data collection phase in which the main objective is to gather information to support the modeling process. Besides traditional tools, on-site measurements and data collection, 3D laser scanning technologies and photogrammetry techniques have become mainstream in the last fifteen years. Often, in archaeological reconstruction, there is neither a picture nor a detailed description of the original palace, and the excavation did not provide enough facts to establish a scientifically valid model. For the Marconi Station, on the contrary, it was possible to achieve a faithful reconstruction, built not only on data arising from the laser scanner survey, but also from the original project drawings and a lot of historical photos, videos and documents. All these bases allow to elaborate hypotheses and evaluate them directly through 3D modelling. [Cacia1998]

The 3D reconstruction process is constituted by several aspects and steps: modelling and shape reconstruction, reduction and balancing of detail such as polygon reduction and mesh optimization, visual and light appearance with texturing and ambient occlusion, and other topics related to the challenges in development of AR and VR three-dimensional browsing. Technical choices and visual results will contribute to define the technological framework mainly based on mobile systems, aiming to offer a realistic virtual experience in order to appreciate this Architectural Heritage.

Mcneel Rhinoceros 3D was used as main software for developing a surface model of the building. Starting from the original drawings and combining them with laser scanner data the basic structure of the reconstruction was modeled. The refinement and the final texturing were done directly from the photographic survey campaign. The level of detail and objects organization are strictly dependent on the final aims of the project.

In Unity 3D it was possible to develop the environment, generating a realistic terrain from heightmaps. It is possible to download a real world satellite survey height map from the website Terrainparty (http://terrain.party/), which simplifies the method of finding and importing heightmap data for any spot on the globe. The exported terrain model was edited to add textures and trees on it, to bring it back to the aspect it had at the time of the radio station according to the historical photos and videos.

4 Using the 3D Model to bring back the first radio station

Restoration will never recreate the perception of the original radio station system, with its towers, marshy lake and iron cables up in the air, at the beginning of the XXth century.

The goal is to communicate a reality that no longer exist of the *Stazione Marconi* at its beginning through a modern technology system. For this reason a system of Augmented and Virtual reality is used to create a memorial milestone, which, at the same time is a dissemination tool and a disclosure of information.

The result of the digital reconstruction process can often represent the starting point of further work that may have several purposes. Diverse multifaceted uses can be identified for a 3D digital reconstruction. On this basis, the proposal is the use of Augmented reality applications overlapping the virtual model on the real site using a portable/wearable devices. The use of game engines and Virtual Reality device allows to navigate and to explore the reconstructed buildings in a virtual environment; including interactive components and metadata, but also recreating the lost environment in an immersive perception.

The dissemination represents the last phase, but not the least important; it can be the main aim of a research project or its final step, where the results of the applications and analysis of the 3D digital reconstruction constitute the main outcomes useful to spread the information to a wider audience for different purposes such as cultural tourism and education.

5 From the 3D Model to Virtual Reality

The main challenge, after the previous modeling phases, is to provide smart tools to enjoy the digital reconstruction. Computer graphics techniques have demonstrated to be effective in increasing the value of cultural heritage. These potentialities should be utilized appropriately, by developing an integrated package of services for improving the visitor experience and enjoyment.

As told, Augmented Reality could be the most appropriate tool for our goal. The AR system is the integration of a computer generated 3D model with the natural environment or an architectural context in real time. This enhanced version of reality can be viewed through several devices, such as head mounted devices. One of the major fields of application of this technology can surely be useful for scientific dissemination in archaeological subjects. In fact the contribution AR gives in this field can increase knowledge-based experiences about Cultural Heritage. The user experience can be improved by imaging the architectural ruins with the ancient landscape, providing non-expert users with useful and effective instruments for the knowledge of artistic and architectural vestiges.

The purpose of this work is to apply the present approach to the Coltano Radio Station, in order to bring the visitors back into the historical landscape where the Radio Station was placed. The aim is to augment the whole area using our 3D models together with other interactive approaches, turning the exploration of these unknown spaces more accessible and enjoyable [Csl2012].

Nevertheless it can be problematic to plan a first person augmented reality experience in the area around the Radio Station, due to the huge size of this complex. To further explore the whole area could be difficult due to the current condition of the terrain, where wheat is cultivated today. The visitor would have to cross this tricky terrain for kilometers, sometimes inaccessible, to be able to see up close and in Augmented Reality the towers or the station. Moreover the state of abandon of the structure makes the access impossible. The two main problems are due to the centenary disuse of the building leading it to ruin, and consequently the growth of vegetation that hides all the structures.

For this reason our project provides to create a panoramic position from which the user can have a good view of the whole area. So, the first step has been the choice of a definite place that can be easily approached by everyone. A key element was identified in the area, in order to set the rigid support: a bridge made of bricks and stones, measuring two meters wide and nine meters long, crossing the "Fossa Fonda" rural canal. From above this bridge it is possible to see the station and the bases of the towers [Bert1922]. This is the perfect place for experiencing a 360° virtual tour. This bridge is halfway among the Marconi's Station and the ex-radio receiving station, today wrecked. At about 250 meters away from the main station itself, the receiving station was originally built to create a pedestrian passage on the Padule Maggiore, before his restoration, to reach the tower number 8 of the so-called "Lato Coloniale" [Bert1922].

The choice of this bridge has multiple reasons, such as the allegorical meaning of the actual information passage, wishing to give back architectural and functional pride to a previous important structure, unusable because of its condition.

On the bridge a panel is installed on which the target and a QR code are printed *(See Fig. 3)*.

Fig. 3: QR Codes Panel, invented for AR/VR experience, and dissemination of general information of the area, such as videos, articles and ancient images

From this point the virtual experience starts. By simply scanning the QR-Code, the user can download our mobile app. The application is structured in two parts. The first one is in augmented reality, it allows users to interact with the panel. For exact tracking we use image-based techniques [ScHol2016].

The software renders in Augmented Reality some historical information about the station and its functioning above the panel: texts, historical images, historical videos and the 3D model of its reconstruction in scale *(See Fig. 4)*.

Fig. 4: A.R. Experience on the panel, with historical images, videos and 3D model

In the second part of the app users can enter inside the virtual reconstruction of the entire environment in VR mode. With 360 degree renderings we built a panoramic video, using Unity3d. This allows everyone to explore the whole area by staying comfortably in place [KipRa2012]. In the video the 360° camera moves across the 3D reconstruction, virtually carrying through the towers to the station. Wearing Google cardboard, or other VR viewers, the experience increases its realism *(See Fig. 5)*.

Fig. 5: V.R. Experience: here a frame of the video, with the reconstruction of Marconi Radio Station at its beginning

A full panoramic tour of the area allows us to perceive the clear transformation undergone by Coltano in the last hundred years *(See Fig. 6)*.

Fig. 6: V.R. Experience with Google Cardboard

6   The idea of a real/virtual museum

The situation of this particular built heritage is quite dramatic, many parts seem beyond any possibility of architectural recovering, but the sense of the place, its particular relationship with landscape and with the story of technology is still present and strong.

As the reason of its building has to be found in the will of scientific progress and continuous innovation, in a similar way, new technologies of simulation may work, enhance the understanding and create a connection between what this place was and its meaning, bringing the surprise of the high antennas, of the great arches of the wires, of what was happened between these walls, of something that cannot be recreated and is to be considered as definitively lost, but can be evoked in our contemporary technologies. The creation of a "new reality" for Coltano and for the Stazione Marconi is a possible step forward recovering, while even if a place decays and is at risk of destruction, it is very important to keep its trace, disseminate its best value and create the condition and the tools for starting reflecting about a real and intelligent recovery.

Literature

[ArchSPI]   Archivio di Stato di Pisa, Genio Civile, Buste 26-27-28.

[Bert1922]   Bertarelli L. V. Terra Promessa: le bonifiche di Coltano, Sanluri, Licola e Varcatauro dell'OperaNazionale per i combattenti, Milano Arti grafiche Modiano e C., 1922

[Cacia1998]   Caciagli C. Disegno e Rilevamento dei monumenti, architettura e costruzione. in laboratorio Universitario Volterrano. Quaderno I, Pacini editore, 1998

[Ciabat1995]   Ciabattini P. Coltano 1945, Mursia, Milano 1995.

[Csl2012]   Communication strategies lab, Realtà aumentate: Esperienze, strategie e contenuti per l'Augmented Reality, Apogeo Editore, 2012.

[KipRa2012]   Kipper G., Rampolla J. Augmented Reality: An Emerging Technologies Guide to AR, Elsevier, 2012.

[Lions2004]   Various Authors. La Stazione Radiotelegrafica Guglielmo Marconi di Coltano, Lions Club Livorno, Pisa 2004.

[Paglia2000]   Paglialunga S. Il Parco naturale Migliarino, San Rossore , Massaciuccoli: alcune notizie su 20 ani di storia, in Ambiente e urbanistica, proceedings of the workshop 9–10 June 2000, Ente Parco Regionale Migliarino San Rossore Massaciuccoli, 2000,

[RuMa1997]   Rupi L.P. , Martinelli A. Pisa Storia Urbanistica, Pacini Editore, Pisa 1997.

[ScHol2016]   Schmalstieg D., Hollerer T., Augmented Reality: Principles and Practice Addison-Wesley Professional, 2016.

[Simoni1911]   Simoni D. Coltano e la Sua Storia, R. Bemporad & F., Pisa 1911.

[Solari1939]   Solari L. Storia Della Radio, Treves 1939.

[Solari1928]   Solari Luigi. Il Grande impianto di Coltano, da Marconi alla borgata di Pontecchio in Australia, Napoli, A.Morano, 1928

[Valluri1924] Vallauri G. Il Centri Radiotelegrafico Di Coltano, In L'Elettrotecnica, 1924

Art++ – Augmenting Art with Technology

Bernd Girod

Robert L. and Audrey S. Hancock Professor of Electrical Engineering
School of Engineering, Stanford University
bgirod@stanford.edu

Abstract

Art++ is a new augmented reality application that enriches and enlivens the in-gallery experience for museum visitors. Developed in collaboration between Stanford engineering students and the Cantor Arts Center, Art++ immerses visitors in the history, context, and importance of selected artworks by overlaying relevant content on a tablet viewfinder. Overlay highlights include historic photos and 360 panoramas that visitors can explore. The experience is interactive and self-guided, encouraging visitors to look at art in new and unexpected ways. It this talk, we review the underlying mobile augmented reality technology that we have explored at Stanford over the last 10 years and review lessons learned from deploying this technology in the context of an art museum.

Digital Curation Tool in the Age of Semantic Technology

Jing He, Novina Göhlsdorf

ART+COM AG

Kleiststraße 23–26

10787 Berlin

jing@artcom.de

Abstract

This paper presents our research process, challenges and findings in designing and developing a semantic technology empowered curatorial application for our in-house knowledge workers in the DKT research project[1]. Based on a user-centered design process, the user evaluations indicate that *information extraction* and *information visualization* can enhance knowledge workers' understanding of a domain by providing effective overviews and the possibility to discover meaningful insights from large-body textual resources.[2]

---

1   DKT (Digitale Kuratierungstechnologien) is a project funded by BMBF (the German Federal Ministry of Education and Research). Further information can be found on the project website http://digitale-kuratierung.de/

2   Parts of this paper have been published in: Rehm et. al, 2017.

1   Technological Background

1.1   Natural Language Processing

"Natural Language Processing (NLP) is an area of research and application that explores how computers can be used to understand and manipulate natural language text or speech to do useful things (Chowdhury, 2003, p.51)." From its inception in the 1950's, the NLP field has in the recent decades made great strides in understanding human speech and text due to the growing computing power of processors, falling prices for data storage, and the availability of big data. The advancement in several subfields includes speech recognition, machine translation, and speech synthesis, etc. (Hirschberg, 2015).

The development of NLP today relies on Machine Learning (ML), a field within Artificial Intelligence (AI). Unlike the previous hand-coded rules-based approach, ML can infer rules by analyzing large bodies of text based on statistical models. In recent years, Deep Learning through Digital Neural Networks (DNNs) greatly refined the process of ML (Hirschberg, 2015).

In this paper, we focus on use cases of Information Extraction (IE), an area of NLP that deals with finding factual information in free text (Piskorski, 2013). The demand for structuring unstructured text is increasing as the amount of available textual data proliferates. We will demonstrate in section 3 of this paper how an NLP task such as Named Entity Recognition (NER) is used to analyze and extract key information from free-text documents.

1.2   Semantic Technology

Semantics is the study of meaning communicated through language. Founded by Tim Berners-Lee, the inventor of the World Wide Web as we know today, the World Wide Web Consortium (W3C) has set out the movement called the "semantic web3" to promote standardization of vastly scattered data formats and semantic content on the web so that the data structure and content are machine-readable (Berners-Lee, 2001).

---

3   https://www.w3.org/2001/sw/

One conceptual model for realizing the semantic web is the Resource Description Framework (RDF). [4] RDF can be thought of as a relational database template that encodes knowledge by expressing how datum also called *entities* relate to each other, i.e., object X is "an instance of" object Y. In the Semantic Web any website which implements such data model will allow machines to extract the semantic content of the site, thus assisting human in searching, querying, and performing other automated services based on acquired knowledge.

As the amount of information grows so does the need to centralize the distributed knowledge. Since the early 2000s there have been several developments of Knowledge Graphs such as DBpedia, Freebase, and Wikidata where semantic data is stored in an RDF based format. In the following section we will describe in detail how the semantic technology is implemented in our application using Wikidata based graph service to extract, look-up, and enrich entities found in documents. [5]

1.3   Semantic Web Visualization

Information visualization is a field of study emerged from Computer Graphics in the late 80s. According to Card's definition: "information visualization is the use of computer-supported, interactive, visual representations of abstract data to amplify cognition (Card, 1999, p.6)." As more institutions and corporations contribute to the Semantic Web, new ways of organizing and accessing large-scale information resources become more relevant for the human users (Geroimenko, 2006). In section 3.2.2 we will discuss in detail some of the information visualization techniques we have explored to represent the different facets of semantic data.

---

4   https://www.w3.org/RDF/
5   https://developers.google.com/freebase/; https://www.wikidata.org; and https://www.wikidata.org.

2 The Use Case: Knowledge Work at ART+COM

2.1 Knowledge Work

Within the last decades, knowledge work has been a widely discussed topic.[6] Connected to postindustrial economies and the emergence of the so called information society, a "shift from manufacturing to knowledge work has occurred," that is, "an increasing amount of work is taken up with the production and distribution of information, communication, and knowledge."[7] Due to digitalization and the World Wide Web, the amount and accessibility of data, information and knowledge has seemingly exploded.

Knowledge work can be defined by the immateriality of its results and the importance of its very process, which is, moreover, often a processing of language in a broad sense – of symbols (Hube, 2005, p.28–29). Knowledge is a resource and an outcome of knowledge work, and its continuous modification, revision and change is inevitable and even desired. In view of the growing "creative class", Richard Florida connects knowledge work with a specific kind of creative labor resulting in "…meaningful forms (Florida, 2002, p.68)". For Florida, knowledge work is not merely the handling or distribution of knowledge but the genuine production of it. Of course, the boundaries between handling and production of knowledge are blurry – which can be demonstrated in view of the knowledge work at ART+COM.

2.2 Creative Knowledge Work at ART+COM

ART+COM is a design studio with an extensive history in creating media-rich exhibition design in cultural and commercial sectors, e.g. a zoo for microorganisms (Micropia) in Amsterdam, an experience centre on Viking history in Denmark or a Product Info Center for BMW in Munich.[8]

For every new exhibition, the in-house knowledge workers need to quickly familiarize themselves with its topic, by sighting briefing material offered by clients, by learning about the context and related aspects of the topic. Eventu-

---

6   see, e.g., Cortada, 1998, ,McKercher and Mosco, 2008.
7   Mosco and McKercher 2008, ix. For the relation of the English term "knowledge work" and the notion of the German "Wissensarbeit" see, e.g., Hube, 2005
8   https://artcom.de/en/

ally, they need to effectively share their key findings with the design team in order to facilitate brainstorm sessions and the emergence of design concepts.

The knowledge workers at ART+COM absorb and structure information in various forms and transform it into an enriched and contextualized kind of knowledge on the base of the processed material. Their work is always curatorial in the wider sense of curation as transforming data of all kinds into content, and it is often curatorial in the traditional sense: developing ideas for exhibitions or visitors centers that will then be expressed by media enriched exhibits. Both types of curatorial activity are complex processes. They involve routine tasks like the fast sighting, highlighting and sorting of material, and they require a creative re-combination of material and thus decision-making or the inclusion of already acquired knowledge or other data.

3 Design and Development of the Digital Curation Tool

With the significant progress in AI driven semantic technology in the recent years and our in-house expertise in user experience design, we are motivated to find out how information extraction and visualization could improve knowledge workers' understanding of the domain and their ability to discover meaningful insights.

3.1 Scope of Work

Our latest prototype focuses upon optimizing the knowledge worker's initial research phase of the entire workflow. [9] The user research conducted during our design phase will be discussed in the later section. In this subsection we will describe the functioning prototype in three parts: overview of the application framework, information extraction service, and graph services.

3.1.1 Application Framework Overview

Our prototype is a web application implemented using RESTful APIs. It allows users to begin their research by importing existing documents, such as briefing materials from the client, or by performing an explorative web search with keywords. In either case, the content is automatically analyzed by first

9   A screen screencast of the prototype is available at https://vimeo.com/182694896

the NLP service which extracts entities from text. Then the Graph service assigns semantic information to the entities. Finally the application performs an entity batch-lookup on Wikidata in order to enrich them with information potentially useful to the user. For instance, the entity "Gorm the Old " – a male person – can be contextualized with the date and place of birth and death, family relations and occupation, etc. The entities are further enriched with top-level ontology labels in order to give the user an overview of the distribution of information in categories, i.e., "person", "organization", and "location".

3.1.2 NLP Service

The NLP service is provided by our research partner in the DKT project, the German Research Center for Artificial Intelligence (DFKI). The specific NLP service used in the prototype is called Named Entity Recognition (NER), which allows information about people, places, and organizations extracted from any given documents. For instance, the historical text about the Vikings that was used in the knowledge workers' research for the Viking Experience Center, when fed through the NLP service, generates a list of entities such as king "Gorm the Old", king "Harald Bluetooth", "Sweden", "Denmark", etc. The NLP service can handle non-domain-specific information; however, the service also provides possibilities to be trained to recognize more domain-specific entities by providing a corpora of sample text.

3.1.3 Knowledge Graph Service

The graph service deals with AI based semantic data extraction. The service preprocesses the entire Wikidata knowledge base in order to generate a graph that approximates how closely Wikidata entries relate to one another. This is done by a ML algorithm such as Word2Vec that generates a set of vectors for each entity. The semantic distance between the entities is encoded in these sets of vectors.[10]

When a list of entities from a document is found via the NLP service, the graph service performs analysis on the entities and retrieves a set of *entity candidates* for each entity. For example, the candidates for the entity

---

10   https://www.tensorflow.org/tutorials/word2vec (Mikolov, 2013)

"Denmark" are "Kingdom of Denmark", "city in South Carolina", "town in Maine" – possible meanings of "Denmark". Through an iterative re-sorting process where candidates for each entity are compared to other entities and their respective candidates in order to calculate a similarity value. Based on this similarity value the candidate for each entity that fits the best in the given context is chosen. "Denmark" resolves to "Kingdom of Denmark" because it relates to king "Gorm the Old" and Harald Bluetooth" better than other suggested candidates.

Some of other techniques addressing entity ambiguity are *term shadowing* and *term construction*. In the text the term "Gorm" and "Gorm the Old" are both mentioned and therefore extracted as separate entities. It is very common that the subject is addressed only with first or last name for the sake of brevity. *Term shadowing* resolves these two entities as one. In other cases an extracted entity has incomplete information, i.e. only "Gorm" is mentioned in the text. *Term construction* completes the identity of an entity. In the chosen case the system would suggest that "Gorm" means "Gorm the Old".

3.2   Design and Design Process

3.2.1   Interface Design: Features and Structures

The prototype is designed with our in-house knowledge workers' iterative work cycle in mind. Since they often deal with multiple projects at the same time, the interface allows the users to switch between projects at any time during their research process while the research materials, whether imported by the users or search results from the web, are saved within the related project. This way the users can continue from where they have left off in the previous research session. The design template for each project's home screen consists of two main areas. On the left side the user can import multiple text files or view imported files, while on the right side the user can start an explorative search on the web with advanced search options such as knowledge sources, depth of search, and amount of returned results (Figure 1). Following the *import file* or *open collections* option, the interface displays the *collection view* and shows imported files. In the future we will develop the option to create new collections by the user, i.e. by topics much like the common usage of the folder structures.

Within each project space there are six main interface areas:

- The current project title and menu dropdown to switch to other projects are located in the *top bar*.
- On the left side, a collection icon offers a shortcut for the user to quickly navigate back to the top level *collection view*. An empty space labeled "workspace " where the users can add shortcuts to collections or documents allows the users to gain quick access to research materials they are currently working on or save their findings from search or imported documents.
- The *search bar* on the far right is where the users can jump over to the search results. For example, the user finds "Gorm the Old" an interesting entity in the imported document, she could start a search from the entity to learn more about it in depth.
- The *header bar* area contains main content navigation structure. A breadcrumb trail displays where the user is located within the project. The three main document-centric views are accessible at all times so that the user can freely toggle amongst: *document view, entity list view,* and *entity visualization view*.
- Within each content view an *interaction panel* is always present on the right-hand side where context-specific interaction options are displayed. Although interaction options change based on the different content views, the functionality of the area remains consistent so that the user can become familiar with different interaction options faster.
- In the *document view* (figure 2), the user can browse through the original text with extracted entities highlighted. In the *interaction panel* area a search field offers search options on any given entities.

The *entity list view* (figure 3) consists of a list of entities which can be sorted by number of occurrences in the text, category types or alphabetic order. A short entity statement accompanies each entity, i.e. "Gorm the Old was the king of Denmark." In the *interaction panel,* a search bar to search for existing entities is available as well as a category filter to filter entities by category types.

The third content view is the *entity visualization view*. Since this is a main focus of our research project it will be detailed in the following section.

3.2.2   Information Visualization

We implemented the visualisations in D3 (Bostock, 2011), a Javascript library optimized for visualizing data with HTML, SVG and CSS. The challenge is to provide intuitive and effective interaction modalities so that the users can gain a quick overview of a specific topic or drill down into the semantic knowledge base to explore deeper patterns or relationships.

We realized several visualizations including a network overview, semantic clustering, timelining and maps (Figure 4-8). While a network is effective for exploring semantic relationships amongst extracted entities, semantic clustering provides a good overview of entities closely related to each other in groups. Timelines and maps, in addition, offer a geo-temporal overview of extracted entities. Combining all of the above-mentioned visualisations for doing research on "Harald Bluetooth", for example, the user can explore the places and people to which he is connected in the network visualization, view his timespan of reign and family lineage along the timeline, and learn about notable events that are highlighted on the map.

In terms of interaction modalities, the user can directly manipulate the graph such as zoom and pan. On highlighting entities, tooltips appear to display entity properties found on Wikidata. The user can also select and focus on the connections between two entities in the *detailed connection view* to investigate how they are related. Harald Bluetooth's connection to Gorm the Old, for instance, is encoded with several connection possibilities. Harald is the son of Gorm and his heir to the throne.

Besides the direct interaction with the visualization, we also implemented interactive filters in order for the user to effectively gain specific information needed. For instance, the category filter allows the user to filter entities that are only "person" or a combination of "person", "location", or other category labels that appear relevant to the user. In the future, the user can also add new category labels, filter by number of occurrence, or by connection types.

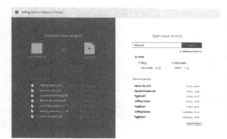

Fig. 1: Project home screen

Fig. 2: Document view

Fig. 3: Entity list view

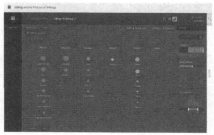

Fig. 4: Entity list visualization

Fig. 5: Network visualization

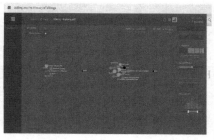

Fig. 6: Semantic cluster visualization

Fig. 7: Detailed connection visualization

Fig. 8: Timeline and map visualization

3.3 User-centered Design Process

The UX design team at ART+COM followed user-centered design principles (Abras, 2004). Our research process began with in-depth interviews and surveys to learn about the knowledge workers, their behavior, goals, motivations and needs. We gained insights into the kinds of tools and environments each user is familiar with and their usage patterns. Moreover, the team acquired an intuitive understanding of the different phases of their workflows, and the goals and expectations for each research step.

The qualitative and quantitative user research formed the basis for creating several *personas* (Miaskiewicza, 2011). *Personas* can be used to synthesize real users' needs, behaviors, and mental models. Julia is our primary *persona*. "She works at a creative agency as a content researcher. Constrained by time and budget, she's quick on her feet in gathering information for many short-term projects, often at the same time. Her research process is open, from one keyword branching into other possibly interesting topics, formulating and refining the "right" questions. Her goal is to be able to quickly grasp a general impression of an unfamiliar topic so that she can focus on meaningful key points to highlight and share with the team. During the research, she constantly weighs in on the validity of the sources found (Rehm, 2017)."

Based on the knowledge about the *personas*, a *task flow* is generated describing the individual steps Julia would take in order to complete an assignment (J.T.Hackos, 1998). The tasks are described intentionally on a high level to focus on her actions rather than being distracted by the current technology she employs. Twelve steps have been defined, which are grouped in the phases "search", "evaluate", and "organize" of her entire workflow. From the *task flow*, a set of user's pain points are identified, such as lacking an overview of her sources, and the inability to identify key information contained in the sources. Based on the identified functional needs, the team therefore decided to prioritize the system functionalities which would optimize the user's *task flow*, namely impart the knowledge they need, and improve the information overview.

3.4 User Evaluation

The curation tool is developed in an agile approach (Beck, 2001), by iterating design, development and user test cycles. We consistently invited our in-house curation workers to participate in the user tests from earlier low-fidelity paper prototypes to the fully interactive prototype.

The last user test was conducted using the latest developed web application. The design team focused on: one, evaluating the usefulness of semantically extracted entities and the information that enriches the given entities, and two, user interaction with the visualisations.

We interviewed five knowledge workers. Each interview took about one hour. We first informed the users about a fictitious scenario: "our design studio has been invited to create a concept proposal for an interactive installation about the Italian artist Caravaggio for an art museum." The users had a few minutes to glance through a printed document about the artist. They were then asked to switch to the web application, in which we presented the printed document digitally with extracted entities highlighted. We asked them to focus on the highlighted words and reflect on their meanings. All the users were able to identify that the highlighted words described people and places. One user questioned why these types of information were highlighted while another user concluded that the people and places must all have connections to Caravaggio.

The users were asked to navigate to the *entity list view* in which the entities are listed based on the number of occurrences, category types or alphabetical order. Each entity is assigned a top-level category and enriched with a short descriptive statement. The users were invited to explore the content and interface freely while *thinking aloud*.[11] Here, the users perceived that the enrichment of the entities seem to come from the web, like "a condensed version of a browser search."

Throughout the evaluation, the users were asked to keep in mind a few keywords that seemed interesting to them as they transition from the *document view*, to the *entity list view*, and finally to the *visualisation view*, in hope that they can keep their focus on exploring the content rather than feeling overwhelmed by a new interface. In the *visualisation view*, the users first began with free exploration while *thinking-aloud*. All of them started by

---

11   Thinking-aloud is a technique used in usability testing where the users verbalize their thoughts as they move through the user interface (Lewis, 1982).

directly manipulating the graph, i.e., dragging the nodes or highlighting nodes to see additional information in the tooltip. We then asked them to perform actions they did not try during the free exploration phase. For example, one user didn't realize that she could zoom into the graph while another user didn't know that she could click on the edge between nodes to explore in depth the relation. In summary, all users found the *entity list visualization* most useful because "it's very structured" and the *Detailed connection visualization*, showing all the connections between two entities intriguing, offered further research directions.

The challenge of the user test was that the users had to familiarize themselves with the interface before they could feel confident enough to use the tool to help them analyze the content. Secondly, our users are content workers who are not familiar with interacting with visualizations. Changing the visual encoding (Yi, 2007) of the node size based on the number of connections an entity has versus the number of occurrences the entity is mentioned in the document was not obvious to them, nor was the concept of cross-filtering to distill down the information they were looking for. [12]

In the users' opinion, the application provided a good overview of the subject. They would use the tool at the beginning of a project, particularly when confronted with massive amounts of text. However, some relevant information from the original text was not highlighted and some extracted information seemed out of context. Regarding the usefulness of extracted information, they confirmed the relevance of the extracted names of people and places and considered the enriched ``general information'' about each entity useful. However, they wished for more relations between entities extracted from the document so that they could deepen their understanding through the document itself as well as through the, more generally defined, Encyclopedia-like information stemming from Wikidata.

---

12 https://square.github.io/crossfilter/

4   Next Steps

ART+COM will continue to improve the visualization-based user interface, allowing for a seamless browsing experience between analysis of entities and the content from which they are extracted. We will evaluate the approach with different knowledge domains as ART+COM's exhibition topics are very diverse, ranging from historical to scientific. We already started exploring image classification as the knowledge workers often work with images. The web search so far is based on search queries from Bing and Wikipedia only. We could, in addition, include sources from other structured knowledge sources. Finally implementing custom annotation features i.e. star or comment on a piece of information, as well as project management features i.e. customize collections would be useful so that the platform can support the users throughout the entire work cycle.

On the semantic technology front, in order to offer our knowledge workers reliable enriched information that is context-specific, we will continue to improve the graph service to optimize the clarification of ambiguous entities. We plan to provide more flexibility within the user-interface so that the system can not only suggest but also learn and adapt based on the user's input and intent. Secondly, in close collaboration with DFKI, more NLP features such as *relation extraction* and *text classification* can be applied. *Relation extraction* improves knowledge workers' understanding of how the extracted entities relate to each other in a given context besides their general relationship in the real-world encoded in a knowledge base. *Text classification* can help pre-sort a large body of documents according to topics or domains.

The future of a digital curation tool lies in the potential to assist the knowledge workers not only in optimizing laborious tasks but also in uncovering unforeseen insights. The digital curation tool is not only a mere workspace for knowledge finding but also an agent which co-curates information. As AI empowered semantic technology learns and "understands" the world ever better, concept-based search /research will become inseparable part of knowledge work.

Literature

Abras, C. M.-K. (2004). User-centered Design. Encyclopedia of Human-Computer Interaction , 37, pp. 445–456.

Beck, K. B. (2001). Manifesto for agile software development.

Berners-Lee, T. H. (2001). The semantic web. Scientific American , 284 (5), pp. 28–37.

Bostock, M. O. (2011). D3: Data-Driven Documents. IEEE Trans. Visualization & Comp. Graphics.

Card, K. S. (1999). Readings in Information Visualization, Using Vision to Think. . San Francisco, CA: Morgan Kaufmann.

Chowdhury, G. G. (2003). Natural Language processing (Vol. 37). Annual review of information science and technology, pp. 51–89.

Cortada, J. W., Ed. (1998). Rise of the Knowledge Worker, Woburn, MA: Butterworth-Heinemann.

Florida, R. (2002). The Rise of the Creative Class And How it's Transforming Work, Leisure, Community and Everyday Life. New York: Basic Books

Geroimenko, V. C. and Chen, C., Eds. (2006). Visualizing the Semantic Web: XML-based Internet and Information Visualization (second ed.). London: Springer.

Hirschberg, J. M. (2015). Advances in natural language processing. Science (349), pp. 261–266.

Hackos, J. T. (1998). User and task analysis for interface design.

Hackos, J. T. and Redish, J.C. (1998). User and Task Analysis for Interface Design, New York: Wiley & Sons.

Hube, G. (2005). Beitrag zur Beschreibung und Analyse von Wissensarbeit, Heimsheim: Jost Jetter Verlag.

Jones, S. K. (2001). Natural language processing: a historical review. In Current Issues in Computational Linguistics: In Honour of Don Walker. Cambridge, UK: Springer Netherlands, pp. 3–16.

Lewis, C. (1982). Using the "thinking-aloud" method in cognitive interface design. IBM TJ Watson Research Center.

McKercher, C. and Mosco, V., Ed. (2008). Knowledge Workers in the Information Society. Lanham, MD: Lexington Books.

Miaskiewicza, T. K. (2011). Personas and user-centered design: How can personas benefit product design processes? Design Studies, 32 (5), pp. 417–430.

Mikolov, T. S. (2013). Distributed representations of words and phrases and their compositionality. Advances in neural information processing systems, pp. 3111–3119.

Norman, D. A. (1986). User-Centered System Design: New Perspectives on Human-Computer Interaction. Hillsdale, NJ: Lawrence Earlbaum Associates.

Piskorski, J. Y. (2013). Information Extraction: Past, Present and Future. In Multi-source, Multilingual Information Extraction and Summarization (pp. 23–49). Springer Berlin Heidelberg.

Rehm, G., He, J., Moreno-Schneider, J., Nehring, J., Quantz, J. (2017). Designing user interfaces for curation technologies. 19th International Conference on Human-Computer Interaction – HCI International 2017. In print, Vancouver, Canada (July 2017)

Spencer, R. (2007). Information Visualization: Design for Interaction (2nd ed.).

Yi, J. S. (2007). Toward a Deeper Understanding of the Role of Interaction in Information Visualization. IEEE transactions on visualization and computer graphics 13(6), pp. 1224–1231.

Enhancement of Printed Content Using Augmented Reality

Julien Letellier[1,2], Florian Pfeiffer[1], Jens Reinhardt[1,2],
Peter Scholl[1], Jürgen Sieck[1,2], Michael Thiele-Maas[1]

[1]Hochschule für Technik und Wirtschaft (HTW) Berlin
Wilhelminenhofstraße 75A
{florian.pfeiffer, peter.scholl}@student.htw-berlin.de,
{jens.reinhardt, j.sieck, michael.thiele-maas}@htw-berlin.de

[2]Faculty of Computing and Informatics
Namibia University of Science & Technology
13 Storch Street,
Windhoek, Namibia

Abstract

While not a new concept, Augmented Reality has gained increasing momentum in the last few years through the widespread propagation of high-performance mobile devices. These powerful handheld devices allow users to see the real world enhanced with computer generated content anywhere at anytime. This has led to a massive rise of Augmented Reality technology; large companies and start-ups are adding affordable Augmented Reality accessories to their product portfolios. In this paper we describe a joint project between our research group and the Konzerthaus Berlin to use Augmented Reality to enrich the Konzerthaus' printed media. With the aid of the Augmented Reality, the readers of the seasonal brochure of the Konzerthaus Berlin are given the opportunity to access additional content complementing the brochure. These contents include images, illustrations, audio, video, simple 2D and 3D animations, interactive media as well as 3D objects. The application was implemented using Vuforia and Unity.

1   Introduction

The paper presents the first results of the APOLLO[1] project. The APOLLO project is a joint project between the Konzerthaus Berlin[2] and the research group INKA[3] at the University of Applied Sciences in Berlin[4] (HTW Berlin). One of the projects goals is the development of various Augmented (AR) and Virtual Reality (VR) applications for the Konzerthaus Berlin.

"Konzerthaus plus" is the name of the first subproject and is an AR system that aims to implement a "living concert hall magazine". In this subproject the printed seasonal magazine of the Konzerthaus Berlin will be augmented with digital content. The team of this subproject consists of musicologists, designers and computer scientists.

In cooperation with the Konzerthaus Berlin we are currently looking for innovative approaches to increase the customer relationship. While we considered many different areas, the print media published by the Konzerthaus Berlin has an vast reach and similar projects proved that the concepts are effective, e.g. the Städel Museum5 has implemented a range of applications, mainly meant to be used inside the museum. Our approach is to provide a variety of additional content to users of the seasonal magazine for the Konzerthaus Berlin. In order to not disturb the layout and design of the magazine, markerless tracking was used. The corresponding page of the magazine is used in the same way as the traditional AR markers for the identification and registration of the corresponding contents. This has lead to a portfolio of barely visible AR markers embedded in the brochure with varying offers of visualisation and interactivity. To make pages recognisable for their additional AR content, every page that can be augmented has a small, subtle icon added. This informs the user of the additional AR content, but otherwise these marker pages are not distinguishable from regular pages. Our long-term goal is to provide a single application that integrates a wide range of mixed reality applications that can be used outside as well as inside the physical building. In addition to the application described in this paper, AR modules for entrance tickets and a guided tour through the Konzerthaus Berlin will be integrated. A digital program booklet will also be part of this application.

---

1   https://inka.htw-berlin.de/inka/de/project/apollo/
2   https://www.konzerthaus.de/en/
3   http://inka.htw-berlin.de
4   https://www.htw-berlin.de/en/
5   http://www.staedelmuseum.de/en

2 Previous Work

The content in print media is based on the presentation of text and images. New media, such as audio, video and various interactive media formats, cannot be integrated directly into a printed newspaper or magazine. Classical print media consist of static content and offer poor or no interactivity [Pere11].

Different approaches such as printing internet links, printing qr-codes or adding additional media such as CD and DVD were used to try and counter this problem in the past. In principle, the desire of the reader to get further information can be fulfilled using these additions. However, the user has to switch from the actual medium, which provides the content and information, to a new medium to retrieve the additional information. The connection of the user to the print medium can quickly be lost. With the use of AR, print media can offer contextual information, make them interactive and give the possibility to include forms of media content that would not be possible by printed media alone.

AR allows the user to view the real world with superimposed computer-generated content. Therefore, AR complements the reality rather than replacing it completely [Azum97]. Since Ivan Sutherland's pioneering work of the 1960s and the development of the first Head-Mounted Display (HMD) up to the present time, the research and development in the field of the AR have been significantly advanced [Krev10]. Advances were made in the main research areas of AR, visualisation, tracking and registration, as well as interaction. All these areas must be addressed by the usage of AR for print media. Tracking is necessary to identify the printed content to be expanded and to register the artificial content geometrically correct. Visualisation techniques are required to present the additional contents to the user. Interactive access gives the user the possibility to control the additional content.

Registration is the process of overlaying the virtual objects in the real scene and is one of the most important research topics in AR [Azum97, Azum01]. The required information for registration is extracted from the characteristics or feature points of the real scene [Pang06]. The authors in [Pang06] define two categories of registration approaches.

Firstly, the sensor based approach, where mechanical, magnetic, ultrasonic or optic sensors are used to gather the information for registration from the real scene. Often a calibration of the sensors is necessary and specialised sensors can be expensive, or lack satisfactory levels of accuracy [Pang06], especially when external sensors are used. Computer vision based approaches avoid the need to calibrate external sensors. They offer the potential for accurate tracking without the use of additional sensors. Different approaches for camera-based tracking are named in [Pang06], which can be used without calibrating the camera. The necessary information for the registration is gained through the tracking.

The use of image recognition in AR for tracking is widespread. Due to their simplicity and accuracy, tracking techniques based on markers are some of the most commonly used techniques in AR [Li15]. The simplicity and accuracy is based on the design of the markers. A predefined shape and the high contrast of the embedded pattern make them easily recognisable in most setups [Li15]. The authors in [Li15] describe a system, which combines tracking of markers with the gyroscope sensor of the mobile device for pose estimation of a mobile AR device. Another example can be found in [Youn16], where the authors use ARToolkit[6] Marker in an interactive AR system to place furniture in a room. In this system, markers are used to define the spatial position of the furniture to be placed. Dibidogs children storybook[7] contains also AR markers to enrich the user experience.

Markerless augmented reality techniques allow the use of natural images as targets or bases for the placement of superimposed virtual objects. The natural images correspond to parts of the real world, which are captured by the camera of the AR-system and are examined for their natural features such as edges, corners or texture patches [Bara09]. The authors in [Kao13] describe a markerless AR application for picture books with the usage of the scale-invariant feature transform (SIFT). The usage of the SIFT-algorithm and associated SIFT-descriptors to match the feature points of the images allows them to use the pictures included in the book included as AR markers and to enrich them with virtual 3D-objects [Kao13]. The authors of [Yang12] describe an approach to speed up the SURF (speeded up robust features) algorithm on mobile devices.

For a long time, most AR interfaces were based on the desktop metaphor or used designs from Virtual Environments Research. A major trend in interaction research, especially for AR systems, is the use of heterogeneous designs, tangible interfaces [Azum01], and multimodal interaction methods. Hetero-

---

6   https://artoolkit.org
7   http://www.dibidogs.com/files/3113/9323/2202/DIBIDOGS_BROCHURE_EN.pdf

geneous approaches blur the boundaries between reality and virtuality and take parts from both worlds. Tangible interfaces emphasise the use of real, physical objects and tools. Similar to AR systems, the user sees the real world and will often interact with real objects; it is expedient that the AR interface has a real component [Azum01]. A major focus in interaction research lies in the use of mobile AR systems (MARS). With the increasing sales of smartphones and their increasing technical equipment and technical possibilities of these, smartphones seem to be the ideal platform for AR. Many AR applications for smartphones and tablets are limited to the visual superposition of reality with additional information. The interaction with the most important content is usually done via the touchpad [Tani15]. A classic example for this kind of application is the mobile AR browser. Interacting with virtual objects in the way one would be interacting with real objects is one of the biggest problems to solve. In order to allow interaction with virtual objects in such a way that the interaction with real objects is emulated, different approaches are pursued [Tani15]. One approach is tangible user interfaces for real object-based interaction. The targeted virtual objects are coordinated with a real object. They allow the user to handle, rotate or manipulate virtual objects by handling and rotating the coordinated real object [Tani15]. By using different tracking methods, changes on the real object in positioning or alignment can be transferred to the virtual object.

Another approach is to track the users hand to interact with virtual objects [Tani15]. With the aid of computer vision, the user's hand is recognised by a camera-mapped AR system. [Kova16] describe in their work a system based on a normal RGB camera to recognise the user's hand and gestures. [Tera09] tracks fingers to realise in-air typing. In [Hagb09] hand-drawn shapes are used to create AR objects. In [Hürs13], a system is presented in which the user's fingertips are equipped with AR markers. This allows recognising the finger gestures of the user and using them for manipulating virtual objects.

The mobile device itself can also be used for interacting with virtual objects due to the configuration of the diverse sensors. [Henr05] describes a system in which virtual objects can be manipulated depending on the orientation of the device. By changing the position and orientation of the mobile device the user gets the opportunity to move and rotate virtual objects.

3   Application Concept

For every concert season the Konzerthaus Berlin publishes an extensive magazine that focuses on highlights of the upcoming season and summarises the former season. This brochure is the most important printed publication of the concert hall and has a far reach. Besides being handed out to visitors to concerts and other events at the concert hall, the seasonal magazine can be obtained free-of-charge at the location by passers-by. The cooperation with the Konzerthaus Berlin provided us with the opportunity to develop an AR application to enhance the contents of their seasonal magazine. However, as the reader base of the magazine is closely correlated with the visitors of the concert hall and the majority around the age of 50 to 70, the expected user base for our AR application will mostly be located in this age range as well. In addition, this application also offers the opportunity to inspire a younger audience for the Konzerhaus Berlin through the use of modern technologies and presentation forms.

This knowledge influenced the general concept of the AR application and led to a cautious approach. First of all, the AR application should only extend existing content of the brochure not replace it, so that users who does not want to use the AR application are not left with the feeling that they are missing out on essential material to understand the content of the brochure. Earlier experiments by the concert hall with modern technologies, e.g. when they published the accompanying information flyer for a concert only online and did not hand out printed versions, were met with distrust and were overall conceived negatively by the older concert guests.

Furthermore, the AR applications handling needed to be as intuitive as possible to enable less technically literate users to use the application. As a result, we discarded the use of any multi-touch gestures or hardware sensors like the accelerometer or the gyroscope. While widely used across mobile applications, we did not want to assume any of them as known nor did we want to congest the user interface by adding a lot of explanatory texts. Ideally any augmentation should only need to be viewed through the mobile devices camera and if interactivity is desired, can be touched using a simple tap.

For the content and the possibilities for interactivity this meant slight limitations, but we were able to use images, drawings, audio, video, simple 2D and 3D animations, and 3D models. For example, the Konzerthaus Berlin had a recent project titled "#klangberlin" (translated: "the sound of berlin"), where they used their orchestra to replicate the sound of typical everyday situations of the city of Berlin, such as the arrival of a train of the S-Bahn or the frying of a Currywurst. The videos where extensively edited and published through the concert hall's Youtube channel[8]. The project is included in the seasonal brochure and the AR application adds the actual videos to the experience (see Figure 1).

Fig. 1: The three augmented video players are placed on the page. In the upper part of the page the currently active video is displayed. The printed page displays a frame of each of the three videos (train station clock simulation is active).

Finally, we decided to use a markerless AR approach as this enables us to use the non-augmented content of the printed magazine to position our augmented content. The printed content is not obscured with typical QR-code-like markers. Every page that can be augmented has a small, subtle icon added, that informs the user of the additional AR content, but otherwise the marker pages are not distinguishable from regular pages.

4   Application Development

The development process involved close collaboration with the existing team of musicians, musicologists, illustrators and designers of the Konzerthaus

8   https://www.youtube.com/watch?v=Dd5BF48LMS0

Berlin to convey the same look and feel through the augmented contents as with the physical magazine and therefore strengthen their conjunction. Originally the development of native applications for Android and iOS devices was planned. Due to a small team of developers and the resulting research to reduce the development effort, it was decided to develop the application using Unity[9]. Unity is a cross-platform game development engine and is used to develop video games for PC, consoles and mobile devices. Using Unity offers the advantage that only one application has to be developed, which can be deployed for different operating systems with only a small increase in overhead. Therefore, the developers were able to focus on one implementation using Unity and did not have to work out multiple separate implementations, e.g. for Android and iOS.

For the augmentation the Vuforia[10] library was be used. The Vuforia platform supports a variety of AR features such as marker-based and markerless tracking and object recognition. It also supports extended tracking, which allows for the visualisation of large objects, models and media even if the corresponding marker is no longer in the field of view of the camera and provides the possibility to view AR contents beyond large areas.

The extended tracking option was further experimented with to evaluate whether this function results in an added value for the end user. However, since only single-sided markers are used in the application and the augmented area extends only slightly beyond the marker page, this technology was discarded as not suitable for the application. Besides the missing benefit of using extended tracking, the algorithm also led to unwanted behaviours in tests, e.g. leaving the augmented content intact after users changed pages which could lead to unwanted the overlapping of independent augmentations from different pages.

Vuforia allows implementing AR applications using either cloud- or device-based marker recognition. The main benefit of cloud-based marker recognition is the related Vuforia Web Service (VWS) API, which allows developers to dynamically change markers for published applications without the need to update the application itself. However, for the cloud-based recognition to work, a permanent internet connection is needed and the recognition time is highly dependent on the speed of the internet connection. For device-based recognition all markers are present in the application and updates to the

---

9   https://unity3d.com
10   https://www.vuforia.com

marker database are only possible through an update of the application. For regularly changing content this may be unfavourable, but the content of the seasonal magazine is fixed and we therefore decided to use device-based recognition for this project. However, looking forward to the addition of an AR indoor guide for the concert hall (see "Future work" below) this decision may have to be re-evaluated.

As the AR application is a debut for the concert hall and they are unsure whether their customers will actually use it, we added a rudimentary, anonymous logging system, which collects usage statistics. Besides general information like the number of application downloads and the number of uses for the different markers, we put special emphasis on the interactive augmentations and are logging if users are experimenting with the interactivity. The logging is used to record how often the application is used, which media are used, how long they are used for, which videos are played for how long, which interactive elements are selected, and whether the application is terminated.

5   Media, Interaction and Interactive Elements

In order to access the AR content, the reader must interact with their smartphone and the magazine. The user has to view the printed page through their phone's camera. For support, a simple graphic user interface is displayed on the smartphone, highlighting the selection of the area graphically. In addition, the user is advised to centre the complete page in the marked area (see Figure 2). If the marker (the corresponding side of the magazine) is detected, the additional elements of the AR application appear as an overlay of the size of the magazine on the display of the mobile device.

Fig. 2: Pass-through camera UI to scan the pages of the magazine

Dynamic media such as audio and video are visualised by a graphical representation of the content with a superimposed play button. A gallery metaphor was chosen for the presentation. Three thumbnails of the corresponding videos overlay the printed content. The user must actively confirm the play by clicking on the play button of the corresponding video. Here the conscious interaction concept of video portals or websites with video was emulated. The user is aware that the media can be started separately by pressing the play button. With acoustic contents of the magazine the procedure is equivalent. 3D models support different themes of the magazine. To display the additional virtual content, the page in the app must be scanned again. Since it is not an interactive element, the 3D model is displayed directly on the display and is visualised perspective-correctly and geometrically upright on the page (see Figure 3).

Overall the application visualises three 3D models on different pages of the magazine: the downscaled model of the concert hall itself, a stylised model of the organ in the large hall and the fish Melos. The latter is the mascot of the concert hall and can be found at around 200 different places inside the building. As one of the criteria for AR is embedding in the real world, a touch-screen-based interaction to the complete or detailed view of the models has been dispensed with. When viewing the models on the screen of the mobile device, it soon becomes clear that the perspective of the virtual representation also changes depending on the distance and the position of the mobile device to the magazine. The user will easily recognise that they can change the position of the virtual content by changing their position.

Fig. 3: Augmented 3D model from different perspectives

Another part of the magazine is devoted to the subject of seasonal highlights and is supported by photographs. Due to the limited space of exactly one page and the layout of this page, not all images that the editorial team wished for can be displayed. In order to fulfil the desire to display more photos, a stack of photos was integrated as an interactive medium into the AR application. After recognition and identification of the corresponding page through the application, 12 pictures are superimposed onto the page. These are stacked above each other. If the user wants to see the individual pictures, they must press the displayed play button as known from the video and audio player. The pictures then spread over the page of the magazine in an animated way. The arrangement of the images takes place in such way that no virtual picture superimposes an image of the printed page. The user can increase the size of any of the augmented images by clicking on them (see Figure 4).

Fig. 4: Stack of photos (left) and the photos distributed on the magazine (right)

As the final interactive element, a Baltic map is displayed within the application. This map corresponds to a respective article in the magazine. On one page of the printed magazine this year's partnership of the Konzerthaus Berlin with different musicians from the Baltic States, which include Estonia, Latvia and Lithuania are be presented. The interactive virtual map expands the information offer and also presents the venues for the partnership. For this purpose, the printed map is superimposed with a virtual map on the screen of the mobile device. The different venues of the partnership are displayed on the virtual map as additional information. The venues are represented by a graphical representation of the participating houses and cultural institutions on the ground. These appear animated and graphically represented in a cardboard cut-out-like look. The graphical representation of the printed map is rotated up. The representation as cardboard holder was chosen to change from the two-dimensional representation of the printed card in the magazine to a three-dimensional representation (see Figure 5). In order to not overload the display on the mobile device with too much information, the user can select the different elements by clicking one of the elements on the display. For the selected items, information about the respective playground appears on the display.

Fig. 5: Augmented map with its interactive elements as cardboard holder

6   Test

A first internal test was conducted on different Android and iOS based devices. For this test multiple mobile devices with varying screen resolutions were used (Samsung Galaxy Note 4, Samsung Galaxy S4, Huawei Nexus 6P, iPhone 6, iPhone 6s and iPad Air 2). All selected markers of the magazine were recognised quickly and reliably. Additionally, with the selected devices, no problems were observed regarding the differences in hardware such as camera, processor and memory or with different operating systems and respective versions. The markers were selected jointly with the concert hall being the driving force, so that they match in content but also meet the criteria for markerless AR. When using markerless AR, care should be taken to ensure that the content which acts as a marker consists of images, which have a lot of corners and edges, high contrast and do not only consist of small-scale type.

A second test, which includes a wider range of devices, is scheduled for the end of March. For this test the concert hall staff will also included.

A final test with the printed magazine is still pending. The markers used for the development correspond to the layout and design of the final magazine. However, at the time of development, the magazine's printing was not completed and so the pages that were used for the application had to be printed out on single pages. In order to check whether the glossy paper of the brochure leads to problems, a magazine from last year was used as test material. The results of this test confirmed that the glossy paper does not appear to influence the detection accuracy.

7 Future Work

Following the publication of the first version of our AR application, we will continue the development by extending the application to further use cases. One of the long time goals is to establish a content management system (CMS) for new AR content that the Konzerthaus Berlin can use to manage the AR application and add new content and alter existing. One of the first new applications to be implemented is an indoor guide that will be used to explain the history of the building and inform about current events. The inside of the concert hall offers vast possibilities for exciting new concepts for AR.

Finally, we will be using the logged data of the current version of the application to evaluate the overall success of the application. The logged data will tell us how many readers of the magazine will download and use the app and if they use it only once or multiple times. Furthermore, we will use this data to determine the intuitiveness of the interactive components of the application and will use the result to decide if more complex interactive approaches can be introduced in the next seasonal magazine.

8 Conclusion

The goal of the development of an interactive AR application for print media could be achieved. With the help of Unity and Vuforia, it was possible for the relatively small developer team to develop a cross-platform AR application in a short time. The application could easily be built for the operating systems iOS and Android. Additional adjustments to the code were not necessary.

The algorithms implemented in Vuforia for detecting the pages of the magazine work reliably, stably and with a high detection speed. All media, defined during the concept stage, could be implemented with the desired high demands on design and aesthetic.

Unfortunately, no statement can yet be made regarding the use of the application. To be able to draw conclusions about the use of smartphone-based AR applications via the obtained data, the developer team hopes for a large number of users.

The "living concert hall magazine" application will be launched together with the new printed season magazine of the Konzerthaus Berlin to the general public as well as to the press, radio and TV stations on 4th May 2017 with a public event in the Konzerthaus Berlin.

9 Acknowledgements

This paper describes the work undertaken in the context of the project APOLLO hosted by the research group Information and Communication Systems INKA and the Konzerthaus Berlin that is generously funded by the European Regional Development Fund (ERDF).

Literature

[Azum01] Azuma, R., Baillot, Y., Behringer, R., Feiner, S., Julier, S., & MacIntyre, B. (2001). Recent advances in augmented reality. Computer Graphics and Applications, IEEE, 21(6), pp. 34–47. http://doi.org/10.1109/38.963459

[Azum97] Azuma, R. T. (1997). A Survey of Augmented Reality. Presence Teleoperators and Virtual Environments, 6(4), pp. 355–385. http://doi.org/10.1162/pres.1997.6.4.355

[Bara09] Barandiaran, I., Paloc, C., & Graña, M. (2009). Real-time optical markerless tracking for augmented reality applications. Journal of Real-Time Image Processing, 5(2), pp. 129–138. http://doi.org/10.1007/s11554-009-0140-2 [Krev10]   van Krevelen, D., & Poelman, R. (2010). A Survey of Augmented Reality Technologies, Applications and Limitations. The International Journal of Virtual Reality, 9(2).

[Hagb09] Hagbi, N., Bergig, O., El-Sana, J., & Billinghurst, M. (2009). Shape recognition and pose estimation for mobile augmented reality. Proceedings of the 2009 8th IEEE International Symposium on Mixed and Augmented Reality.

[Henr05] Henrysson, A., Billinghurst, M., & Ollila, M. (2005). Virtual object manipulation using a mobile phone. Proceedings of the International Conference on Augmented Tele-Existence, pp. 164–171. http://doi.org/10.1145/1152399.1152430

[Hürs13] Hürst, W., & Van Wezel, C. (2013). Gesture-based interaction via finger tracking for mobile augmented reality. Multimedia Tools and Applications, 62(1), pp. 233–258. http://doi.org/10.1007/s11042-011-0983-y

[Kao13] Kao, T. W., & Shih, H. C. (2013). A study on the markerless augmented reality for picture books. IEEE International Symposium on Consumer Electronics (ISCE), pp. 197–198. http://doi.org/10.1109/ISCE.2013.6570182

[Kova16] Kovalenko, M., Antoshchuk, S., & Sieck, J. (2016). Visual hand tracking and gesture recognition for human-computer interaction. Proceedings of International Conference on Culture & Computer Science ICCCS'16

[Li15] Li, J., Slembrouck, M., & Deboeverie, F. (2015). A hybrid pose tracking approach for handheld augmented reality. Proceedings of the 9th International Conference on Distributed Smart Camera – ICDSC '15. http://doi.org/10.1145/2789116.2789128

[Pang06] Pang, Y., Yuan, M. L., Nee, A. Y. C., Ong, S.-K., & Youcef-Toumi, K. (2006). A markerless registration method for augmented reality based on affine properties. Proceedings of the 7th Australasian User Interface Conference, 50. http://doi.org/10.1145/1151758.1151760

[Pere11] Perey, C. (2011). Print and publishing and the future of Augmented Reality. Inf. Services and Use, 31(1-2), pp. 31–38. http://doi.org/10.3233/ISU-2011-0625

[Tani15] Tanikawa, T., Uzuka, H., Narumi, T., & Hirose, M. (2015). Integrated view-input AR interaction for virtual object manipulation using tablets and smartphones. Proceedings of the 12th International Conference on Advances in Computer Entertainment Technology – ACE '15. http://doi.org/10.1145/2832932.2832956

[Tera09] Terajima, K., Komuro, T., & Ishikawa, M. (2009). Fast finger tracking system for in-air typing interface. (pp. 3739–3744). Presented at the CHI '09 Extended Abstracts on Human Factors in Computing Systems, New York, New York, USA: ACM. http://doi.org/10.1145/1520340.1520564

[Yang12]   Yang, X., & Cheng, K.-T. T. (2012). Accelerating SURF detector on mobile devices. ACM International Conference on Multimedia, 569–578. http://doi.org/10.1145/2393347.2393427

[Youn16]   Young, T. C., & Smith, S. (2016). An Interactive Augmented Reality Furniture Customization System. International Conference on Virtual, Augmented and Mixed Reality, pp. 662–668. http://doi.org/10.1007/978-3-319-39907-2_63

Archiving Ephemeral Knowledge –
Hong Kong Martial Arts As a Strategy for the
Documentation of Intangible Cultural Heritage
為權時知識存檔 –
香港武術作為記錄非物質文化遺產的策略

Harald Kraemer
Jeffrey Shaw
School of Creative Media
City University of Hong Kong
H.Kraemer@cityu.edu.hk, j.shaw@cityu.edu.hk

CHAO Sih Hing 趙式慶
International Guoshu Association, Hong Kong
hing@orochenfoundation.org

Sarah Kenderdine
National Institute for Experimental Arts
UNSW Australia
s.kenderdine@unsw.edu.au

Keywords

Martial Arts, Motion Capture, Documentation Standard, Intangible Cultural Heritage, Long Term Preservation

Abstract

Different martial art styles and schools have influenced Chinese culture, philosophy, folklore but also medicine and sports. Especially Hong Kong has a long tradition in martial arts with its diverse and rich kung fu styles. With the traditional methods of documentation by photos, drawings or video, the different models of body mechanics are insufficiently recorded.

Therefore the School of Creative Media of City University has started in 2013 a collaboration with the International Guoshu Association Hong Kong to install the Hong Kong Martial Arts Living Archive. Using high-definition and high-speed 3D video capture of sequences, the activity of annotation itself will be transformed to include such physical data for: speed, torque, torsion and force (momentum and acceleration). 4D analysis of kung fu necessarily includes time. Meanwhile, in the fall 2015, twenty Kung Fu styles and over 120 weapon sets in form of 3D motion data (MOCAP) but also stereoscopic video with panoptics from six points of view, panoramic video, stills photography, HD high-speed video sequences, spatial audio files as well as video interviews with contemporary witnesses have been recorded.

In 2014 the Documentation Committee (CIDOC) of ICOM had established the CIDOC Intangible Cultural Heritage Working Group because the existing data field catalogues used in museums and archives lag often behind the demands made by intangible heritage. At the moment there is no existing model or data field catalogue based on museum documentation standards for the archiving of martial arts.

In our talk we will report about our recent research project funded by General Research Fund of the Research Grants Council of Hong Kong (GRF Project No. 11671416) and show the way how martial arts related forms of intangible cultural heritage like performance art and performing arts like dance get documented by MOCAP technology and how their digital data can be used for data visualisation as well as get prepared for long-term preservation.

1   Background

Continued political instability in China from the late 19th to mid 20th century triggered several migration waves to Hong Kong, which engendered the development of Hong Kong's unique culture, including martial arts. Cantonese martial arts had the greatest influence on the development of Chinese martial arts and sports [Chao09; Chao16; MaMD09]. Some of the most important styles of Southern Chinese martial arts are best preserved in Hong Kong, including Hung Kuen and Wing Chun, as the most important masters of these styles moved to Hong Kong. However, Northern Chinese martial arts mixed with local/Southern styles of martial arts to develop unique traditions which are found nowhere else [Wile95; Fran06]. For Hong Kong authors like Hing Chao, Duncan Jepson or Bono Lee have analysed the influence of Martial Arts on the regional, national but also international culture [Chao15; Chao 16; Zhao11a; Chao09; Lee09; Fran06]. In the 1960ies and 1970ies with the leading figure of Bruce Lee, Kung Fu made in Hong Kong became a main export commodity and had a strong influence in Martial Arts movies as well as American/Western culture. [Lee09; Zhao11b]. Facing this success of popularity we should not forget that like other forms of mostly orally transmitted ephemeral knowledge the diversity and the origin of Martial Arts is in danger of becoming lost [Chau12; Lee09].

Significantly, different martial art styles/schools make use of different models of body mechanics which until now are mostly orally transmitted, often in a language crouched in esoteric terms [Chao15; Kenn05]. With dwindling number of practitioners in some styles, this knowledge is now in danger of becoming lost. Therefore the School of Creative Media of City University has started in 2013 a collaboration with the International Guoshu Association Hong Kong to install the Hong Kong Martial Arts Living Archive [Kend13; Chao16]. The project encompasses the first-ever comprehensive digital strategy of archiving and annotating a living Kung Fu tradition using state-of-the art data capture tools. Using high-definition and high-speed 3D video capture of sequences, the activity of annotation itself will be transformed to include such physical data for: speed, torque, torsion and force (momentum and acceleration). 4D analysis of kung fu necessarily includes time. Meanwhile, in the fall 2015, twenty Kung Fu styles and over 120 weapon sets in form of 3D motion data (MOCAP) but also stereoscopic video with panoptics from six points of view, panoramic video, stills photography, HD high-speed video sequences, spatial audio files as well as video interviews with contemporary witnesses have been recorded. With this fundament of collected data and material the Martial Arts Living Archive has reached a point where the structure of the archive as well as the data fields should be discussed and defined. But during the recording of the data it has been shown that the documentation of Martial Arts is much more complicated than assumed. The finding of a structure of the archive based on museum documentation has encountered difficulties.

The transient process of Martial Arts is comparable with process-related works of art like performance art, kinetic art as well as other forms of intangible heritage of performing arts like dance or folklore. Due to the complexity of their occurrence, works of intangible cultural heritage like Martial Arts or Performing Arts as well as works of Contemporary Art call for documentation in an extended sense if they are to be the object of academic questioning and historicizing by those who were not present at their production, presentation or performance [Sere13; Tan09; Krae16]. Using the traditional means of documentation, it is not usually possible to register such decisively eventual and site-specific works in an adequate way [Rine04; Krae09]. In the fields of Performance Art and Performing Arts several projects for the archiving and documentation have been realised so that it seems obvious what documentation means here [Schr09].

2 Oral History

The primary orientation of existing text and image databases is descriptive, placing emphasis on iconographic indexing. In the case of Martial Arts, this form of linguistic description often reaches its limits. So there is a necessity of consulting a Martial Artist on matters concerning the origin, the technique, as well as the philosophy of his style. For Contemporary Art E. Gantzert-Castrillo has demonstrated this in an exemplary way by creating an archive of interviews with artists concerning the needs of conserving their works of art [Gant96]. His documentary form of oral history was continued in the renown International Network for the Conservation of Contemporary Art (INCCA) [Weye99].

3 Learning from Performing Arts and Performance Art

Performing Arts are art forms in which artists use their voices and/or the movements of their bodies to perform in front of a live audience, mainly distinguished itself from purely visual arts. They are primarily skills-based and happen in set places, such as dance, opera, circus in concert halls, opera houses or theatre spaces. In his dissertation "The use of martialacrobatic arts in the training and performance of Peking Opera" Hai-Hsing Yao gave an insight how motion sequences and exercices of Martial Arts have influenced the dance sequences in the classic Peking Opera gear together [Yao90].

By contrast to the Performing Arts, Performance Art is primarily concept-based, it's a term usually reserved to refer to conceptual arts which convey artistic thoughts and often challenge the audience to think in new and unconventional ways. Performance art like several of the works of Kinetic Art emphases on the interactivity with viewers, it can be any situation that involves four basic elements: time, space, the performer's body, or presence in a medium, and a relationship between performer and audience [Jone12; Dreh01; Krae09].

- From 1994 to 1999 choreographer William Forsythe and Ballett Frankfurt have produced in cooperation with ZKM Center for Art and Media the CD-ROM Improvisation Technologies. A Tool for the Analytical Dance Eye. By linking the explanations of W. Forsythe (theory) and performing them (practice) this excellent interactive learning tool offers a rich and complex insider perspective on the methodologies of creative process.[1]

- In 2000 Nomura Mansaku, the grand master of kyogen and best-known performer in his field, produced in cooperation with ZKM the DVD-ROM "That's Kyogen" to document this traditional Japanese theatre. The DVD-ROM enables users to select various chapters on theory and practice conveying in direct and vivid form the entire range of kyogen theatre, and to call up videotapes with abridged versions of pivotal kyogen plays.[2]

- With his project "Capturing the Art of Motion" Tim Glenn has addressed the urgent need in the dance field for documenting and preserving cultural expression as displayed in the form of concert dance. This site includes a look at dance-specific considerations for documentation projects and the development of new documentation models using video as a medium.[3]

---

1   http://on1.zkm.de/zkm/werke/ImprovisationTechnologiesAToolfortheAnalyticalDanceEye
2   http://on1.zkm.de/zkm/projekte/kyogen
3   http://dancedocumentation.com/Home.html

- Like in the history of teaching Martial Arts there is a long tradition in systems of notations. The New York based Dance Notation Bureau's mission is to advance the art of dance through the use of a system of notation. DNB does this by creating dance scores using the symbol system called Labanotation. This allows the dances to continue to be performed long after the lifetime of the artist. Dance scores function for dance the same way music scores function for music.[4]

- In 2009 Alison Kotin from the Dynamic Media Institute at Massachusetts College of Art and Design has examined in her investigation Documentation of Live Performance and Variable Media Artworks the impact of documentation on performance artists' approach to creating new work, and she analysed the role that digital documentation is playing in shaping our experience of live performance.[5]

- Stephen Gray, Project Manager of Curating Artistic Research Output (CAiRO) of the University of Bristol has shown on the performance work "Becoming Snail" of Paul Hurley in 2009 how a detailed record with more than 50 individual digital documents can become a standard for the documentation of transitory art.[6]

- The following projects show in spectacular ways the visualisation of data in the Performing Arts. In some of them the dancers appear as animated 3D sculptures, in other ones the dancer disappears completely in a rhythm of colours. One challenge for the documentation of Martial Arts will be to define a high quality form of visualisation of the recorded data sets.

- "Digital Studio's" (2010) made by Angelos Chronis investigates the interaction of a body with a screen through the manipulation of a "pixels" field and the generation of sound. A "pixels dance" is thus generated, translating the gestures of the performer to an evolving visual and music performance.[7]

---

4   http://dancenotation.org
5   http://www.dynamicmediainstitute.org/projects/documentation-live-performance-andvariable- media-artworks
6   http://www.vads.ac.uk/kultur2group/casestudies/Bristol2011.pdf
7   https://vimeo.com/9473801

- "Dance Dance Ribbon" (2012) by Joshua Noble and David Gauthier explain how to use software as a tool of expression and how to visualize dance by tracking the body of the dancer and tracing their movements with trails of ribbons using Microsoft's Kinect and Processing.[8]

- "Presence" (2013) by Universal Everything consists of a series of large-scale video pieces of motion-captured dance performances that create abstract forms with a human presence. This project collaborates with choreographer Benjamin Millepied and the LA Dance Project, enquiring into the essence of choreography, movement and the human form.[9]

- "As·phyx·i·a" (2015) is a collaborative effort and experimental film created by Maria Takeuchi with Frederico Phillips and performed by Shiho Tanaka in 2015 to explore new ways to use and/or combine technologies.[10]

- "Tai Chi" (2013) is exploring into the limits of abstract representation and the fundamentals of the human form. The five different digital costumes explore a variety of textures and techniques, drawing from architectural influences, randomized drawing, laser beams, glass sculpture and ceramics.[11]

- In "NUVE" (2010) Joao Martinho Moura aims to explore the artistic possibilities offered by the digital dance performances in the interaction between the individual and his virtual double.[12]

- "Hong Kong Performance Art Research Project" (2005) was carried out by Asia Art Archive in 2005. It consisted of latitudinal and longitudinal studies of the development of performance art in Hong Kong and included extensive documentation as well as a chronology of Hong Kong performance art since the mid-1970s.[13]

---

8   https://vimeo.com/37743091
9   http://www.universaleverything.com/projects/presence/
10 http://www.asphyxia-project.com
11 http://www.universaleverything.com/projects/tai-chi/
12 http://jmartinho.net/nuve/
13 http://www.aaa.org.hk/Programme/Details/224

4 Data field catalogues and the demands of intangible cultural heritage

For the recorded data especially the 3D and 4D material and their integration into the complexity of Martial Arts as intangible cultural heritage the traditional data field catalogues are not extensive enough. Existing data field catalogues used in museums and archives – structured for the traditional documentation of individual traditional works of art – lag often behind the demands made by intangible cultural heritage [Krae14b; Mata11; Tan09]. Therefore CIDOC – the worldwide renown leading organization for documentation in museums and archives – has decided to establish the CIDOC Intangible Cultural Heritage Working Group at their annual conference in 2014. Because there is no existing model like Museumdat or the Conceptual Reference Model of International Documentation Committee (CIDOC CRM) [Crof09] or data field catalogue based on museum documentation standards like Lightweight Information Describing Objects (LIDO), Spectrum of the British Collections Trust (Spectrum XML scheme) or Categories for the Description of Works of Art (CDWA Lite) for intangible heritage and ephemeral cultural heritage the registrars, archivists and experts in museum documentation of CIDOC have started to create a vocabulary and define standards and guidelines.

By analyzing existing Museum documentation standards like CIDOC Information Categories, SPECTRUM, CDWA Lite, CIDOC CRM, Museumdat, LIDO, and the Dublin Core Metadata set as well as discussing data models used for the documentation of Performance Art, Dance and Kinetic Art, the needs of the Martial Arts Archive will get defined [Krae01; Mart08]. In this research project leading experts in the field of the documentation of performance art, kinetic art, performing arts and martial arts will share their experiences and their knowledge to define criteria for the archiving of ephemeral knowledge by using technologies like MOCAP. By defining the Martial Arts Living Archive the results of this research will have an impact on the ICOM/CIDOC guidelines on documentation of intangible heritage as well as for the long-term preservation of digital museum data [Dekk10]. Therefore this project will support the work of ICOM/CIDOC and their working groups in several ways: the CIDOC Documentation Standards Working Group and the CIDOC Intangible Cultural Heritage Working Group by creating a vocabulary and defining standards and guidelines for the documentation of Martial Arts as well as the

CIDOC Digital Preservation Working Group by discussing aspects of long-term preservation of digital data esp. MOCAP. By using CIDOC as a multiplicator of international reputation the process and the results of this project will have the best chance to become a case scenario for the documentation of intangible heritage worldwide.

Literature

[Alls15]   Allsop, Amelia and Clement Cheung (2015): "Preserving Corporate Memory in Hong Kong", in: Preserving Local Documentary Heritage, ed. by Patrick Lo, Hong Kong: City University Press, 2015, pp. 99–120.

[Buck10]   Buck, Rebecca A. and Jean Allman Gilmore (Eds.) (2010): MRM5: Museum Registration Methods, Washington, DC: AAM Press, American Association of Museums, 5th ed.

[Chao09]   Chao, Hing and Duncan Jepson (2009): "Chinese Martial Spirit: 1900-1950s", in: Spirit of a Nation. Development of Chinese Martial Arts 1900 to Present, Hong Kong: International Guoshu Association, pp. 16–31.

[Chao13]   Chao, Hing (2013): "Hung Kuen in Late Imperial South China", in: Chun Fai Lam and Hing Chao: Hung Kuen Fundamentals: GUNG GEE FOK FU KUEN, Hong Kong: International Guoshu Association, pp. 13–24.

[Chao15]   Chao, Hing (2015): "Keeping Traditional Martial Arts Alive", in: Preserving Local Documentary Heritage, ed. by Patrick Lo, Hong Kong: City University Press, pp. 277–292.

[Chao16]   Chao, Hing; Sarah Kenderdine; Jeffrey Shaw (2016): 300 Years of Hakka Kung Fu. Digital Vision of its Legacy and Future, Hong Kong Heritage Museum (2.–30.9.2016), City University of Hong Kong., AC3 Gallery (27.10.2016–28.2.2017), Hong Kong: International Guoshu Association.

[Chau12]   Chau, Hing Wah (2012): "Community Engagement: Key to the Safeguarding of Intangible Cultural Heritage", in: NODEM Conference 2012 Hong Kong. https://www.youtube.com/watch?v=Gv1bnPWTUJM

[Chen03]   Chen, Ya-Ping (2003): Dance History and Cultural Politics: A Study of Contemporary Dance in Taiwan, 1930s–1997, Dissertation, New York University, Department of Performance Studies, January 2003, Microfiche.

[Crofts09]   Crofts, Nick; Martin Doerr; Tony Gill et. al. (2009): "Definition of
             the CIDOC Conceptual Reference Model". http://cidoc.ics.forth.
             gr/official_release_cidoc.html

[Croi11]   Croitoru, Michael (2011): The Movement Factory: The Bridge
             between Dance, Martial Arts and Athletics, Master Thesis, Arizona
             State University, December 2011, Microfiche.

[Dekk10]   Dekker, Annet (Ed.) (2010): Archive2020: Sustainable Archiving
             of Born-Digital Cultural Content, Rotterdam: Virtueel Platform.

[Dreh01]   Dreher, Thomas (2001): Performance Art nach 1945. Aktions-
             theater und Intermedia. Munich: Wilhelm Fink.

[Fran06]   Frank, Adam D. (2006): Taijiquan and the Search for the Little
             Old Chinese Man: Understanding Identity through Martial Arts,
             Basingstoke: Palgrave-Macmillan, 2006.

[Gant96]   Gantzert-Castrillo, Erich (1996): Archiv für Techniken und Arbeits-
             materialien zeitgenössischer Künstler, Stuttgart: Enke.

[Gree10]   Green, Thomas A. and Joseph R. Svinth (Eds.) (2010): Martial Arts
             of the World. An Encyclopedia of History and Innovation, 2 Vols.,
             Santa Barbara CA: ABC-CLIO.

[Henn13]   Henning, Stanley E. (2013): "Chinese Martial Art", in: Demy-
             stifying China: New Understanding of Chinese History, ed. by
             Naomi Standen, Washington DC: Rowman & Littlefield, pp.
             89–98.

[Jone12]   Jones, Amelia and Adrian Heathfield (Eds.) (2012): Perform,
             Repeat, Record. Live Art in History, Bristol: Intellect.

[Kenn05]   Kennedy, Brian and Elizabeth Guo (2005): Chinese Martial
             Arts Training Manuals: A Historical Survey, Berkeley CA: North
             Atlantic Books.

[Kend13]   Kenderdine, Sarah and Hing CHAO (2013): "Hong Kong Martial
             Arts Living Archive: A comprehensive digital archival strategy
             for intangible heritage", in: MWA2013: Museums and the Web
             ASIA 2013, http://mwa2013.museumsandtheweb.com/proposals/
             martial_arts/

[Krae16]   Kraemer, Harald (2016): „Sammeln ohne Zugriff: Sammeln ohne
             Sinn! Über den zunehmenden Verlust hypermedialer Wissens-
             räume im Zeitalter ihrer elektronischen Speicherbarkeit", in:
             Sarah Schmidt (Ed.), Sprachen des Sammelns. Literatur als
             Medium und Reflexionsform des Sammelns, Paderborn: Wilhelm
             Fink, pp. 295–311.

[Krae14a]   Kraemer, Harald and Norbert Kanter (2014a): "Use and Re-Use
             of Data. How Collection Management Systems, Transmedia and
             Augmented Reality impact the Future of Museum", in: Virtual
             Systems Multimedia, IEEE Conference Publications, 2015, DOI:
             10.1109/VSMM.2014.7136693, www.ieeexplore.ieee.org

[Krae14b]   Kraemer, Harald (2014b), "What is less or more than a touch? Multimedia Classics – Hypermedia Hermeneutics", in: Curator. The Museum Journal, January 2014, Vol. 57, No. 1, pp. 119–136. www.curatorjournal.org/less-touch-multimedia-classics-hypermedia-hermeneutics/

[Krae11]   Kraemer, Harald (2011), "Interdependence and Consequence. En Route toward a Grammar of Hypermedia Communication Design", in: Oliver Grau, Thomas Veigl (Eds.): Gazing into the 21st Century, Cambridge MA: MIT Press, 2011, pp. 289–312.

[Krae09]   Kraemer, Harald (2009): "A Pale Reflection. The Limitations and Opportunities of Extended Documentation, Referring to the Example of Kinetic Art", in: Sigrid Schade, Anne Thurmann-Jajes (Eds.): Artists Publications, Cologne: Salon, pp. 116–127.

[Krae07]   Kraemer, Harald (2007): "Art is redeemed, mystery is gone: the documentation of contemporary art", in: Sarah Kenderdine, Fiona Cameron (Eds.): Theorising Futures for the Past. Cultural Heritage and Digital Media, Cambridge MA: MIT Press, 2007, pp. 193–222.

[Krae01]   Kraemer, Harald (2001): Museumsinformatik und Digitale Sammlung, Vienna: Wiener Universitätsverlag, 2001.

[Lee09]   Lee, Bono (2009): "Hong Kong Kung Fu Culture", in: Spirit of a Nation. Development of Chinese Martial Arts 1900 to Present, Hong Kong: Intern. Guoshu Association, pp. 92–109.

[MaLZ09]   Ma, Lian-zhen (2009): "The Confucian Tradition of Martial Studies: Ma Fengtu & Tongbei Martial Studies", in: Spirit of a Nation. Development of Chinese Martial Arts 1900 to Present, Hong Kong: International Guoshu Association, pp. 70–81.

[MaMD09]   Ma, Ming-da and Lian-zhen Ma (2009): "China's National Studies (Guoxue) and National Sports (Guoshu)", in: Spirit of a Nation. Development of Chinese Martial Arts 1900 to Present, Hong Kong: International Guoshu Association, pp. 32–55.

[Mart08]   Marty, Paul F. and Katherine Burton Jones (Eds.) (2008): Museum Informatics. People, Information, and Technology in Museums, New York: Routledge.

[Mata11]   Matassa, Freda (2011): Museum collections management. a handbook, London: Facet Publishing.

[Rine04]   Rinehart, Richard (2004): "A system of formal notation for scoring works of digital and variable media art", in: Archiving the avant-garde. Documenting and preserving digital/variable media art: project documents and papers, University of Berkeley. http://www.bampfa.berkeley.edu/about/formalnotation.pdf

[Sche05]   Scheurer Vincent (2005): "Adapting Existing Works for Use in Games", in: Developing Interactive Narrative Content, ed. by Brunhild Bushoff, Munich: High Text Verlag, pp. 296–321.

[Schr09]   Schroeder, Franziska (ED.) (2009): Performing Technology: User Content and the New Digital Media: Insights from the Two Thousand + NINE Symposium, Newcastle upon Tyne: Cambridge Scholars Publishing.

[Sere13]   Serexhe Bernhard (2013): "On System Change in Cultural Memory and the Conservation of Digital Art", in: Digital Art Conservation, ed. By Serexhe Bernhard , Karlsruhe: Center for Art and Media Karlsruhe, pp. 75–84.

[Smit07]   Smith, Laurajane (2007): Cultural Heritage: Critical Concepts in Media and Cultural Studies, London: Routledge.

[Tan09]   Tan, Guoxin, Tinglei Hao and Zheng Zhong (2009): "A Knowledge Modeling Framework for Intangible Cultural Heritage Based on Ontology", in: Knowledge Acquisition and Modeling, KAM'09. 2nd International Symposium on 30.11.2009. http://ieeexplore. ieee.org/xpls/icp.jsp?arnumber=5362170

[Weye99]   Weyer, Cornelia and Gunnar Heydenreich (1999): "From Questionnaires to a Checklist for Dialogues", in: Hummelen, Ijsbrand and Dionne Sillé: Modern Art: Who Cares?, Amsterdam: Foundation for the Conservation of Modern Art/Netherlands Institute for Cultural Heritage, pp. 385–388. www.incca.org

[Wile95]   Wile, Douglas (1995): Tai Chi's Ancestors: The Making of an Internal Martial Art, New York: Sweet Chi Press.

[Yao90]   Yao, Hai-Hsing (1990): The use of martial-acrobatic arts in the training and performance of Peking Opera, Dissertation, Department of Theater Arts, University of Minnesota, January 1990.

[Zhao11a]   Zhao Shiqing (2011): "Blue House Memories: Fighting for Heritage in Hong Kong", in: Journal of Chinese Martial Studies, Issue 5, pp. 76–87.

[Zhao11b]   Zhao Shiqing & Hao Gang (2011): "Bruce Lee & His Legacy in China", in: Journal of Chinese Martial Studies, Issue 4, pp. 34–41.

Mixed Reality Sandbox

Toolkit to Involve Users in MR Application Development

Felix Brennecke
Creative Director
Danziger Str. 41, 10437 Berlin
info@felixbrennecke.com

Pablo Dornhege
Universität der Künste Berlin
Fakultät Gestaltung/Visuelle Kommunikation
Institut für Transmediale Gestaltung
Grunewaldstr. 2-5, 10823 Berlin
pablo@dornhege.com

Abstract

Since Mixed Reality will have a growing impact on our lives and may soon become a major communication interface for leisure, business and culture it is important to find ways to involve a wider public in the development of MR applications so that MR will become a vehicle for cultural discourse rather than just another way to sell merchandize. Due to the complex interactive and technical dimensions of MR applications and the lack of experience with such applications on the side of the client today many service providers (s.a. communication agencies) end up moderating the initial concept to their clients, while the client has a hard time understanding and putting together flowcharts, customer journey maps and storyboards in relation to space and user interaction. Communicating and approving the project development within large organizations becomes a real challenge. From the author's experience this situation is not ideal as the ownership sometimes shifts and content is not adequately presented. The MR Sandbox is a first step to develop a toolkit for non-pros to quickly and remotely sketch their vision of a Mixed Reality user experience within a cultural institution. Combining the HTC Vive, Google`s Tilt Brush software, an imported 3D model and a library of symbols the MR Sandbox project allowed even complete novices to mock up the augmented layers for a space and document this in a short video.

1   Mixed Reality Sandbox

1.1   Is Mixed Reality a game changer?

There is little doubt that Mixed Reality applications offer great potential to communicate, learn, work, play, sell and give access to many wonders of this planet and our human culture. As wearable devices "will become the fastest ramping technology devices", our physical and digital realities are connected further, therefore it is to be presumed that wearables entail the "beginning of an even bigger change in behavior and culture than smartphones". [MoSt14a] It is likely that we will use them to perform many functions currently executed with smart phones or personal computers, once products like the Microsoft Hololens become more affordable and suitable for daily routines. "Of the digital convergence technologies, it is mixed reality (MR) that has fundamentally changed the environment of human experience."[ChYi12a] Merging our digital and physical worlds poses a set of new challenges for development teams as interfaces now respond to human interaction as well as to the physical location they are used in. Interconnected these applications can potentially become very effective, overpowering and even dangerous tools as the provocative vision "Hyper Reality" of the artist Keiichi Matsuda shows. [Mats16a] Unfortunately a higher level of complexity to design, approve and deliver MR applications arises.

Mixed Reality can become a game changer, because if combined with widely distributed wearables, it will change our entire perception and communication.

1.2   What is the reality of Mixed Reality?

With numerous, affordable Virtual Reality consumer products (s.a. Oculus Rift, Samsung Gear VR etc.) introduced to the market and the first wearables being launched, Mixed Reality has caught the attention of communication experts around the globe. Currently there are a lot of solitary applications being developed for commerce and culture. Unfortunately these applications require elaborate and expensive content, media and software productions and involve a variety of experts [Gonz17a]. "These [Mixed Reality Applications] new learning environments are complex from a design and development point of view." [KiTo17a]. Therefore Mixed Reality poses new challenges for the development process between clients and producers.

Each application must integrate technical, didactic, content-related, legal and commercial specifications into a seamless user experience to be accepted by users and the provider. In regard of this complexity it is difficult to define the specifications as a solid basis for development. In the professional experience of the authors, interdisciplinary development teams often spend a lot of time presenting, explaining and understanding certain features and their implications on the underlying technology, usability, content or business model. This predicament is multiplied, as the team has to present preliminary results to third parties needed for expertise. This makes Mixed Reality productions costly, time consuming and often leads to solitary solutions for lack of integrative development. At the same time the complex and technological production often results in a process that is based on decision templates provided by experienced service partners rather than on the specific briefing of the client himself. Therein the dedicated user of the application is following a process rather than actively steering it.

In reality there are no established standards or tools available to manage/ moderate an integrated development process. This means Mixed Reality applications are often planned as stand-alone applications following technical rather than strategic objectives, while taking too much time and burning to large budgets.

1.3   Are Mixed Reality applications viable for cultural institutions?

Mixed Reality Devices offer location based and personalized information and service and enable us to implement new learning strategies and value chains. The potential for convenient and enhanced visitor experiences is vast and should not be ignored e.g. by museums. Since most users will select and operate Mixed Reality applications on their own private, mobile devices (i.e. *wearables*), these applications are destined to become a part of cultural experiences. "Since museum exhibitions are under greater spatiotemporal constraints than any other environment, they urgently need digital technologies that allow the augmentation of visitor's experiences" [ChYi12b] Adding value to a museum visit, Mixed Reality can allow users to handle and explore precious artifacts, add contextual media and offer customization of details, language and service. At the same time Mixed Reality applications running on visitor devices relieve museums of the pressure to purchase, maintain and update expensive hardware and use their resources for the preservation, research and communication of their respective fields.

A good Mixed Reality application is an intuitive and personal gateway for visitors to contents and services offered by its provider. [WiNo17a] Cultural institutions present great but complex contents and operate in value networks to offer their products.

Future Mixed Reality applications will enhance cultural experiences through: Offering location based information, enabling gamified and customized information linked to personal data profiles and support visitors with navigation. Moreover e.g. within a museum context Mixed Reality applications will allow visitors to interact and explore objects that are currently not accessible. They can also offer new services creating additional user benefit and institutional revenue. On our way to successful and user-friendly applications it is vital to integrate interdisciplinary professions and provide a common basis for discussion and decision-making.

For Example: While rather secretive at first sight an antiquarian tube radio, can be a very narrative object. A Mixed Reality Application enables visitors to virtually work the controls to scan for stations, listen to original broadcasts or even dismantle the object and inspect its components. Furthermore a holographic expert can explain the object and its context tailored to the users own experience and interests.

Powerful Mixed Reality applications provide experiences and services that exceed the classic audio and media guides and are able to engage and connect the visitor to the provider as well as affiliated partners. It is therefore vital that the development process for a Mixed Reality application starts with the clients vision, rather than with the assumption of an external supplier well versed in the development of Mixed Reality, but foreign to the institution. The project Mixed Reality Sandbox made an attempt to place the authorship in the hands of the provider.

There will be viable Mixed Reality applications for cultural institutions. The development process of these applications may pose exceptional challenges as complex contents, limited technical expertise and tight budgets of cultural institutions are faced with the developer's need for a detailed briefing they can transcribe into a project backlog.

1.4   How can Mixed Reality projects be developed together with laymen?

As previously shown we are currently missing suitable and user-friendly tools and methods to mock up and test visionary Mixed Reality applications. "An increasing number of systems are exploiting mixed reality but to date there are no systematic methods, techniques or guidelines for the development of such systems." [DuGrNi12a] Combining time based, process driven, location based and ergonomic interfaces designing for Mixed Reality requires a process that unites the classic mock-up methods such as interaction-storyboard, wireframe, flowchart or click-journey. The objective of the project Mixed Reality Sandbox was to provide a simple yet conclusive mock-up scenario allowing professionals and laymen to remotely sketch and test Mixed Reality experience concepts at an early stage.

Ambition of the Mixed Reality Sandbox was to enable every member of a project team to quickly walk through the designated space, mark relevant touch points and label and explain the intended user experience. This walkthrough is recorded from the test person's point of view and, together with the spoken explanation saved as an .mpg file. Additionally a virtual 3D model with all the allocated markers is saved, documenting the position of each touch point and its features. Using a 3D model as the basis of walkthrough and mock the development process can happen remotely for different team members and be applied for buildings that are still under construction.

The key idea is to involve everyone on the team. In a quick walkthrough everyone describes the most important features of their imaginary user experience inside the simulated space. By offering a user-friendly sketch method that can be applied remotely and documented in a video and a 3D model, the Sandbox will enable multilateral decisions and make communication with third parties easier.

1.5   How can we build a sandbox for Mixed Reality?

In order to be able to evaluate our method the project was developed alongside a fictional usecase for a real site. Cooperating with the Museum Neukölln and its staff we assembled and tested a Mixed Reality toolkit for virtual walkthroughs. The Gutshof Britz is a historic monument making local farming history accessible. Offering multiple leisure and cultural programs the Gutshof is home to a restaurant, music school, an open-air stage, a model farm and the museum itself. Cooperative services are in the mutual interest of all residents and Mixed Reality would be a great asset in promoting the history of the site, the synergy between the residents and the appeal of the museum.

The sandbox is based on four components:

1. As the hardware for the sandbox we decided to use the HTC Vive, because the spatial tracking of controller and helmet movement allow for a very intuitive yet immersive experience and workflow. Furthermore the helmet has an integrated microphone and is able to capture the narrative of the test person. [Fig.1]

2. To navigate and work inside the mockup we used Google's Tilt Brush program, as it is very user friendly and can load externally prepared images and 3D models. The program allows for recording the interaction and exporting the modified 3D models.

3. We modeled the Gutshof as well as the museum's interior using Cinema4D and imported the model in Tilt Brush. The model allows museum employees to feature within the imagined user experience of the space. [Fig.2]

4. Starting with a large chart we assembled a list of possible digital service, media and control features needed within a possible application and possible physical components that may be required. [Tab.1] The list in the chart was then translated into a small icon library. All icons were exported and imported to a library in Tilt Brush. [Fig.3]

After a brief introduction into the handling of HTC Vive, Tilt Brush and our icon library we asked the museum staff to move within the space, place labels and verbally describe their visitor journeys across the relevant visitor touch points of the museum (such as e.g. reception desk, shop, and special exhibits). Recording the mock up process itself we documented the journey in a video file and virtual model. [Fig.4] Thereby presenting a solid decision basis to identify the functions and services of a future Mixed Reality application for the Museum Neukölln or if desired use it as a basis to discuss a wider application with site partners.

The project Mixed Reality Sandbox shows how VR can be used as an effective tool to bridge the complex combination of physical spaces and digital contents at an early stage of a Mixed Reality production. The case study indicates the potential Mixed Reality offers for cultural institutions and when non-techies participate in the briefing and discussion about the key features. The project further demonstrates how costly efforts can be reduced within an interdisciplinary development team using a simple but meaningful test setup.

2 Images and Tables

2.1 Images

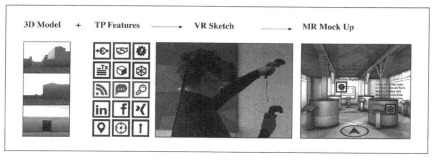

Fig. 1: HTC Vive as a tool to generate a virtual walkthrough

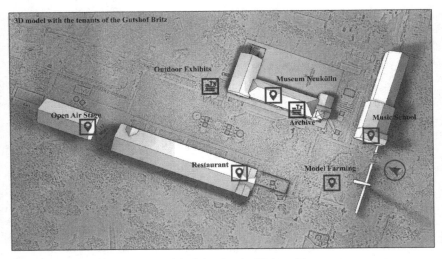

Fig. 2: 3D Model of the Gutshof Britz with tenants

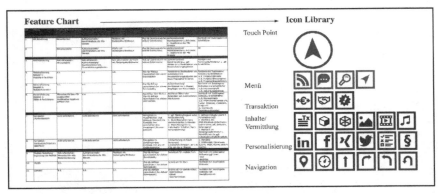

Fig. 3: Feature chart translated to library of icons

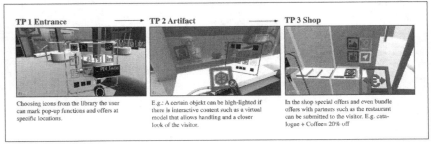

Fig. 4: Screenshots of a mock up application created with the sandbox

2.2 Tables

MR Sandbox   Stand   15.03.17
Toolkit Development   Autor   P.Domhege / F.Brennecke

Touchpoint bezogene MR Dienste und Darstellung de Dienste im Toolkit

NR	Dienst	Physische Komponenten			Virtuelle Komponenten		
Aktivierung							
1	MR Aktivierung	Hinweisschild	Aufmerksamkeit/ Kenntnisnahme der MR-Dienste	Rechteck mit Texteingabe/Bildtextur	Pop-Up (automatisch bei aktiver Schnittstelle)	Aufmerksamkeit/ Kenntnisnahme u. Aktivieren o. Deaktivieren der MR-Dienste	Rechteck mit Texteingabe und Schaltfläche
2		Attraktorobjekt	Aufmerksamkeit/ Kenntnisnahme der MR-Dienste	Würfel mit Texteingabe/Bildtextur	Pop-Up (automatisch bei aktiver Schnittstelle)	Aufmerksamkeit/ Kenntnisnahme u. Aktivieren o. Deaktivieren der MR-Dienste	AR
Personalisierung							
3	Personalisierung	falls erforderlich: Hinweisschild	falls erforderlich: Aufmerksamkeit/ Kenntnisnahme von Personalisierungsoptionen	falls erforderlich: Rechteck mit Texteingabe/Bildtextur	Pop-Up (automatisch bei aktiver Schnittstelle)	Aufmerksamkeit/ Kenntnisnahme o. ggf. Aktivieren o. Deaktivieren von Personalisierungsoptionen	Rechteck mit Texteingabe/Bildtextur u. ggf. Schaltfläche
4	Personalisierung Beispiel 1: Tracking & Analytics	s.o.	s.o.	s.o.	Pop-Up Abfrage (automatisch bei aktiver Schnittstelle)	Aktivieren o. Deaktivieren von automatisierten Personalisierungsoptionen auf Basis freigegebener Daten	Rechteck mit Texteingabe & Schaltfläche: -z.B. Freigabe Kontakte -z.B. Freigabe Shoppingchart -z.B. Freigabe Browserhistory
5	Personalisierung Beispiel 2: Selbstinformation	s.o.	s.o.	s.o.	Pop-Up Abfrage (automatisch bei aktiver Schnittstelle)	Aufmerksamkeit/ Kenntnisnahme u. Nutzen/ Einpflegen von Nutzerdaten	Rechteck mit Texteingabe/Bildtextur und Schaltfläche: -z.B. Interessenprofil -z.B. Zeit-/ Budgetrahmen
6	Personalisierung Beispiel 3: Teilen & Partizipieren	Hinweisschild kann für ausgesuchte Partizipative Angebote sinnvoll sein	s.o.	s.o.	Anwählbar über Menü o. Pop-Up Abfrage (automatisch bei aktiver Schnittstelle)	Aktivieren Teilen oder Einspeisen von Autorendaten des Nutzers	Rechteck mit Texteingabe/Bildtextur & Schaltfläche: -z.B. Kamerainhalte -z.B. Profilinhalte/ Kanäle (FB, Twitter, Pinterest, Instagram, Snapchat) -z.B. individuelle Exportschnittstellen
Navigation							
7	Navigation (Aussenbereich)	nicht erforderlich	nicht erforderlich	nicht erforderlich	Navigation im Aussenbereich folgt gängigem Standard z.B. Kompass Icon ansteuerbar über Hauptmenü (Blossom Gesture)	1. ggf. Trackingfreigabe siehe Personalisierung 2. Bietet Navigation nach standardisierten Funktionen 3. Bietet Navigation zu individuellen Inhalten (bei 3 Personalisierung)	1. Abfrage Freigabe (siehe 3 Personalisierung) 2. Rechteck mit: -POI Standards (Information, Gastronomie, WC, Babycare, Notausgang) 3. Rechteck mit Texteingabe/Bildtextur u. Schaltflächen für ggf. individuelle Inhalte/Angebote
8	Navigation (Innenraum/Anbieterspezifisch)	nicht erforderlich	nicht erforderlich	nicht erforderlich	Navigation im Innenraum über Kompass Icon und AR-Gebäudestruktur	1. Orientierung im Raum (Kompass) 2. Konkrete Direktion (AR z.B. Pfeil auf Tür o. Treppe)	1. Kompass 2. Pfeilsymbole (Geradeaus, Zurück, Hoch, Runter, Links & Rechts)
Medien							
9	Mediale Vertiefung/ Ergänzung der Realität	falls erforderlich: Hinweisschild oder Bodenmarkierung	Aufmerksamkeit/ Kenntnisnahme der MR-Dienste	Rechteck mit Texteingabe/Bildtextur	Pop-Up Abfrage (automatisch bei aktiver Schnittstelle)	Individuell für mediale Form	Rechteck mit Texteingabe/Bildtextur ggf. Icon: -Film -Bild-Text
10	Storify	s.o.	s.o.	s.o.	Pop-Up Abfrage (automatisch bei aktiver Schnittstelle)	Individuell für Story	Rechteck mit Texteingabe/Bildtextur
11	Gamelfy	s.o.	s.o.	s.o.	Pop-Up Abfrage (automatisch bei aktiver Schnittstelle)	Individuell für Gamekonzept: -Schnitzeljagd -Rätsel -Geschicklichkeit	Rechteck mit Texteingabe/Bildtextur ggf. Navigationsicons
12	Nichtkommerzielle Partnerschaft	ggf. sinnvoll	s.o.	s.o.	Pop-Up Abfrage (automatisch bei aktiver Schnittstelle)	Individuell für Partnerschaft	Rechteck mit Texteingabe: Verweis/ Downloadoption
Steuerung/ Menü							
12	Suche	-	-	-	kein eigener Marker da über Menü aufgerufen z.B. Blossom Gesture	Keyword Suche	Icon Lupe
13	Teilen/Kommunizieren	-	-	-	kein eigener Marker da über Menü aufgerufen z.B. Blossom Gesture	Individuell über: -Social-Media-Kanäle -Messaging/TK/Mail -andere	Icon Sprechblase + Icon Kanal
Transaktion/ Kommerziell							
13	Angebote Crosselling/Upselling	falls erforderlich: Hinweisschild oder Bodenmarkierung	Aufmerksamkeit/ Kenntnisnahme der MR-Dienste	Rechteck mit Texteingabe/Bildtextur	Pop-Up Abfrage (automatisch bei aktiver Schnittstelle)	Individuell aus Such-/Kundenhistorie	Rechteck mit Texteingabe/Bildtextur
14	Angebote Bundle intern/extern (Partnership)	s.o.	s.o.	s.o.	Pop-Up Abfrage (automatisch bei aktiver Schnittstelle)	Individuell aus Such-/Kundenhistorie	Rechteck mit Texteingabe/Bildtextur
15	Bonussysteme/ Redemptionsysteme	s.o.	s.o.	s.o.	?	?	?
16	Cashless Payment	s.o.	s.o.	s.o.	Icon ansteuerbar über Hauptmenü (Blossom Gesture)	Individuell	Icon Euro

Tab. 1: Chart of relevant features for an MR application in the museum case

Literature

[ChYi12a]   Choi, Hee-soo affiliated (Sangmyung University) Yi, Dong-Suk (M&C Maru Co., LTD): Mixed Reality in Museum Exhibition Design, in: Publisher: Springer (Hrsg.) Computer Applications for Bio-technology, Multimedia and Ubiquitous City 2012, http://link.springer.com/chapter/10.1007/978-3-642-35521-9_40 visited: 19/3/2017

[ChYi12b]   Choi, Hee-soo affiliated (Sangmyung University) Yi, Dong-Suk (M&C Maru Co., LTD): Mixed Reality in Museum Exhibition Design, in: Publisher: Springer (Hrsg.) Computer Applications for Bio-technology, Multimedia and Ubiquitous City 2012, http://link.springer.com/chapter/10.1007/978-3-642-35521-9_40 visited: 19/3/2017

[DuGrNi12a] Dubois, Emmanuel; Gray Philip; Nigay Laurence: The Engineering of Mixed Reality Systems (Human–Computer Interaction Series) (Hrsg.) Publisher: Springer; Edition: 2010 (14. March 2012)

[Gonz17a]   Gonzalez, Juan G. (User Experience Designer, Product Designer): The UX Workflow for Hololens & Mixed Reality, https://www.linkedin.com/pulse/ux-workflow-hololens-mixedreality-juan-guillot-gonzalez, visited: 12/1/2017

[KiTo17a]   Kirkley, Sonny E. Ph.D.; Tomblin, Steve; Kirkley, Jamie (Information in Place, Inc.): Instructional Design Authoring Support for the Development of Serious Games and Mixed Reality Training, in Interservice/Industry Training, Simulation, and Education Conference (I/ITSEC) 2005, http://citeseerx.ist.psu.edu/viewdoc/download?doi=10.1.1.91.7385&rep=rep1&type=pdf, visited: 18/3/2017

[Mats16a]   Matsuda, Keiichi: Hyper Reality 2016, http://hyper-reality.co/, visited: 19/3/2017

[MoSt14a]   Morgan Stanley: Wearables The "Internet of Things" Becomes Personal. Blue Paper, New York 2014, p.18

[WiNo17a]   Dr. Wienrich, Carolin (TU Berlin) & Noller, Felix (UseTree Berlin): vrguideline.org – Open platform for collaborating on scientific VR research, http://vrguideline.org/ visited: 18/3/2017

Should We Be the Shortcut on the Homescreen?

How to Attract Visitors Digitally for an Authentic (Analogue) Museum Experience

Sebastian Ruff

Stadtmuseum Berlin

Ruff@stadtmuseum.de

Abstract

The Stadtmuseum Berlin collects and presents Berlin history since 1874. The four exhibition venues are located right at the city centre where a lot of museums and historical sites compete for visitors.

This paper is presenting a pilot project using Augmented Reality as a marketing instrument in order to attract visitors of the Nikolaikirche to see the nearby Märkisches Museum as well. The project is presented from the conceptual beginnings in early 2015 up to the first months into operation in early 2017 with special regards to practical issues and visitor reactions.

1   The Stadtmuseum Berlin – locations right at the heart of the city

1.1   The Märkisches Museum – a cornerstone of citizen engagement

In 1929, a revolution took place in Berlin when the director of the *Märkisches Museum* Walter Stengel introduced artificial lighting at the exhibition place. Stengel however had to fight hard in order to get some modernity into a building which was erected in 1908 primarily to put an architectural antithesis to the modern city Berlin had become. The need to collect the artefacts of the history of city and the Berliners was expressed even earlier in the 1860s. The Biedermeier Berlin rapidly shifted into a modern metropolis which attracted a great number of new citizens and led consequently to old buildings and places being torn down. In 1874, the magistrate chose to bring the *Märkisches Provinzial-Museum* to life. The aim of this organization was to collect objects from the past and present of Berlin which otherwise would be lost or forgotten. The cornerstone of this new collections have always been the citizens of Berlin who donated thousands of objects - *high-culture* and *low-culture*. Only 15 years later, the collection had grown to an extent that a dedicated museum building was needed.

In 1896, Stadtbaurat Ludwig Hoffmann was contracted as the leading architect. Hoffmann who was already known for his programmatic and iconic buildings, put an intense review of the museum collection first on his agenda. Additionally, Hoffmann travelled through Berlin and the Mark Brandenburg in search of architectonical elements to be incorporated to the new museum building. When the citizens of Berlin celebrated the opening in 1908, the Märkisches Museum presented itself as a mixture of different architectonical styles on the outside and on the inside as an orchestration of historicist rooms, however without any electricity. The introduction of Mixed Reality or Virtual Reality at the Stadtmuseum Berlin in 2015/16 is not as revolutionary as the artificial lighting in 1929, but it raises the question of how technology can help to make the visitors enjoy their analogue museum experience.

1.2 Three historical venues where Berlin was born

Today the Märkisches Museum is part of the Stadtmuseum Berlin, the city museum of Berlin. The Stadtmuseum was founded in 1995 in order to consolidate the city museums of former East-Berlin and West-Berlin as well as many other museums and collections. In 2017, the Stadtmuseum consists of 4 historical exhibition venues at the city centre plus one open-air museum in the southwest of Berlin. In addition to the Märkisches Museum, the other 3 historical buildings of the stadtmuseum are located at the Nikolaiviertel in immediate vicinity to the Town Hall, the Museumsinsel and the Humboldt-Forum:

1.2.1 Knoblauchhaus

Located right at the historical city centre, the Knoblauchhaus gives an insight to the Biedermeier-era in Berlin. The house was built in 1761 for the wealthy Knoblauch-family which were silk traders and politicians. The house was reconstructed on the occasion of the 750th birthday of Berlin in 1989 and has been used as a museum ever since.

1.2.2 Museum Ephraim-Palais

Built in 1766 for the Prussian moneyer Veitel Heine Ephraim, this beautiful Rokoko-Palais dominated the scene at the historical border between the cities of Berlin and Kölln. Though it was torn down in 1936 in order to make room for a wider road, the facade could be saved in a storage in West-Berlin. The Ephraim-Palais was rebuilt in the 1980s and opened as the venue for temporary exhibitions in 1987.

1.2.3 Nikolaikirche

The Nikolaikirche is one of the cornerstones of the historical city centre of Berlin and the oldest remaining church of the town. The church suffered from heave damage after air strikes in 1944. However, it took nearly 40 years to start the reconstruction which lead to a reopening in 1987. Since then, the church has not been used for liturgic purposes, but for exhibitions, concerts and important political events. The second major reopening was celebrated in 2010, when the Stadtmuseum opened a permanent exhibition.

2   Using VR/AR to get more visitors at the museums

2.1   The situation

The Stadtmuseum Berlin today is a player in the complex and dense museum environment in Berlin. The German capital offers more than 160 museums and dozens of memorial sites with more than 16.5 million visits in 2015[1]. Especially for tourists visiting the city centre, there are multiple high class museum venues and exhibitions to visit. The area between the Brandenburger Tor and Alexanderplatz offers within a radius of 1.5 km memorial sites such as *Topographie des Terrors* (1 Mio visitors/year)[2] and the *Denkmal für die ermordeten Judens Europas*, historical sites such as the *Brandenburger Tor*, the *Checkpoint Charlie* and the *Neue Synagoge Berlin* and big museums such as the *Deutsches Historisches Museum* (850.000 visitors/year)[3], the *Jüdisches Museum* (750.000 visitors/year)[4] and the several museums at the *Museumsinsel* (2.4 Million visitors/year)[5]. The four venues of the Stadtmuseum Berlin are also within this radius of 1.5 kilometres and attracted more than 266.000 visitors in 2015[6]. Within this touristic and cultural ecosystem in the city centre, there is high visitor potential as well as high competition. The aim for the Stadtmuseum in this environment should be to make the visitors aware that our museums are only a 10 minute walk away and offer an insight to the history of the city in an authentic environment.

2.2   Mixed Reality, but how and where?

The project *Mixed Reality at the Nikolaikirche* started in early 2015 when a Berlin-based startup presented the idea of using VR in cultural contexts. There were several possibilities discussed:

a) **Adding VR to the special exhibitions at the Ephraim-Palais in order to convey additional information**

   After several discussions with our staff and the curators, we decided

---

1   Materialien aus dem Institut für Museumsforschung, Bd. 70, 38.
2   https://www.berlin.de/sen/archiv/kultur-2011-2016/2013/pressemitteilung.94192.php
3   https://www.dhm.de/fileadmin/medien/relaunch/presse/presseinformationen/
     Pressemeldungen_2015/20151230_DHM_Besucherzahlen_2015.pdf
4   https://www.jmberlin.de/sites/default/files/jahresbericht_2013-2014.pdf
5   https://www.preussischer-kulturbesitz.de/fileadmin/user_upload/documents/presse/
     pressemitteilungen/2016/160126_JPK_02_Zahlen.pdf
6   https://www.stadtmuseum.de/sites/default/files/pressemappe_mm_paul_spies_web_0.pdf

not to use VR within the special exhibition "Dancing on the volcano" simply due to the lack of time and pre-produced content.

b) **Using VR to offer a look behind the scenes of our museum depot at Berlin-Spandau**

We decided to build a prototype in order to present some behind-the-scenes footage of our museum depot and the preparation of the upcoming exhibition based on 360-degrees-photospheres. This prototype has only been used once at the Lange Nacht der Museen in August 2015.

c) **Using VR as a marketing tool to raise interest in museum offers**

In May 2015 we decided to put the efforts to renew the information desk at the Nikolaikirche together with an Augmented Reality installation at the church. The following information describe the preparation of the projects and the first weeks after the launch.

3 What can we do best and where to tell everyone?

In order to attract more visitors to the museums, especially to the Märkisches Museum, the Stadtmuseum is focussing on two messages to convey:

a) We are the experts for the history of Berlin. Visit our locations to get to know the city.

b) Experience history emotionally by discovering our historical museum buildings.

The starting point in order to put those messages into marketing actions is the Nikolaikirche. This venue is visited by many tourists as it is listed in most of the tourist guides as a must see. As the Nikolaikirche is not used as a church, but as a museum, visitors have to pay an entrance fee. However, every visitor is able to get a first impression of the church interior without having to pay anything. This leads to 60.000 visitors paying the admission to see the whole church and additional estimated 40.000 visitors only paying a short visit.

In 2015, the Stadtmuseum Berlin decided to use this potential of nearly 100.000 visitors/year in order to make them aware of the other Stadtmuseum venues, especially of the Märkisches Museum. The Nikolaikirche was used as a kind of *portal* for the Stadtmuseum Berlin. The aim of this offer of information was to give short information and to create an impulse to visit the other museums.

In order to get the attention of a big variety of visitor types, we decided to convey information in three different media types:

a) classical analogue flyers and brochures,

b) mobile website on three stationary iPads

c) a Virtual-Reality installation

All those information were summoned at one central piece of furniture, available for every visitor coming to the Nikolaikirche.

3.1   Content and technology

The crucial point preparing the app was to choose the right amount of content in order to make the AR-installation a short but enjoyable experience. We wanted the visitors to use the devices for a maximum of 5 minutes, so the content had to be short and exemplary. The first aim was to inform the user of the 4 locations belonging to the Stadtmuseum Berlin. The second aim was to put 4 or 5 highlight-objects of each location on the stage and add some material such as video or audio. The third aim was to stimulate a visit to those locations by pointing out the location and the short walking distance which is especially relevant for the Märkisches Museum.

The basis of the content production were spherical panorama photographs taken at the inside of the exhibition buildings. Those panoramas were taken in the most popular exhibitions rooms and were expanded by 3 POIs per scene. Those POIs were produced as short film clips, audios or still images. The most important thing was to choose those museum objects which were a showcase for the whole exhibition house and the topics. As we wanted the visitors to see the objects and venues in reality, there was only 1 line of information given per POI.

In addition to those 6 scenes with a total of 15 POIs, there were Steadicam clips as well as drone flights in order to give the information about where to go next in the city in a very emotional and entertaining way. Those drone flights were the most important pieces of content as they put us in the position to show the visitors the short walking distance in order to get to the Märkisches Museum. The second advantage was an entertaining way of showing the historical museum sites from an unknown viewpoint. In total, the application used one Steadicam video and 5 different drone flight videos.

All the content was produced within 6 months and put into a specially designed Android-application.

Dealing with technology in a public space like a museum foyer needs a lot of preparation. We chose to use two units consisting of Samsung Gear VR and Samsung Galaxy S6 phones. The devices were continuously powered through the USB cable of the Gear VR. In addition to those devices, we added a large screen showing a tutorial of how to use the device.

In the final weeks before the launch we had spent a lot of time researching suitable anti-theft methods for the VR-devices and the smartphones. As the devices were not continuously supervised by the museum staff, we needed special security measurements. This was especially important as the devices were only connected to the information desk via the USB-cable.

3.2   What we learned

After testing the information desk and the AR-devices for 2 weeks, we officially launched the whole "Portal" project in October 2016. So far, we have learned some important things concerning content, technology, feasibility and visitor reactions.

a) Content

As stated before, we have offered 6 scenes and 5 different drone flights. We have learned that this might be too much content as the surrounding interior of the Nikolaikirche and other members of the visiting groups prevent single users from taking their time.

Regarding the content types, the spherical photographs were used quite often, especially watching the small video clips from concerts at the church made a huge impression on the users.

b) Technology

Using VR-consumer technology in an autonomous environment without supervision did not go well for us. On the one hand, the smartphones used tend to overheat or to reboot. On the other hand, the materials used for the Gear VR do not react well on heavy usage from dozens of people a day.

The biggest setback however is the lack of out-of-the-box anti-theft solutions. In the end, we produced our own anti-theft devices by adding an alarm devices to the Gear VR. However, this does not prevent anyone from cutting the cables.

c) Feasibility

In addition to the large screen right next to the VR-devices showing a tutorial video, we also produced small printed tutorials in English and German. However, after 2 weeks we started to put one of the staff members to take care of the users a bit more. Like other technical devices, the VR devices tended to shut down after a while or to produce problems. Especially at the testing stage, we had to supervise the devices daily which is not possible in a normal exhibition use scenario.

d) **Visitor reactions**

However, the visitor reactions were very good. When entering the Nikolaikirche, most of the visitors were immediately attracted by the screen and the devices were recognized. We could see the desired effect that the visitors split up depending on their media skills: some of them went to the brochures, some of them used the iPads and some of them – especially the young users – went to the VR devices and used them without hesitation.

We have learned that using VR technology in a visitor group is a highly communicative and motivating thing to offer. We could also notice the visitors to stay longer at the Nikolaikirche and to take away more brochures of our other exhibition houses.

e) **Technology in historical sites**

We have noticed that we have to be very careful of how much visible technology can be used in an historical museum environment. During our test stage, there were whole groups of young visitors not taking the least notice of the 800-year old church but only using the VR-devices and leaving the place afterwards.

4   The future

a) Short-Term future of the project

After several months of offering the AR-devices at the Nikolaikirche, they are now into a general overhaul. In addition to making new content available, we are working on better anti-theft methods together with Samsung Germany and hope to make progress here very soon.

Nevertheless, we believe in AR/VR to be a good choice in an orchestrated marketing strategy for museums. We have seen that VR/AR-content can bridge the gap between classical museums and younger audiences by using attractive technology. We would also add some features of active visitor feedback and monitoring.

The most interesting question will be whether the visitors are getting along with the media discontinuity when it comes to digital marketing measures advertising analogue museum experiences.

b) Long-Term future – The Humboldt-Forum

In 2019, the Humboldt-Forum is going to be opened as a massive new player in the field of culture at the centre of Berlin. Many of the museums within the previously mentioned radius of 1.5 kilometres are going to have to react on the expected shifting tourist activities around the Forum.

The Stadtmuseum Berlin is dealing with the Humboldt Forum on a very special level, as the director of the Museum Paul Spies is also the curator of the Berlin-exhibition at the Humboldt-Forum.

It will be interesting to see, how the tourists and Berliners are finding their way to the other museums when leaving the Humbolt-Forum. Maybe the Stadtmuseum Berlin can attract new visitors for the Märkisches Museum based on the things we have learned from our current AR-project. One thing is sure: Turning on artificial lighting just like 90 years ago won't be enough.

Digital and Analog Distribution of the Records of the Sound Archive of the Humboldt Universität zu Berlin

Jochen Hennig

Hermann von Helmholtz-Zentrum für Kulturtechnik
Humboldt-Universität zu Berlin
10099 Berlin
jochen.hennig@uv.hu-berlin.de

Abstract

The Humboldt-University's Sound Archives are a collection of speech and voice recordings that date back to systematic recording activity in World War I prisoner of war camps. Between 1999 and 2007 the collection was digitized and made accessible in a database, and since 2007 the catalog has been researchable online. In view of this relatively early digitization, begun in the late 1990s as a pilot project for opening up university collections, it is well suited for a review of – and a reflection on – the influence that digitization has had on utilization scenarios and on how the status of the collection and of individual recordings has changed. Today, for instance, detached from the project's original linguistic ambitions during World War I, the recordings are seen as transcultural objects approached from a wide range of perspectives as scientific and cultural projects and as part of educational formats. What part did digitization play in the changes observed and which other factors played a decisive role?

The analysis was based – in addition to evaluation of publications—on interviews with former Sound Archives employees and users and on correspondence they made available. In order to encompass changes in epistemic and ontological status, technical and infrastructural entities such as the digital catalog were considered in connection with objects, discourses, persons, conventions, institutional logic, communication situations, and contexts.[1] Analysis of these manifold factors reveals that digitization and digital development have contributed toward the Sound Archives' change in status since 1999, but that other forms of exchange such as in connection with travel, book publications, film distribution, etc. have not become obsolete. Cultural science-oriented, postcolonial theory embedding of the Sound Archives and documentary film practices played a key role in bringing about the change in the Archives' status. It became clear that the data model on which the metadata from the time when the recordings were made could not be adjusted to the dynamics of the use to which it was put. The digital side of the Sound Archives – their representation in the form of a data model lagged – behind the science history and cultural theory innovations and the respective knowledge generation.

These results thus have a marked science policy dimension. It is not only a matter of ensuring the digitization, opening up and permanent storage of cultural assets but one of thinking about strategies for the distribution of capacities and alignment of infrastructures in order to keep data modeling and its related knowledge spaces lastingly dynamic and flexible.

---

1   Cf. Jochen Hennig: Wechselnde Formate. Zur rezenten Geschichte der Sprachaufnahmen des Berliner Lautarchivs – ein Bericht. In: Manuela Bauche, Christian Vogel (ed.): Mobile Objekte. Special Issue of "Berichte zur Wissenschaftsgeschichte" 4/2016, pp. 350–366

Henry Fair Augmented: "Hidden Costs"

A Touring Exhibition by the Museum für Naturkunde Berlin and the New York Based Photographer J. Henry Fair

Ronald Liebermann

shoutr labs UG

Wolfener Str. 32-34

12681 Berlin

rl@shoutrlabs.com

Valentin Henning

Museum für Naturkunde Berlin

Invalidenstr. 43

10115 Berlin

valentin.henning@mfn-berlin.de

Abstract

Touring exhibitions and pop up museums have become more popular over the last decades and are able to reach a huge audience. Unlike regular museums, touring exhibitions travel around and "come" to their visitors. These exhibitions tend to be smaller because they need to be able to be transported and set up at different locations. Thus they contain also fewer information and especially multimedia installations are more expensive and complicated to install. With the exhibition "hidden costs" the Museum für Naturkunde Berlin wants to set new standards for multimedia usage in touring exhibitions.

1   The Exhibition

1.1   Henry Fair

"Art can tell a story that pedagogy and dialog cannot. In our hi-speed hyperlinked world, only an image can make us pause, put aside our preconceptions, and consider the meaning. To show an image that prompts curiosity opens a door into the viewer's mind.

If we tell someone something, especially if it contradicts their belief, they are unlikely to hear or consider it. If we can inspire curiosity and provide a compelling narrative response, possibly a person might consider alternatives". – J. Henry Fair

J. Henry Fair is a photographer and environmental activist based in New York. He wants to draw attention to social and environmental problems around the globe. He captures the footprints of human actions on the surface of the earth from an aerial perspective.

1.2   Hidden Costs

"Hidden Costs" is a photo exhibition, curated by the Museum für Naturkunde Berlin and the photographer J. Henry Fair that mixes the art of photography, environmental science and technology. It shows the viewer a reflection of the results of human – and therefore the viewer's – behavior in their day-to-day life.

Henry Fair's images are rather abstract. They are made up of patterns and organic forms combined with vivid colors and intensive contrasts. His aerial images show the environmental damage and thus the hidden costs of human's everyday life: The amazing colors are created by toxic waste, the interesting patterns are what's left of opencast mining sites. In his work he creates superficially stunning images – only on the second gaze they reveal their destructiveness.

Fig. 1: Fort McMurray, Canada

1.3 The exhibition

The exhibition consists of 30 images and two free-standing illuminated columns.

The issue was how to show further pictures, videos and information about Henry Fair and the sites on the images especially in several languages. From early on the idea of using multimedia technology was in the curators' minds – but due to the costs and the size of exhibitions they had to find different ways how to deal with those issues.

2   Technology

2.1   Idea

The curators wanted to show a lot of additional content in several languages without the use of printed texts or catalogues by using modern technologies like augmented reality. It was also important to let the visitors experience the exhibition with their own devices (BYOD = bring your own device) because providing multimedia devices involves extra costs.

A new way to store and stream content had to be found. An app would need a lot of space which doesn't fulfill the needs preconditioned. They also had to find a way to make the exhibition independent from the infrastructure at the venue. It had to able to be placed anywhere.

2.2 Solution

To provide a special WIFI solution for the exhibition that works independent from the internet at the site of the exhibition, the museum cooperated with the company *shoutr labs* who also installed their system with ten shoutr.Boxxes (fig. 2) in the exhibition "Tristan, Berlin zeigt Zähne" in Berlin.

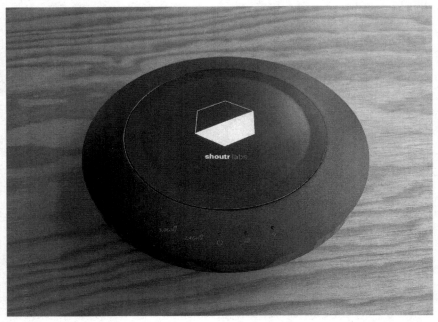

Fig 2: shoutr.Boxx

The shoutr.Boxx-system is an information system for visitors that provides position based interactive content for in- and outdoor purposes. The content is transmitted by an autonomous high-speed Wi-Fi onto the smart devices of visitors (BYOD – Bring Your Own Device) and does not need an internet connection for visitors. This Wi-Fi infrastructure is provided by the shoutr. Boxx. Their unique feature: content with high bandwidth can be made available in places where it is hard to get a mobile internet connection and without using the user's data volume.

2.3 How it works

Visitors have to download a small app approximately 15 MB in size. This app connects the user's device automatically with the shoutr.Boxx that is implemented in the exhibition. The whole content is saved on the shoutr.Boxx and streamed to the visitors device without actually downloading any content.

2.4 Augmented Reality

Augmented reality is a special feature of the exhibition.

Fig 3: example for augmented reality on flyer of the Museum.

All 30 pictures are defined as markers who can be detected by the app. The visitors can focus them with their smartphone cameras and additional content is triggered automatically. This additional content can be videos, maps, satellite views, information in several languages or more pictures from the series.

The content is made by the Museum für Naturkunde Berlin in cooperation with Henry Fair.

Virtual Orchestra: an Interactive Solution for a Concert Hall

Mykyta Kovalenko[1], Svetlana Antoshchuk[2]
Institute of Computer Systems
Odessa National Polytechnic University
65044 Odessa
{[1]kov.nikit, [2]asgonpu}@gmail.com

Jürgen Sieck
Hochschule für Technik und Wirtschaft Berlin
12459 Berlin &
Namibia University of Science and Technology Windhoek
j.sieck@htw-berlin.de

Abstract

This paper presents a Virtual Orchestra system – a pose- and gesture-recognition based system that can recognise when a user is imitating playing a musical instrument with their hand movements. The system uses Augmented Reality technology to add a virtual musical instrument into the scene, both visual and auditive: the visual representation of the instrument is placed into the user's hands and the sound of the corresponding instrument is played. An additional functionality is that the user can control the intensity and the pitch of the sound by changing the speed of his hand or finger movements.

1   Introduction

The development of information technologies in the last decade was able to bring new possibilities and challenges into many aspects of life. This is especially true for the cultural aspects like art and music, where the introduction of information technologies attracts newer and wider audiences.

Experiencing classical music at a live concert has always been popular with masses. This is true even today in the age of digital recordings and internet-streaming services like Spotify, iTunes or YouTube. Unfortunately, many concert halls and music theatres cannot be open 24 hours a day and have to stay empty if there is no live performance. This may in some cases have a negative effect on the profitability of such establishments.

Augmented Reality, which becomes more and more popular, has an excellent potential to keep the interest of visitors and even to introduce more people to the world of classical music – either as listeners, or even as new performers. The Kinect device, developed by Microsoft, is an excellent tool for bridging the gap between reality and virtuality, and provides an easy and intuitive way for people to interact with the virtual content.

We have developed an interactive system that uses a Kinect device to detect if a user is imitating playing a musical instrument in front of the screen. Our system will then recognise the pose and use Augmented Reality to overlay the corresponding musical instrument so that it is placed in the user's hands, as well as to play the sound of the instrument.

2   Related work

A popular medium for creating virtual musical instruments is the use of Augmented Reality and object detection [Sera16]. An example of this is the use of in-air gestures, as with Lages, Nabiyouni, Tibau and Bowman's Interval Player [Lage15]. The system uses a Leap Motion controller. The developed virtual instruments employed the use of both hands to play notes and chords. The dominant hand specifies intervals between successive notes, while the non-dominant hand plays the chords. However, the interface has not been able to handle half step intervals, such as sharps and flats, and it cannot handle intervals greater than five.

Another group [Kank12] modified the existing drumstick so that it outputs sound when the drummer strikes a virtual drum. They have equipped drumsticks with an accelerometer, a gyroscope, a PC and a Musical Instrument Digital Interface (MIDI) sound generator. The data measured by the sensors are sent via Bluetooth. The PC sends MIDI messages to the MIDI sound generator when the system recognises that the virtual drum is being struck. The proposed system is designed to be used with physical drums because only less frequently used parts such as the cymbal and the cow bell are being simulated by the Airstic.

A further interesting research [Sara15] features "Drum", a virtual instrument using the Microsoft Kinect and Arduino. The researchers employed the 3D sensing framework OpenNI as the driver and API to communicate with the Kinect. When the wrist enters the region of the virtual drum sets, their program triggers static WAV sound files corresponding to the virtual drum. The researchers were only able to create virtual drums for the Snare, Tom, Crash Cymbal and Ride Cymbal. The foot pedals were simulated using the Arduino and a cantilever switch. They programmed the Arduino to register signals from the cantilever switch and to play a sound whenever a trigger signal is received.

In one of our recent publications [Kova16], we proposed a gesture-recognition system that uses a simple colour camera for colour segmentation, hand tracking and fingertip extraction. The approach uses contour analysis to extract and track the coordinates of the fingertips, which allows controlling an Augmented Reality object or a Virtual Reality environment using simple gestures. The main idea behind the approach was to use a probabilistic network to predict and recognise different gestures, described with an ontology.

Sensors are one of the most fundamental things in developing a virtual system. One of these systems is described in a research article by Liu, Fan, Li, and Zhang [Liu15]. Using the particle filter model, they developed a hand tracking and gesture-recognition system that has a high tracking accuracy. The researchers utilised formulas that identify hand-skin colour, temporal motion and depth to identify the hand in the presence of background. Initialisation happens during start-up when the actor is asked to place the hand above the actor's body. The system described is only able to detect hand gestures when the actor is in a static position (sitting down in front of the camera), and is only able to track one hand.

3   System description

The proposed interactive system consists of the following fundamental steps: grabbing the colour and depth images from the Kinect camera; recognising the user's pose; extracting detailed information about the pose; and finally augmenting the video by adding the visual effect of a musical instrument and the corresponding instrument's sound (Fig. 1).

The Kinect device does all the necessary calculations to track people in front of the camera and extracts the coordinates of their skeleton joints (up to 20 joints), as well as provides an easy to use API. However, the Kinect in itself does not have any embedded functionality to estimate and recognise the user's pose or any other information about their movement and gestures.

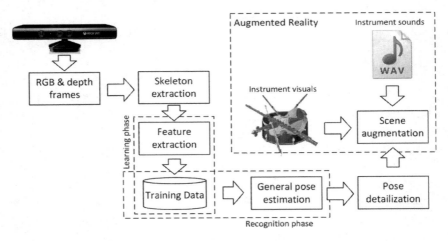

Fig. 1: The schematic overview of the system

Therefore, we have developed a simple but efficient approach to recognise poses and match them to the corresponding musical instruments and sounds. Our system uses the OpenNI framework to interact with the Kinect [Opni17], as well as the OpenCV for image processing and frame augmentation [Opcv17].

4   Pose estimation

The main principle is the use of the k-Nearest neighbours algorithm we developed and used in the real-time hand tracking and gesture-recognition system [Kova14]. For every possible pose that can be recognised by our system, we have at least a dozen training samples pre-recorded. The training samples are provided from multiple people for each pose. The training data are recorded from positions in front of the Kinect device and significant features are extracted.

4.1   Feature extraction

The biggest problem is choosing the right set of significant features to use as training data. We have to consider that the users in front of the Kinect device are of different size or stand in different positions from the camera. More importantly, the users might not be facing the camera directly, i.e. their bodies might be at a slight angle in relation to the camera. This eliminates the possibility of directly using the coordinates of the joints or using the distances between them or using the relative positions of the joints.

In order to solve that problem we decided to use relative angles and relative directions as features. More specifically, we are using the angles between the forearm and the upper arm on each side (α and β on Fig. 2a), as well as the angles between the body's centre of mass and the four essential joints of the arms: wrists and elbows (*AB* on fig. 2b).

 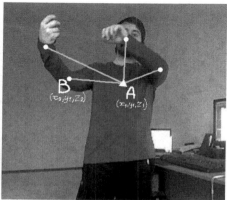

a)   b)

Fig. 2: The main features used in the system: elbow angles (a) and relative joint angles (b)

To calculate the angles α and β between the forearm and upper arm on each side we use the formula (1) for the angle between two 3D-vectors:

$$\cos(\alpha) = \frac{\vec{x} \cdot \vec{y}}{\|\vec{x}\| \, \|\vec{y}\|} \tag{1}$$

The vector coordinates and vector norms are easily calculated from the 3D-locations of the joints. The vector $\vec{x}$ is the vector from the shoulder to the elbow and $\vec{y}$ is the vector going from the elbow to the wrist.

The angles between the body centre of mass and the joints are calculated as the angles between the vector going from the centre of mass to the joint (vector AB on Fig. 2) and the normal vector to the user's torso (at the point A on Fig. 2).

To calculate the normal vector we assume that the three points, corresponding to the locations of the two shoulder joints and the torso joint, form one planar surface. Then the normal vector coordinates $N(x_N; y_N; z_N)$ can be expressed as (2):

$$N(x_N; y_N; z_N) = N \begin{pmatrix} (y_2 - y_1)(z_3 - z_1) - (y_3 - y_1)(z_2 - z_1); \\ (x_2 - x_1)(z_3 - z_1) - (x_3 - x_1)(z_2 - z_1); \\ (x_2 - x_1)(y_3 - y_1) - (x_3 - x_1)(y_2 - y_1) \end{pmatrix}. \tag{2}$$

With this calculation, we can then use the equation (1) to calculate the angle between the normal vector and the "joint" vector.

4.2　Pose classification

During the training stage we calculated all these angles, we built the feature vector for every training sample of every recorded pose and saved all the vectors for future use in the recognition process. When the user stands in front of the Kinect device, the system once again detects the user's skeleton joints and extracts the pose features. After that we use the k-Nearest neighbours (kNN) algorithm to classify the pose in the current frame of the video. Considering the number of training samples, the Kinect's framerate of 30 fps and the fact that our system is supposed to work in real time without any delay (also 30 fps), we determine that $k = 5$, also the 5 nearest neighbours provide the best recognition accuracy.

Furthermore, our algorithm has to deal with possible noise, jittering and false positives caused by the fluctuations in the joint coordinates provided by the Kinect device. The idea behind the algorithm is using a queue of "tumblers" of a fixed length N. At every frame, after we extract the features and use the kNN algorithm to classify the pose, we push the recognition result to the back of the queue. If the queue is full, we also add the element to the front of the queue, so that the size of the queue is always kept lower or equal to N. After some experiments, we have found the most optimal values of N to be between 3 and 5.

When the tumbler queue is full, then

- if all N values in the queue are the same (i.e. the pose classification result was the same in N consecutive frames), or
- if M of N values in the queue are the same (i.e. the majority of the classifications results in the previous N frames were the same).

We can then conclude that the pose was recognised and we can continue with the visual and auditive augmentation of the scene. Here, the first option allows us to eliminate false positives caused by joint jittering and measurement noise, making sure that our system is certain about the recognition result, although this may result in the system taking slightly longer to arrive to a conclusion. The second option allows us to make our system more fluid and forgiving toward sudden measurement noise; however, this requires setting a good enough M to N ratio.

The experimental testing shows that the proposed pose-recognition approach provides a high recognition accuracy. The test results are summarised in Table 1.

The average response time for a switch between different poses is 268 ms.

Pose name	Tumbler queue type		Response time (ms)
	Full N ($N = 4$)	M of N (3 of 4)	
Flute	0.98	0.97	240
Violin	0.94	0.93	320
Drums	0.96	0.95	235
Cello	0.89	0.90	360
Trombone	0.93	0.94	270
Clarinet	0.97	0.98	260
Guitar	0.96	0.97	230
Triangle	0.92	0.93	290
Conductor	0.97	0.94	210

Table 1: Summary of the pose recognition accuracy testing

4.3   Pose detailing

It is clear, that simply standing in a position matching the musical instrument is not enough for playing an instrument as that process is normally much more dynamic. For instance, playing a flute requires moving fingers, while playing a violin involves moving the hand holding the bow. To solve this problem, we add the pose recognition system with an additional hand-gesture recognition subsystem described in [Kova16].

When a pre-recorded pose is successfully recognised and maintained for several consecutive frames, we run a gesture-recognition procedure that consists of several key elements:

- calculate the movement speed and direction of each hand
- extract the fingertips on both hands (if possible) and counting the number of outstretched fingers.

To calculate the movement speed and direction of the hand we only require the coordinates of both wrist joints. Using the coordinates of the joints, we can calculate the track line of the hands and their average speed, velocity and movement direction (Fig. 3). This information is used to control the speed and intensity of the musical instrument, e.g. the force with which the user bangs the drums or the movement speed of the bow while the user is playing the violin. In our system we use three gradations for the hand movement speed (slow, medium, fast) as well as the four main movement directions (up, down, left and right).

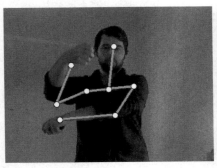

Fig. 3: Tracking the wrist joints and calculating the movement speed and direction

To extract the fingertips we also use the coordinates of the wrist joints. However, in this case we also use the information from the colour frame in order to estimate the average colour of the user's skin and then use colour segmentation to get the hand contours. This give us the ability to perform a contour analysis [Kova14] to extract the positions of the fingertips by executing a clockwise contour traversal and calculating the angles between points of the contour (Fig. 4).

Fig. 4: Extracting fingertips

The total number of detected fingertips will correspond to the total number of outstretched fingers, which means that we can easily calculate the number of fingers that are applied to the instrument. This information can be used to control the pitch of the instrument, e.g. pressing fingers to the holes of a flute or a clarinet.

Our chosen approach for pose- and gesture-recognition allows to identify a multitude of instruments. In addition the system also recognises the user's gestures, specifically the speed of the hand and finger movements to control the sound of the instruments. It should be noted, that there are many instruments that use very similar poses and similar gestures in order to be played. An example of such a group of instruments are wind instruments (clarinet, bassoon and oboe). This may also apply to some other instruments that are not similar in nature, but use seemingly similar movements (e.g. playing drums and playing a piano). The Kinect device unfortunately does not provide enough information to differentiate between such cases. That is why in this paper we limit ourselves to only one instrument out of such a group of similar instruments, i.e. out of the wind instrument group we only choose the clarinet.

5   Scene augmentation

By this point we have gained the following information from the Kinect device: the positions of every skeleton joint; the pose; the movement speed and direction of the hands; and the number of fingertips. This information can be used to augment the scene visually as well as auditively by adding the visual effect of an instrument in the hands of the user as well as adding the sound of the corresponding instrument [Bern16]. The auditive part of the augmentation can be further supplemented by adding variation of the sound according to the movements of the hands and the positions of fingers.

In particular, we can easily modify our system, i.e. the speed of the hand movements will control the intensity of the sound for the violin, cello and drums, while the finger positions will change the pitch for the flute or clarinet. Finally, both the hand movement and finger positions will control the loudness and the pitch for the trombone. An example of scene augmentation is show in Figure 5.

Fig. 5: Example of visual scene augmentation

Additional information is displayed for clarity, such as the name of the instrument, as well as information about each hand, i.e. movement direction, movement speed and number of fingers.

As for the sound augmentation, our system includes a collection of WAVE sound files that contain the sounds of every instrument on the system. For each instrument we keep several sound files. For movement-based instruments we have three sound effects for every movement speed gradation. For the "finger movement" instruments the system has up to five sound effects with different pitches that match different finger positions. For example, there are three sound files for the violin (one for each movement speed) and five sounds for the flute (here we are only counting the number of fingers on the left hand). After the pose is recognised, our system decides whether it should take into account the hand movements or the finger positions. Then the system extracts the additional features (movement or fingers) and plays the matching sound.

6   Conclusion

We have proposed an interactive system that uses a Kinect and is able to recognise user's pose as well as hand and finger movements. In addition, the system provides Augmented Reality to overlay the instrument that matches the recognised pose so that an image of the instrument is placed in the user's hands. The sound of the corresponding musical instrument is played, with its speed and intensity depending on the movements of the user, as well as the positions of the user's fingers. This means, if the user is imitating playing drums, faster hand movements will result in a faster and louder drum sound or while moving the fingers to play the flute the sound will change corresponding to the position of the fingers and the speed of the movement.

7   Acknowledgment

This paper describes the work undertaken in the context of the project APOLLO hosted by the research group "Information and Communication Systems" INKA that is gratefully funded by the European regional development fund (ERDF).

Literature

[Bern16]   Berthaut, F., Hachet, M.: Spatial Interfaces and Interactive 3D Environments for Immersive Musical Performances. In IEEE Computer Graphics and Applications, Vol. 36, No. 5, P. 82–87, 2016.

[Kank12]   Kanke, H., Takegawa, Y., Terada, T., and Tsukamoto, M.: Airstic drum: a drumstick for integration of real and virtual drums. In Advances in Computer Entertainment, P. 57–69. Springer., 2012.

[Kova14]   Kovalenko, M., Sieck, J., Anotshchuk, S.: Real-time hand tracking and gesture recognition using a semantic-probabilistic network.

16th International Conference on Computer Modelling and Simulation, Cambridge, P. 269–274, IEEE 2014.

[Kova16]   Kovalenko, M., Sieck, J., Anotshchuk, S.: Markerless Augmented Reality Approach Based on Hand Posture and Gesture Recognition. In: Kultur und Informatik: Augmented Reality, P. 171–182, 2016

[Lage15]   Lages, W., Nabiyouni, M., Tibau, J., and Bowman, D. A.: Interval player: Designing virtual musical instrument using in-air gestures. In 3D User Interfaces (3DUI), 2015 IEEE.

[Liu15]   Liu, W., Fan, Y., Li, Z., and Zhang, Z.: Rgbd video based human hand trajectory tracking and gesture recognition system. Mathematical Problems in Engineering, 2015.

[Opni17]   Open-source SDK for 3D sensors – OpenNI, Retrieved January 18, 2017, from http://www.openni.ru/

[Opcv17]   Open Computer Vision Library, Retrieved January, 17, 2017, from http://opencv.org/.

[Sara15]   Sarang, P., More, A., Gaikwad, A., and Varma, T.: Air drum using Kinect and Arduino. International Journal of Computer Science and Information Technologies, Vol.6 (2), P. 1153–1155, 2015.

[Sera16]   Serafin, S., Erkut, C., Kojs, J., Nilsson, N. C. and Nordahl, R.: Virtual Reality Musical Instruments: State of the Art, Design Principles, and Future Directions. In Computer Music Journal, Vol. 40, No. 3, P. 22–40, 2016.

Heritage Imaging Solutions for the Real World

Michael Maggen

Israel Museum Jerusalem

Derech Ruppin, Jerusalem, Israel

michaelm@imj.org.il

Moshe Caine

Hadassah Academic College Jerusalem

37 Hanevi'im Street, Jerusalem, Israel

mosheca@hadassah.ac.il

Abstract

In this paper, we have attempted to map, compare and suggest three affordable imaging approaches for the documentation, conservation, maintenance, analysis, and presentation of tangible cultural heritage objects. The starting hypothesis for this work is that most cultural institutes lack the funding to adopt the high end and expensive solutions available on the market today. For this purpose, we have limited ourselves to such which may be achieved at little or in some cases even at no cost.

The conclusion of this empiric research suggests that such solutions are indeed practical and within reach, but do not in any way alleviate the users from the necessity of obtaining a high level of proficiency in the use of such technologies. Likewise, we suggest that there is not one overall solution which could be considered suited to all conservation needs and that a careful and objective prior approach to defining the needs is essential as a prelude to choosing the right imaging approach for each chosen cultural heritage object.

1   Introduction

ICOM is not aware of the accurate number of museums in the world. However, in its 21st edition (2014), the most comprehensive directory *Museums of the World* published by De Gruyter covers more than 55,000 museums in 202 countries. (http://icom.museum/resources/frequently-asked-questions/) Likewise, the number of material heritage conservation institutes is not clear either, however its number too must be in the many thousands. All these institutes face the daily challenge of curatorial activities, all of which involve a vast range of considerations.

The big question is how many of these centers have the financial ability to carry out these essential needs in times of economic stress and continual budget cuts.

This paper focuses on one such area, that of visual inspection for curatorial management, public display, quality maintenance, degradation assessment and as an aid in conservation records and considerations.

Today's market demands low cost and practical solutions to combat the dangers of losing out to the ravages of decay, war, vandalism destruction, terrorism and time. (Reznicek, Pavelka 2007).

Over the past decade, great improvements have been made in visual technologies for imaging. Unfortunately, most of these technologies lie outside the reach of most museums and conservation institutes, due to cost of the hardware as well as to the level of expertise required for the running of such equipment. As a response to this challenge, in this paper we have chosen to perform a comparative analysis of three low cost imaging technologies:

- RTI (Reflectance Transformation Imaging),
- Photogrammetry – Structure from Motion
- Low cost 3D scanning.

Currently, as technology is becoming more complex and sophisticated, there is a danger of a gap widening up between the content specialists and the technological and scientific community. Many heritage curators, historians, conservation specialists and content specialist and relatively ignorant or simply intimidated by the tools on offer today. They are therefore in danger of missing out on the assistance these can offer in their work. Therefore, some researches, argue the value of simple methodologies and advocate bridging the gap between technologists and content specialists (Hassani 2015) (Scopigno et al. 2011).

This consideration, along with the financial considerations has led to us purposely limiting our hardware and software solutions to a bare minimum, to keep them both relatively simple as well as within an affordable price range. In this research, we have used, the highlight method of RTI imaging. The photogrammetry was shot in various conditions, sometimes in a studio environment and in other cases on location, using different cameras and software solutions. Likewise, the 3D scanning has been performed in accordance with the dictates of the brief and context of the objects, using either a low-cost laser or depth sensing hardware. The purpose here is to suggest these technologies as readily available and financially manageable aids to the above needs, whist comparing their relative strengths and weaknesses in various real world conditions.

2   Test Cases

Whilst our research over the past years has involved the imaging of well over one hundred objects, we have focused here on a limited number of samples. These have been chosen in consideration of their diversity in respect of size, texture, materials, their environment, lighting conditions and in the practical limitations of imaging them.

The materials tested include: Stone, marble, clay, jade, wood, bronze, various alloys, paper, Papier-mâché, parchment, leather, string, pigments & gold-leaf. Sizes imaged ranged from a 1-cm coin to a life-sized marble statue and from a 13-mm clay bulla to a 3-meter-high Torah Ark.

Imaging environments ranged from outdoors (tombstone, bronze sculpture), museum gallery (various objects) and studio environment (bulla, coin).

It is believed that these objects fairly represent a cross-cut of the obstacles and needs of the cultural heritage institutes today.

3   Working Hypothesis

The working hypothesis for this work is that there will not be a "one size fits all" solution. Not all heritage objects are equal in terms of size, materials, intricacy, colour fidelity, texture, ease of access, etc. Therefore, it is not reasonable to expect one imaging solution to answer all visual documentation needs. Instead, it is hoped that this paper and empiric research will offer practical guidelines and best practice outlines for the many institutes who lack the luxury of high end imaging services.

4   Technology Overview

Following is a short overview of the technologies used. This is but a simple introduction aimed at those less familiar with digital imaging in cultural heritage. More in-depth information may be found online and in the references provided below.

4.1   Reflectance Transformation Imaging

RTI is a unique digital photographic technique aimed at enhancing the surface detail of objects through an algorithmic rendering of multiple registered digital images of the object, shot with controlled, varying, yet known light positions.

Originally termed Polynomial Texture Mapping (PTM), Reflectance Transformation Imaging was invented by Tom Malzbender at the Hewlett Packard Labs. The seminal paper describing the method was published in 2001b (Malzbender, Gelb, Wolters 2001). Today the technology continues to be developed by a dedicated international team, supported by the *Cultural Heritage Imaging Corporation (CHI)*.

The power and beauty of RTI is in its ability to enhance surface detail of a wide variety of materials by changing the apparent direction of light falling upon it – post factum. i.e. after the photographic session has been completed and at the leisure of the researcher in the comfort of the lab.

During photography, the light sources are positioned at a constant radius from the subject and surround it at incremental angles, forming a dome or hemisphere of light positions.

There are two basic methods to creating RTI images. The Highlight Method and the Dome Method. The photographs, anywhere between 40–70, are fed into software which calculates the light positions (L.P. file) and forms the basis for the creation of the final PTM file, essentially a virtual three-dimensional digital image light source that is controlled interactively. The final image, viewed with a Java based viewer (RTI viewer), initially looks like a flat, normal photograph. The magic however starts with the ability of the user to intuitively and interactively move the virtual light source around the image by moving the mouse in a manner that MacDonald terms a "virtual torch" (MacDonald 2011), zoom in and out, and change sharpness, contrast and other light and surface properties through a series of real time filters, thus often revealing surface details not visible to the naked eye under normal viewing conditions. Screen snap shots can be record as JPEG images any moment the user wishes to do so.

As we shall see in the tests carried out here, this technology is very flexible, relatively easy to master and yields remarkable results.

4.2   Photogrammetry – Photo Modelling

Photogrammetry is the "science of measuring in photos", and is most commonly used in remote sensing, aerial photography, archaeology, architecture and other fields where we need to determine measurements from photographs.

It is based on the principle that while a single photograph can only yield two-dimensional coordinates, height and width (X–Y), two overlapping images of the same scene, taken slightly apart from each other can allow the third dimension (Z) to be calculated through the process of triangulation.

Photo modeling is the process of creating a true 3D model via a combined methodology of photographic and true vector modeling techniques.

A photo model combines the elements of shape, texture and lighting of the object and stores them as a combined vector and raster file, thereby providing the combined advantages of mathematical accuracy and flexibility, along with photographic exactitude of colour and texture. This process lends itself especially to 3D reproduction and representation of existing real things, rather than the creation process of new objects, based on copying or imagination. Industrial objects, museum artifacts, merchandise, buildings, even people. and so on.

Furthermore, certain objects may prove immensely difficult to recreate in conventional 3D, especially objects with soft, amorphous, non-geometric shapes. This is where photo modeling stands out.

The past several years have seen a great advancement in this field, due both to improvements in algorithms and software, as well in the proliferation of high quality DSLR cameras and even high end phone cameras. Consequently, there is today a growing argument that for many purposes, image based photogrammetry can equal and often surpass laser and SL imaging.

(Skarlatos, Kiparissi 2012). Moreover, Pavelka argues that with good configuration and quality photos taken by digital camera, the accuracy (standard
deviation) reaches from 0.2 to 1mm from distances 1–5 meters. In larger and
more distant objects the accuracy is worse, but still acceptable. (Pavelka et al.
2013)

4.3   Low cost 3D Scanning

3D scanners are essentially not all that different from conventional flatbed
scanners. Their big advantage is that unlike the flatbed scanner which can
only measure the 2D dimensions, the X and Y coordinates of an object, the
3D scanner captures the third, the Z coordinate, the depth.

Conventional 2D Flatbed scanners are basically a digital camera without a
camera optical system. The image data is gathered by light beamed on and
reflected off a (usually) two-dimensional subject. The gathered light intensity
is translated into pixel density. Thus, very high resolution bitmap images can
be created, albeit of static subjects which can fit into the scan area.

However, because 2D scanners have no optical system to speak of, they can
focus only on a set distance and measure only the X and Y coordinates of
the points. Thus, they are not suitable for three dimensional objects of any
considerable depth. This is where 3D scanners differ. They also gather the Z
coordinate.

Today there are a growing number of 3D scanner technologies, however, in
principle these break down into the following categories.

4.3.1   Laser Scanners

The term Laser scanning has become synonymous with 3d scanning.
However, the laser is but one of the technologies in use today. Furthermore,
there are many laser scanning technologies around and the technology is
continually developing. Simply put however, laser scanners project a point or
beam of light onto the subject surface and measure the reflection of the light,
thereby calculating the position and distance. Each point of light data is then
aligned with the other multitude of points (possibly millions) to form a point
cloud, similar, but usually of greater accuracy than that created by the photo
modelling method.

Laser scanners are usually divided into two main groups: Contact Lasers and
Non-Contact Laser.

As the name implies, contact lasers come into direct contact with the surface area of the object scanned. For industrial design prototyping, reverse engineering and many other uses this allows extremely high levels of accuracy. However, this system is not always acceptable or even possible for some objects. For example, many cultural heritage objects are far too fragile to allow for this kind of treatment.

"Time of Flight" scanners measure the time it takes for the light to reflect from the subject. This is useful for measuring large objects at a distance, such as architectural structures, archaeological sites and the such. Their accuracy however is limited, usually to within a few millimeters. Some laser scanners calculate point by point. Others shine a narrow beam or strip of light to speed up the data gathering process.

Like all technologies, Laser scanners have their advantages and disadvantages. Wachowiak, B.V. Karas argue the advantages of using advanced 3D laser and structured light scanners such as the Breuckmann triTOS-HE due to their high accuracy, yet even these scanners fall short when good quality colour texture is required. In addition, their high cost place them well outside the scope of the conditions set in this article. (Wachowiak, Karas 2013)

In this research, we have used the NextEngine scanner which is recognized as being a leader in the low end low cost range. This scanner includes a 3D colour capture capability, but as we shall see, it is if very low quality and not of much practical use for the fidelity required for heritage documentation.

Because 3D scanners map points in space only, they do not create highlights or shadows. Whilst this may seem a limitation for 3D viewing, it is in fact an advantage, as many if not most 3D viewing platforms offer a controllable lighting, thus allowing a fully interactive relighting of the object as needed.

Research into the comparative qualities of SfM and 3D scanning in various applications is growing, such as in archaeology (P. Bourke) and cultural monuments (B. Bayram et al.).

4.3.2   Structured Light Scanners

Structured-light 3D scanners are similar in principle to triangulation scanners. However, they do not use a laser, but rather white (or blue) light.

Structured light scanners project a line or a pattern of light on the subject and look at the deformation of the pattern on the subject. The line is projected onto the subject using either an LCD projector or a sweeping laser. A camera, offset slightly from the pattern projector, looks at the shape of the line and uses a technique like triangulation to calculate the distance of every point on the line. This technique offers the advantage of greater speed.

A camera is used to look at the deformation of the pattern, and an algorithm is used to calculate the distance at each point in the pattern.

Unlike the time of flight scanners, triangulation scanners usually work best at relatively short distances and on small to medium sized objects.

It is argued that the use of structured light is better suited to cultural heritage objects than laser light (Akca 2012) It reduces speckle noise and provides better surface smoothness (Blais 2004). Furthermore, unlike laser light, it does not penetrate the object surface, thus making it better suited to the imaging of textures such as marble (Godin et al. 2001). On the other hand, being based on projected light, the structured light systems are not effective in daylight and must be performed in a darkened environment.

4.3.3 Depth Scanning

While laser scanning, whether by point or by line, and white light "structured light" scanning comprise the main streams of non-invasive, non-contact 3D scanning technologies around today, the search is on for new innovative approaches, which will bring 3D scanning to the masses both in price and simplicity. No doubt the years to come will bring many such developments, however one direction which is already showing promise is the harnessing of consumer game console based technologies, chief amongst these the Microsoft Kinect.

As we have already learned, the key to 3D scanning is a visual capture system which includes depth perception, together with software which can interpret this information and translate it into a point cloud or polygon mesh.

The Kinect sensor, now in its second generation, is in fact a game-oriented RGB-D camera, the visual receptor of the Microsoft X-Box. Whilst the 2nd generation Kinects is based on Time of Flight technology; the original Kinect was the first general consumer-grade structured-light camera. (Orrego 2012) composed of RGB and IR sensors with an IR pattern projector. (Comb`es et al. 2011)

To gauge the depth, the system uses stereo triangulation. However, whereas stereo triangulation requires two images to get depth information, the uniqueness of this technique lies in the fact that there is only one projection system, the infrared sensor. The second pattern is hardcoded into the chip logic. The images which result are not identical as there is some distance between the two. The software recognizes the images as originating from different camera positions, thus allowing stereo triangulation to calculate the Z axis position for each point.

4.3.4 Limitations of 3D Scanners

Clearly, any system based on viewing reflected light will suffer the same limitation as photography, namely, that it can record only that which it can see. Therefore, 3D scanners must overcome this limitation by either revolving the object and scanning from multiple directions, or by rotating around the object.

A second, and more serious limitation of laser scanning lies in the type of material it can record. Due to the technique being based on reflected light, laser scanners are notoriously problematic at scanning shiny surfaces, especially glass, silver, gold, marble and other reflective materials.

This limitation is often partially overcome by spraying the subject with an anti-reflective powder, much to the chagrin of museum curators and conservation specialists.

5 Overview of Results

Following is an overview of results and conclusions. Limitations of space in this paper prevent providing a detailed analysis of each object. Therefore, we have attempted to give an overall evaluation of each technology in respect to the various contexts of size, material, imaging environments, regarding geometry and texture accuracy, with specific references to the test objects where possible. Unless stated otherwise, all objects included in this research come from the permanent collections of the Israel Museum Jerusalem. The remaining objects come from private collections or public domain.

5.1   Reflectance Transformation Imaging

Figure 1

When it comes to harvesting fine texture information, nothing can beat the price performance of RTI. It works equally well on small or large objects, on parchment or jade. Like any technique, absolute attention must be placed on accuracy in shooting perfectly aligned shots, positioning the reflective ball and so on. However, with the camera sensor and lens quality available today, incredible surface details may be achieved and information invisible to the human eye may be clearly brought out. Such is the case of the Mexican Olmek jade figurine (900–600 BCE) (Art of the Americas The Israel Museum) in which the virtually indecipherable fine chiseling can be made out, thus determining its authenticity and setting it apart from forgeries in which the details were created by metal tools (Yvonne Fleitman/Benjamin Weiss Curator, Art of the Americas) (figure 1.1). A similar result is manifest in the faded texts on a Hellenistic Stele transcript of correspondence in Greek between Antiochus III(223-187 BCE) and Ptolemy son of Thrashes Hefzibah, Beth Shan Valley, 201-195 BCE limestone Israel Antiquity Authority (IAA) collection (Heinrichs) (figure 1.4). In the 18th century Ethiopian medical book (collections of Arts of Africa and Oceania The Israel Museum), RTI revealed previously undetected marks of an earlier binding, raising questions about its lineage (figure 1.3).

In the case of the Lachish bulla (collection of IAA), "RTI enabled considerable improvements in deciphering the faded texts, well beyond that which was achievable during the earlier research in the 1960's" (Mendel) (figure 4.5–4.6). Whilst strong daylight can interfere, camera aperture and shutter controls can overcome this limitation too, as in the case of a faded tombstone (Unsleben, Germany) (figure 1.2).

RTI is cheap and flexible. Admittedly, building a sophisticated computer controlled LED lighting dome is beyond the scope of many institutions, but cheap alternatives can work equally well, even if less efficiently.

On the downside, as each RTI demands 48–70 images and processing, if we wish to examine the surface texture details from multiple directions it can prove impractical. This is where a true 3D object proves superior.

5.2   3D Scanners

Figure 2

Active 3D laser scanners such as the NextEngine excel in surface geometry and give good detail (figure 2.4) within the above-mentioned limitations.

However, their effectiveness is limited to small – medium sized objects and the shooting environment must be highly controlled, i.e. no daylight. Due to the laser scan's relative geometric accuracy, one practical advantage lies in its ability to provide noninvasive data for the creation of custom-made accurate packaging for transportation of fragile objects.

In terms of our defined cost parameters they are not cheap and lie at the very top scale, possibly outside the budget of many small institutes. Generally speaking, laser scanners offer relatively poor and sometimes even no RGB texture. Therefore, it is important to define what our needs are and whether our priorities lie in accuracy of geometry, necessary for conservation and research, or the overall aesthetic photographic appearance necessary for public display.

In our tests, too, scanner results were greatly dependent on the material quali-ties. Shiny, translucent and reflective surfaces such as marble, gold leaf or jade proved virtually impossible to capture by active scanning because the laser is reflected in multiple directions (figure 2.3). Likewise, dark objects (figure 2.1 figure 2.2) absorbed the light and very little was reflected. The usual solutions such as powders or sprays are not practical as they both change the apparent surface properties of the object and in addition can cause highly unwanted responses from the heritage community!

One way of overcoming the inferior texture quality is through overlaying textures created separately with a DSLR camera. There are several ways of doing this and the results are good (figure 2.5). However, this technique, while offering the best of both worlds, is neither simple nor quick.

It should be noted that this field is developing rapidly and as of the writing of this paper there are literally tens of scanners available within this price range or below. Some use laser technology, others structured light, such as the excellent David scanner (Now the HP 3D Scan). The Kinect and Sense scanners can indeed work in subdued soft light but in our tests their overall quality was constantly inferior and frankly impractical for anything other than quick and basic curatorial 3D documentation.

The new Kinect 2 works on the principle of TOF (time of flight) and boasts a higher resolution and sensitivity. We however did not have the opportunity to test it. Today, with the attention focused upon depth sensing technologies by the likes of Apple and Microsoft, we may expect great improvements in the not too distant future.

5.3   Structure from Motion – Photogrammetry

Figure 3

In our practical tests, photogrammetry proved itself to be a general all-rounder in terms of performance. With today's cameras and software such as Agisoft Photoscan, 3D SOM or Autodesk Remake, one can achieve remarkably highly detailed point-clouds, meshes and solid surfaces. However, it should be noted that fine smooth surfaces may in some cases yield a mottled rough and false texture.

Photogrammetry works equally well on virtually any size, be it a large archaeological site recorded by drone photography, a medium sized statue (figure 3.7) or a macro object such as a coin or tablet (figure 3.2). The shooting environment too is flexible. Thus, an outdoor tombstone (figure 3.4), gallery terracotta (figure 3.6) or studio controlled shot (figure 3.3), all proved equally receptive.

The basic rule is "let there be light", preferably soft light. Visual appreciation of texture information and 3D surface modelling is dependent on controlled directional light. Therefore, it is highly advisable to strive for a shadow less shooting environment. This however is not always possible. Where there is strong directional light, such as in the terracotta figure (figure 3.6) it is baked onto the model, whereas if the lighting is soft and equal (Ethiopian medical book) it may be controlled interactively post factum (figure 3.1) rather akin to RTI, through software such as the excellent open source Meshlab. In this respect the 3D model has a clear advantage over RTI in that not only can the light direction be controlled but also the position and orientation of the model. Where this technique stands out is of course the photographic texture or UV map. Nothing comes close to the near perfect photo rendering that can be achieved if care is taken with proper lighting, camera control and shooting technique (figure 3.4). Like all things, nothing is as simple as it may seem at first. Practice and attention to detail are as always the essential imperatives to yielding a good result.

6   Evaluation, documentation, sharing and management

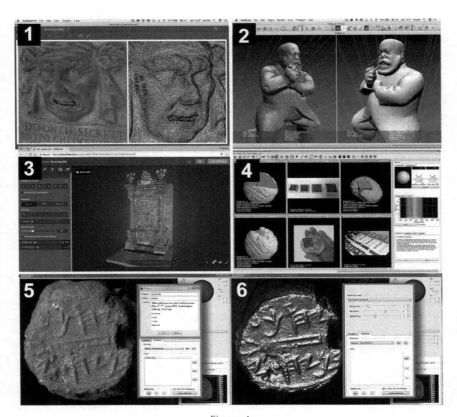

Figure 4

A somewhat overlooked aspect of the technologies outlined above is that of gathering and harvesting the data. One of the major advantages in 3D and

RTI lies in the fact that these are interactive technologies, allowing for a virtually infinite combination of viewing, lighting and filtering parameters. Infra red, Ultra violet and multispectral analysis (not discussed here) also yield vast amounts of information. Even relatively simple and common place 2D photographic technologies include a rich meta data. Much of this is embedded into the file itself and is accessible, yet not necessarily easily available to the non-technical content specialist.

Therefore, it is felt that a comparative analysis of the empiric value of the technologies should also relate to the usability, not just of the technology itself, but also to the data that it yields.

6.1   Reflectance Transformation Imaging

RTI, as explained above gathers the light values (colour and direction) from the multitude of images and builds a virtual interactive light source for the user. The light values themselves are stored in a LP (light position) text file, however those are but the source data of the photographic stage. What is relevant to the end user is the ability to store the data which yielded the exact visual result that was found to be most revealing for the defined purpose. This would include the X & Y positions of the virtual light, the pan and zoom of the image, as well as the specific parameters of the rendering modes: Default, Diffuse Gain, Specular Enhancements, Unsharp Masking, etc. (figures 4.5–4.6)

In the past, such data had to be manually recorded. However, it the later versions of the wonderful RTI viewer all this information can be stored as a bookmark and recalled at will. Likewise, any visual result may be exported as a JPG snapshot. This is a great improvement and advantage.

6.2   3D Models

All 3D models, regardless of whether they are created by a variety of scanning methods or by photogrammetry, are ultimately saved in one of several 3D formats. Depending upon their designated ultimate use these formats vary. Some, such as the ubiquitous .obj are multi purpose. Others, like .stl, .vrml, .u3d, etc. Are designed for more specific purposes, such as printing, virtual displays, pdf embedding, and so on.

As with the RTI files, 3D files too include a vast list of alphanumeric data, defining the vector properties of the point clouds, mesh and texture. These however are of less practical use to the content specialists than to the scientist. What they need as with RTI is the ability to control the viewing parameters, save particular visual displays, lighting, direction, size, etc. and to annotate them with relevant information.

Several solutions are available, some free and open source, others at an affordable price.

6.2.1 Meshlab

The extremely popular Meshlab software, initially created at the University of Pisa in late 2005 is today developed by the ISTI-CNR research center. Meshlab is a tour de force. It offers a vast range of tools for 3D acquisition: Aligning, Visualization and Presentation, Color Mapping and Texturing, cleaning, scaling, positioning and orienting, simplification, refinement and remeshing, measurement, and analysis, colour processing, visualization and presentation. Nevertheless, Meshlab is not for the fainthearted. It is complex to use with a steep learning curve (figure 4.2).

6.2.2 Sketchfab

Sketchfab is a brilliant platform for online storage and presentation of 3D models. Developed by a small team in Paris in 2012, it today hosts over half a million creators contributing over a million models, of which the cultural heritage sector boasts a large slice. Sketchfab offers support for a vast array of 3D formats as well as many post processing tools for lighting, colour balance, tone mapping, depth of field, animation, contrast, orientation, etc. All these greatly enhance to visual quality of the display online. However, to our mind the major asset of this platform lies in the ability to annotate the model with hotspot based texts. This enables the content specialist to enhance the visual information with readily accessible textual data.. The models may be shared or kept private, embedded into other web sites, protected or downloadable, made accessible to searches and galleries by including relevant titles, descriptions, tags, and categories (figure 4.3).

6.2.3 Acrobat – PDF

The major advantage of the Adobe Acrobat PDF format is its universality and popularity.

Adobe Acrobat is not new. I fact it has been around since the early 1990s and for the past ten years it supports the display of 3D models. Surprisingly, this is not well known and its use has been limited primarily to the fields of indutrial design and architecture, much less in the cultural heritage community.

Adobe has developed a specific 3D format for Acrobat, U3D. However it should be pointed out that the 3D capabilities are only supported by the original Adobe Acrobat reader and web plugin, not by the multitude of other PDF readers on the market.

Nevertheless, the advantages of the PDF format are not limited to 3D display alone. A single PDF file can also support a multitude of media. Images, text, video, sound. In this way a PDF can contain a multifaceted multimedia data sheet of an object, compact, searchable and versatile.

Furthermore using either the Acrobat Pro software or various 3rd party software, buttons may be embedded into the PDF, allowing interactive viewing of the object from various angles, dighting, textures, etc. (figure 4.1).

6.2.4   CHER – OB

Developed by Yale researchers in the Department of Computer Science and the Institute for the Preservation of Cultural Heritage (IPCH) at Yale's West Campus, CHER-Ob is an open-source software program designed as a single virtual environment for collaborative cultural heritage research, accommodating many kinds of media (figure 4.4).

CHER-OB is the first dedicated software platform to offer full support for all commonly used 2D and 3D data types, as well as RTIs and CT. It offers full annotation, automatic report generation, bookmarking, screenshots, searching, sorting and filtering options. Recently released from beta, the software is available for download and may well soon prove to become the de facto standard for collaborative cultural heritage research.

7   Conclusions

Comparing the relative merits and weaknesses of the three technologies above is akin to comparing apples and oranges. Each have advantages over the other as well as clear disadvantages.

It is the opinion of this paper that all heritage institutions should make the effort to familiarize themselves with all three technologies and not form prior conclusions as to the preference of one over the other.

Furthermore, whist all the techniques are affordable, it must be stressed that attention to detail and quality in all stages of production are essential. Mastering the techniques demands time and endless testing. In RTI and SfM, the digital images should be initially captured at the highest possible resolution and in RAW format. Always remember that the final quality will be determined by the weakest link.

As for 3D scanning, price performance currently undermines its effectiveness. Lasers offer good mesh quality but poor texture. Good structured light offers better texture but at a price. the stage is set for major developments soon. Companies such as Dell, Microsoft and Apple are introducing 3D sensing technology into their computers and smart phones. Demand pushes the quality up and the prices down. So, whereas currently, laser and depth-sensing scanners are less cost effective than the alternatives, it is felt that this situation may change dramatically

8   Acknowledgements

Chelsea Graham. Institute for the Preservation of Cultural Heritage. Yale University. RTI image of tombstone, Germany.

CHER-OB. Yale Institute for the Preservation of Cultural Heritage in collaboration with Yale Computer Graphics Group through a generous grant from the Seaver Foundation. Software authors: Weiqi Shi, Eleni Kotoula, Kiraz Akoglu, Ying Yang, and Holly Rushmeier

Yvonne Fleitman. Benjamin Weiss Curator, Art of the Americas, Israel Museum, Jerusalem.

Johannes Heinrichs. koeln University, Germany

Anat Mendel-Geberovich. Institute of Archaeology and School of Physics and Astronomy. Tel Aviv University

Literature

Agisoft Photoscan. http://www.agisoft.com (retrieved 4 February 2017).

Akca, D. (2012) 3D modeling of cultural heritage objects with a structured light system. Mediterranean archaeology and Archaeometry, vol. 12, no 1, pp. 139–152.

Autodesk ReCap 360. www.autodesk.com/products/recap/overview (retrieved 4 February 2017).

Autodesk Remake. https://remake.autodesk.com (retrieved 4 February 2017).

Bayram, B., et.al. (2015) Comparison of laser scanning and photogrammetry and their use for digital recording of cultural monument case study: Byzantine land walls-Istanbul. isprs annals of the photogrammetry, remote sensing and spatial information sciences, Volume II-5/w3, 25th international cipa. Taipei, Taiwan.

Boehler, W., Marbs, A. (2004) 3D scanning and photogrammetry for heritage recording: a comparison. Proc. 12th Int. Conf. on Geoinformatics – Geospatial Information Research: Bridging the Pacific and Atlantic University of Gävle, Sweden.

Bourke, P., (2016) Report: Comparing laser scanning to 3D Reconstruction http://paulbourke.net/miscellaneous/laservs3d/.

CHER-Ob. http://graphics.cs.yale.edu/site/sites/files/paper1026_CRC.pdf.

Cultural Heritage Imaging. http://culturalheritageimaging.org/Technologies/RTI(retrieved 14 February 2017).

Grussenmeyer, P. et al. (2008) Comparison methods of terrestrial laser scanning, photogrammetry and tacheometry data for recording of cultural heritage buildings. the international archives of the photogrammetry, remote sensing and spatial information sciences, vol. XXXVII, part b5. Beijing.

Hassani, F., (2015) Documentation of cultural heritage techniques, potentials and constraints. the international archives of the photogrammetry, remote sensing and spatial information sciences, volume xl-5/w7. 25th international cipa symposium. Taipei, Taiwan.

HP. 3D Scan. http://www8.hp.com/us/en/campaign/3Dscanner/overview.html. (retrieved 2 March 2017).

Kadobayashi, R, Kochi, N., Otani, B., Furukawa, R. (2004) comparison and evaluation of laser scanning and photogrammetry and their combined use for digital recording of cultural heritage. National institute of information and communications technology, seika-cho, soraku-gun, Kyoto 619-0289, Japan.

Macdonald, L.W., (2011). Visualising an Egyptian artefact in 3D: Comparing RTI with laser scanning. EVA'11 proceedings of the 2011 international conference on electronic visualisation and the arts, London.

Malzbender, T., Gelb, D., Wolters, H. (2001), "polynomial texture maps", proc. acm siggraph, 28, pp. 519–528.

Meshlab. P. Cignoni, M. Callieri, M. Corsini, M. Dellepiane, F. Ganovelli, G. Ranzuglia MeshLab: an Open-Source Mesh Processing Tool Sixth Eurographics Italian Chapter Conference, pp. 129–136, 2008.

Pavelka, K. et al. (2013) Non-expensive 3D documentation and modelling of historical object and archaeological artefacts using close range photogrammetry. geoinformatics fce ctu.

Payne, E.M., (2013). Imaging techniques in conservation. journal of conservation and museum studies. 10(2), pp. 17–29. doi: http://doi.org/10.5334/jcms.1021201.

RAW format. https://en.wikipedia.org/wiki/Raw_image_format.

Reznicek, J., Pavelka, K. (2008) New low-cost 3D scanning techniques for cultural heritage documentation. The international archives of the photogrammetry, remote sensing and spatial information sciences. vol. xxxvii. part b5. Beijing

RTI viewer. http://culturalheritageimaging.org/What_We_Offer/Downloads/index.html. (retrieved 8 January 2017).

Scopigno, R. et al. (2011) 3D models for cultural heritage: beyond plain visualization, published by the IEEE computer society.

Skarlatos, D., Kiparissi, S., (2012) Comparison of laser scanning, photogrammetry and sfm-mvs pipeline applied in structures and artificial surfaces. Annals of the photogrammetry, remote sensing and spatial information sciences, volume i-3.

Wachowiak, M.J., Karas, B.V. (2009) 3D scanning and replication for museum and cultural heritage applications, jaic 48.

Experiencing Artwork with Augmented Reality

Interactive Perception of Historical Statue "Belvedere Torso"

Victoria Batz, Finn Blümel, Jonas Falkenberg, Elisa Haubert, Dominik Schumacher, Michael A. Herzog

Institute of Industrial Design
Magdeburg-Stendal University
Breitscheidstraße 2, 39114 Magdeburg
{dominik.schumacher,michael.herzog}@hs-magdeburg.de

Abstract

Augment Reality conquers the art world. This paper seeks to examine a context-based use of Augmented Reality regarding cultural heritage presented in museums and at exhibitions. Custom-made hardware is supposed to help visitors to overcome inhibitions when dealing with technology. Also advantages and disadvantages of portable Augmented Reality devices versus a fixed installation are discussed.

The "Belvedere Torso" is an antique statute lacking all limbs and the head. The statue inspired art historians up until now to analyze, whom this "Torso" is supposed to represent. The interpretations are based on a classification of the "Torso" as a figure of the Greek mythology. Johann Joachim Winckelmann was the first to describe this artwork in such great detail. This installation is intended to mediate the complexity of all these interpretations to the visitor in an enjoyable way. It consists of an interactive book, which includes relevant quotes from different interpretations. The visitor flips through the book while the "Torso" is being extended with virtual arms, legs and head. The augmentation is shown on a screen between the visitor and the exhibit. The visualization provides an idea of what art historians described as the true identity of the "Torso" and makes those visible to visitors of the museum.

1   Phenomenon of the "Belvedere Torso" and its Interpretation

The "Belvedere Torso" is a statue of a muscular naked male body in sitting position, of which only the trunk and the thigh are preserved. The marble body rests on a predator's skin, which is swung over his left thigh. The statue contains the inscription: "Apollonius, son of Nestor, made it from Athens." It has been suspected to have its origin in the first century BC. The statue is missing all limbs: arms, legs and the head. The missing body parts are a great inspiration for many artists and scientists. Winckelmann's description of the "Torso" in 1759 has been the first scientific interpretation of the statue, where he concluded it to be the body of Hercules. Many other historians interpreted mythological figures onto the "Torso", such as Polyphemus, Skiron, Marsysa, Aias, Philoktet [Adam03]. The interpretations differ depending on the position of arms, legs and how the head is turned.

The "Belvedere Torso" has been completed with limbs and head as plaster casts and bronze statues in different positions; but not yet with an Augmented Reality device. When visitors study the statue in a museum, there is no seamless way to relate the different views of the original artwork to each other and making the variations visible to the visitor [EWZ98].

2   Art Projects with AR and interactive Books

Augmented Reality (AR) is defined as a live expansion of a physical element by overlapping the real environment with computer-generated information. AR was developed and used in the beginning of the early 1990s.[1] It has been applied to many industry sectors like navigation systems, medical environments, commercials, education purposes, video games and many more. Rather recently, the fields archaeology and art started to understand the opportunities of overlaying digital content, historical heritage and artworks [DJ16]. AR makes it possible to impart different perceptions of the piece of art and make them accessible for the viewer.

The "Belvedere Torso" in particular has not been virtually augmented and also Winckelmann's vivid descriptions and following analyses of the "Torso" have not been visualized yet. Mobile AR guides were introduced in some

---

1   Siehe Wikipedia: Augmented Reality

galleries and museums as a guide system that gives the visitors an individual tour through the exhibition. Visitors reacted positively towards the AR guide systems, seemed to spend more time with single pieces and are more engaged in the artworks [QPFB16]. As an example the Augmented Reality App from Stanford University should be named. The App recognizes the individual art pieces from different angles within 2 seconds. It offers a new way to look at art. The project A++ gives visitors of a museum more insights about an image for example information is presented either as an overlay or a panoramic view of a historical site.[2]

Ancient landscapes, historical architecture and even social situations are already virtually displayed and therefore tangible to visitors. This technology is referred to as CyberARchaeology or Virtual Archaeology. It was also applied to archeological locations where 3D graphics of ruins, buildings and landscapes were mapped onto the present scenery. A project to mention in this field is the MAR experience [QPFB16]. 3D models of historical architecture, downloaded from open source platforms, show the reconstructions on site as AR and also as VR with VR glasses. This way long buried theaters, orchestras and other monuments are brought back to life.

There are several projects experimenting with interactive books. Most of them focus on turning pages with hand gestures using motion sensors. Other projects install technology into the book and therefore use it just as an optical frame. The Monkeybook for example, which was invented for an exhibition entitled "The Alchemical Quest", has an acrylic body in shape of an open book with an integrated screen. This screen controls the content via touch interactivity and projects it onto an angled mirror reflecting upward. A camera tracking system with an infrared sensor grid reacts to swipe gestures and turns the pages virtually [Muse12].

3   Design Research Process

The project presented here was created to develop an interactive access to the interpretation of the "Belvedere Torso". This was conducted on the basis of the Design Science paradigm regarding Hevner [HMPR04] and the DSRM process model of Pfeffer et al. [PTRC07] (fig. 1).

---

2   http://artplusplus.stanford.edu/

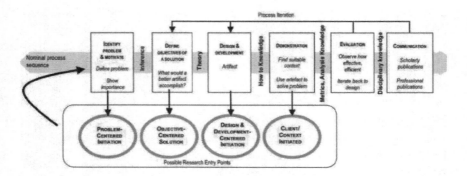

Fig. 1: Design science research methodology (DSRM) process model [PTRC07]

Problem centered entry point was defined by the demand to improve the reception of a specific art object within the complex museum redesign. The desired solution should stand for solving the generic problem of a user centered interaction dealing with different text based interpretations of an artwork.

Design and development of the underlying artefact has been realized after the principles of a User-Centered Design process [ISO9241]. Starting with intensive research about the Winckelmann museum, his live and work, we met with the museum curators and got exclusive tours through the exhibition. Workshops were organized to involve the future plans with the museum into the design process. The target group had to be categorized and a user context analyzed, resulting in a list of user requirements for a modern, interactive experience as a visitor of the Winckelmann museum. At the interim presentation, different concepts and prototype drafts were introduced to the museum management. Similar concept ideas were merged and further elaborated. With the first functional and designed prototypes user testing was performed to exclude problems. Design methods like interview, research, observation, a cognitive walkthrough, thinking aloud were useful for our study. After having real visitors using the installation at "Werkschau Design 2017" for three days some following adjustments had taken place.

4 Interacting with "Belvedere Torso"

Johann Joachim Winckelmann, born in Stendal 1717, is regarded the founder of classical archeology and documented art history. Through the formulation of his concept of beauty in art and his appreciation for the aesthetics of antique objects, he became the intellectual founder of classicism in the German-speaking region [Pott94]. The goal of the underlying project was to develop media aspects of the exhibition at the Winckelmann Museum in Stendal to celebrate the archeologist's anniversaries in 2018/19. A digital, interactive access for the visitors of the exhibits should improve the transmission of Winckelmann's work. Historical artifacts, found in the ancient cities of Herculaneum and Pompeii, had a key function for Winckelmann's work. He discovered the exposed statues while he was traveling around Italy and arranged a transfer to Germany, where they can still be seen today in the Dresden State Art Collection. He studied the three women of Herculaneum, the Laocoon-Group, Apollo and "Belvedere Torso" in particular.

The current exhibition shows all sculptures in one room. Visitors do not get an immediate connection between Winckelmann's writings and the statues. The goal was to create a more seamless level between exhibits and Winckelmann's description of them, as his meaning in relation to the statues, might not become obvious. The role model became the "Belvedere Torso", because of its potential to stimulate the visitor's imagination.

The project enlivens Winckelmann's description by giving the "Torso" the appearance of Hercules. The posture of arms and legs, in which angle the head is turned, the look on his face and what the "Torso" is carrying is very important when projecting a real figure on a stone statue. On a permanently installed screen the "Torso" is overlaid with skin, partly dressed and extended with limbs. This way the visitors get an idea of what Winckelmann had in mind, when he studied the statue for such a long time. The perception of a real-life "Torso" seems to be within reach. Still, the visitors see the statue in its original size at the same time in all its impressive appearance. The gaze can wander between the historical legacy and the inner eye of an art historian and his/her vision of the artifact. It becomes vivid what the artifact could have looked like in former times.

The goal is to mediate the complexity of the artwork and the depth of interpretations referencing the piece. The AR installation provides the visitors with alternate means while experiencing the statue. It is a new approach to work on Winckelmann's writing and hopefully raises the visitor's curiosity and interest to explore the texts more profoundly. The installation also demonstrates several examples of interpretations and shows the "Torso" from different perspectives. The augmented artwork allows the user to become part of the analyzing process.

5   Implementation

The setup for the museum provides a stele, with a good viewing distance to the statue; a book with original excerpts from Winckelmann's descriptions is displayed. Relevant text passages are highlighted and imply possible interactions. The visitor senses how Winckelmann has looked at the artwork and examines them in a similar way by painting across the highlighted phrase with a quill, which is provided in an inkwell on the stele. An interaction between statue and word takes place.

In addition, the installation is equipped with a permanently installed screen between viewer and artwork. The camera included is filming the "Torso" in real time (figure 2). Winckelmann and his imaginative eye saw more than just a trunk watching the "Belvedere Torso". The visitor is given the chance to see the "Torso" like Winckelmann described it in a virtual way. Winckelmann made a detailed description of the individual body parts of the "Torso", how they might have looked like in the Hercules myth. Each muscle on the chest or shoulder is synchronized with the demigod. The visitor can select a text passage in the book by underlining it and the "Torso" will come to life. As soon as the viewer highlights words of the description, the missing limbs are projected onto the "Torso" in Augmented Reality on the screen.

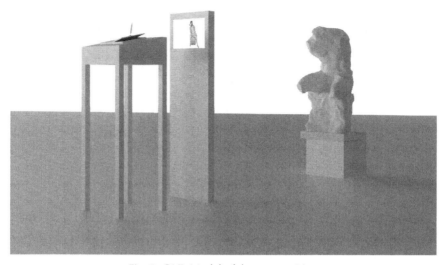

Fig. 2: CAD Model of the composition

A further level of interaction is offered by flipping the pages. The visitor triggers a change of topic. By turning a page – a sensor is activated. A combination of Processing code and an Arduino board makes it possible to show different content on every page. Driven by a very content-based design process a specialized system had to be developed. An interactive book was designed with needed features. The sensors hidden in cardboard pages recognize which page is open. Sensors also support the highlighted areas of the text. The correlation of sensor and magnetic field activates the exchange of information and passes it to the Arduino board. A quill was determined as the input tool. Both interactions, the page detection and the active areas on every page, were set up with hall-effect sensors. Each page got a magnet and a sensor for indexing and four more for the active areas. The positioning of those sensors was determined by single words in the text and triggered with a small magnet at the tip of the quill. In order to make the pages as thin as possible and having the built-in technology disappear, a flexible printed circuit board (PCB) and surface mount components (SMD) were installed in the book (figure 3). Evaluations of the sensor-generated data are replaced from the book in a separate circuit and passed on to a computer. Based on the sensor data, the content was sorted and augmented onto a real-time webcam video of the statue.

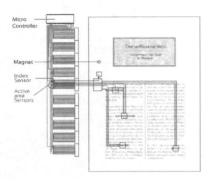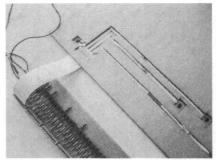

Fig. 3: Sensors and wiring

Not only Winckelmann has dealt with the "Torso" intensively. After his work on the "Torso" historians and writers continued to provide new analyses. The interpretations, reaching into modern times, are briefly presented with quotes and relevant statements are highlighted. The "Torso" on the screen turns into different interpretations visually. The projection on the screen shows a mirror of the represented beauty ideals at the respective time, different body postures and the positioning of arms and legs. The visitors of the Winckelmann museum receive a comprehensive insight of the statue "Belvedere Torso" The prototype of the interactive book with a physical "Torso" mock-up was presented as a functional demonstrator for user evaluation.

6 Evaluation

Fig. 4: The prototype with book-AR interaction at the exhibition ground

The Winckelmann Museum Stendal has a very heterogeneous target group: art enthusiasts, people living in Stendal, German tourist, group excursion with seniors, school trips, etc. The majority has little knowledge of Winckelmann and its origin before the visit. Access to the exhibition must be easy and intuitive. An intensive instruction is not possible.

Since most visitors of the museum are native German speakers, multilingualism is irrelevant. Three main aspects are being investigated.

6.1 Tools for interacting with the book

By flipping the pages, different interpretations are shown on the screen – one per page.

Thesis to be proven: The setup does not need any explanation in advance. The handling of a book is usually familiar. Tested were different tools to interact with the book.

Finger: Tapping on relevant information.

Pen: A pen is often used as a "pointer" to make text locations easier to find, for example when comparing text passages.

Bookmark: A popular way to marking the page where you stopped reading is also used by some people (especially children) to "underline" a particular line, so you do not shift while reading

Quill: In Winckelmann's time, a quill was a common tool for writing.

Very quickly the user recognizes the possibility of selecting highlighted text areas with the pen.

The pen is more likely to be used as a pointer. The bookmark as an interaction item created confusion. The finger was not used as a selection tool – maybe more likely, if highlighted phrases were more raised like a real button. The quill works, but should be noticeably modified to be identified as a special interaction tool.

The drawings of the respective gods on every page were the first eye-catcher and detracted too much from the text. So we decided to scale them down a little.

6.2 Layout book

Three different aspects of the layout were tested: amount of text on every page, two different designs and which content elements are relevant. The test person was asked to perform a Cognitive Walkthrough, so we could observe the handling with different types of the book. Therefor a designer simulates working with the book as a hypothetical visitor of the museum and speaks out loud whatever strikes him. At the same time the test person must answer specific questions about the layout, arrangement, fonts, typesetting and how much of the text he was actually reading. We observed that the user does not read the continuous text; just single sentences in highlighted boxes are being noticed. The test person prefers a modern font without serifs. The layout should be a combination of modern typesettings and antique design.

6.3 Gamification

The last chapter of the book is supposed to become the interactive game section. The visitor can combine the various visualizations of textual interpretations with each other. In other words, arms, legs and head on the "Torso" can be mixed up according to the principle of Cadavre Exquis. The usability test was performed with a paper prototype and an interview afterwards. It had to be determined whether the user understands the principle of the game, if an explanation is necessary, how long the user is involved in the game and if it is possible with multiple players. The evaluation showed that the game was understood without any introduction. The test person had a lot of fun combining the different interpretations and would spend at least 2 minutes easily. It was suggested to extend the game and also use own arms, legs and head to augment the statue.

6.4 Usability testing at the exhibition

To evaluate the final and functional prototype, a few visitors were asked to observe the installation at "Werkschau Design 2017" in Magdeburg (figure 4). The prototype wasn't equipped with any instructions. Based on the results of earlier testings an intuitive access was expected. During the exhibition, a few details were noticed and changed in the code for more intuitive usage. Also a few setup changes would be necessary for a final exhibition layout at the Winckelmann Museum in Stendal.

7   Findings and Perspectives

The main difference to existing projects is the seamless interaction between visitor and artwork. Despite all benefits of AR applications, usually the user has to take the effort and download an app to discover the interaction. One main goal of augmenting the "Belvedere Toro" was an easy and fast access for everyone. A permanently installed setup has been found to be the perfect solution in order to achieve that goal.

Putting the screen on a fixed position had the advantage of a very precise and steady projection on the statue. Also the camera is always in the right spot for showing the exact size, scale and distance of the body parts on the "Torso". The evaluation has shown that the connection between book and quill, as an interactive tool, is not obvious to everyone. The handling still needs some explanation or must be visualized on the desk.

The prototype has been a low budget setup. The visitors desired a more unobtrusive stele as a cover for the screen. The main focus should be on the artwork. Therefor the stele must nearly become invisible, so the visitor can look up from the book and see the augmented "Torso" on the screen and the real statue at the same time. The screen could either be attached to the desk or be inserted into a transparent stele of glass as cover material for example.

The text in the book included a short introduction about the "Belvedere Torso", where it was found, who made it and when it was created. In the second chapter relevant excerpts from Winckelmann's description of the statue are found. Also, the three other major interpretations of the "Torso" as Aias, Philoktet and Hercules are included and the interpretation game. Unfortunately, the visitors mostly overlooked the content – only headlines and single phrases in info boxes were read. The effort to engage with the text has to become more attractive. The installation must encourage the user to first get some background information and then use the interaction tools to immerse deeper into their meaning. Maybe an auditory level of mediation will be added at a later stage.

The general opinion was entirely positive. The augmented "Torso" enhanced the visitor's attention and learning effectiveness. They spent an extended amount of time focusing on the exhibit. The AR installation attracts visitors when passing the installation.

The visualizations are another step towards a deeper interpretation of the archaeological source. 3D graphics of the limbs would make the effect even more realistic and tangible. The visitors get an idea of what the artist and art historians wanted to mediate with or about the exhibit at the same time. Along with these perceptions the visitor creates an own experience with the statue.

8 Conclusion

Augmenting the "Belvedere Torso" is an affordable alternative to extent the statue with missing body parts. The virtual reconstruction of damaged artworks and showing the variety of interpretations at the same time is a great chance for art-historical science and culture heritage. The project demonstrates on site restoration of artwork. The potential to influence the artwork with AR and even influence its appearance creates a memorable experience. The innovation is a combination of augmented artwork influenced by an interactive book. Visitors become part of the process of creation. The technology does not push the actual artwork into the background rather then offering a new, innovative way of experiencing a museum. A relationship between exhibition, artwork and context is established by the installation. AR is considered to preserve history and also includes a new, younger target group. The visit and the experience with the exhibit give visitors something to think about. The functional prototype of the interactive book with a printed live-size model of the "Torso" will be presented at the conference.

9 Acknowledgements

We would like to express our deep gratitude to Prof. Dr. Dieter Schwarzenau, for technical support. Our grateful thanks are also extended to Dr. Michael Minge for his help with the design process and evaluation procedure. Also, curators of the Winckelmann Museum, Dr. Kathrin Schade, Dr. Stephanie-Gerrit Bruer and Prof. Dr. Max Kunze, should be mentioned for their great support and inspiration. Thanks to the people of Unity Design we were able to use their workshop and equipment to build parts of our prototype on short notice before the first exhibition.

Literature

[Adam03] Adam, W.: Kanon und Generation. Der Torso vom Belvedere in der Sicht deutscher Italienreisender des 18. Jahrhunderts: 855. Euphorion: Zeitschrift für Literaturgeschichte, 97(4), p. 419. 2003

[DJ16] Tom Diecka, M. C., & Junga, T.: Value of Augmented Reality to enhance the Visitor Experience: A Case study of Manchester Jewish Museum. e-Review of Tourism Research, p. 7. 2016

[EWZ98] Ewel, M., Wünsche, R., & von Zur Mühlen, I. (Eds.): Der Torso: Ruhm und Rätsel; Glyptothek München, 1998

[HMPR04] Hevner, A. R., March, S. T., Park, J., & Ram, S.: Design science in information systems research. MIS quarterly, 28(1), pp. 75–105, 2004

[ISO9241] ISO 9241-110:2006 Ergonomics of human-system interaction – Part 110: Dialogue principles. https://www.iso.org/standard/38009.html (2017-03-16)

[Muse12] Case Study: Museum Interactive for The Alchemical Quest. Rare Books Interactive. 2012 https://de.scribd.com/document/234869740/Case-Study-Museum-Interactive-for-The-Alchemical-Quest-Exhibit# (2017-03-16)

[Pott94] Potts, Alex.: Flesh and the ideal: Winckelmann and the origins of art history. Yale University Press, 2000.

[PTRC07] Peffers, K., Tuunanen, T., Rothenberger, M. A., & Chatterjee, S. (2007). A design science research methodology for information systems research. Journal of management information systems, 24(3), pp. 45–77.

[QPFB16] Quattrini, R., Pierdicca, R., Frontoni, E., & Barcaglioni, R. (2016). Virtual Reconstruction of Lost Architectures: from the Tls Survey to AR Visualization. ISPRS-International Archives of the Photogrammetry, Remote Sensing and Spatial Information Sciences, pp. 383–390.

Weitere Titel aus dem vwh-Programm (Auszug)